Contemporary Landscapes of Contemplation

"Contemplative landscape" and "contemplative space" are terms often heard in the design world, but what actually constitutes a contemplative realm? What definitions, theories, and strategies guide their creation, and how do we evaluate their effectiveness?

Rebecca Krinke and her contributors, Marc Treib, John Beardsley, Michael Singer, Lance Neckar, and Heinrich Hermann, all highly regarded scholars and designers, have produced a pioneering investigation into contemplative landscapes. The essays explore the role of contemplative space in a postmodern world, and examine the impact of nature and culture on the design and interpretation of contemplative landscapes. Through numerous case studies, the authors disclose principles used to create successful contemplative landscapes. Relationships and differences between contemplative and commemorative space are highlighted, as well as the links between contemplative landscapes and restorative landscapes (those landscapes that provide measurable benefit to human health).

Rebecca Krinke is an Associate Professor of Landscape Architecture at the University of Minnesota, and has a practice focused on the design of contemplative space. She has also taught at the Harvard Design School and the Rhode Island School of Design. She was a primary contributor to *Manufactured Sites: Rethinking the Post-Industrial Landscape*, edited by Niall Kirkwood (Spon Press, 2001).

Contemporary Landscapes of Contemplation

Edited by Rebecca Krinke

Routledge
Taylor & Francis Group

LONDON AND NEW YORK

First published 2005
by Routledge
2 Park Square, Milton Park, Abingdon, Oxon OX14 4RN

Simultaneously published in the USA and Canada
by Routledge
270 Madison Ave, New York, NY 10016

Routledge is an imprint of the Taylor & Francis Group

© 2005 Rebecca Krinke, selection and editorial matter;
individual chapters, the contributors

Typeset in Univers by
Florence Production Ltd, Stoodleigh, Devon
Printed and bound in Great Britain by
TJ International Ltd, Padstow, Cornwall

All rights reserved. No part of this book may be reprinted or reproduced
or utilised in any form or by any electronic, mechanical, or other means,
now known or hereafter invented, including photocopying and recording,
or in any information storage or retrieval system, without permission in
writing from the publishers.

British Library Cataloguing in Publication Data
A catalogue record for this book is available from the British Library

Library of Congress Cataloging in Publication Data
    Contemporary landscapes of contemplation/edited by Rebecca Krinke.
  – 1st ed.
      p. cm.
  1. Sanctuary gardens. 2. Spiritual retreats.
  I. Krinke, Rebecca
  SB454. 3. S25C66 2005
  712–dc22   2004026543

ISBN 0–415–70068–X (hbk)
ISBN 0–415–70069–8 (pbk)

Contents

Illustration credits	vi
Notes on contributors	vii
Preface	xi
Acknowledgements	xiii
Introduction: contemplation, landscapes of contemplation, contemporary *Rebecca Krinke*	1
Attending *Marc Treib*	13
On the transcendent in landscapes of contemplation *Heinrich Hermann*	36
Map of memory, an interview *Michael Singer with Rebecca Krinke*	73
Contemplative landscapes, restorative landscapes *Rebecca Krinke*	107
Berlin: topology of contemplation *Lance Neckar*	139
Filling a void: creating contemporary spaces for contemplation *John Beardsley*	174
Index	196

Illustration credits

Collections of The New York Public Library, Astor, Lenox and Tilden Foundations © 1.4
Dia Art Foundation © (Photograph by John Cliett) 6.6, plate 4
Heinrich Hermann © 2.1, 2.2, 2.3, 2.4, 2.5, 2.6, 2.7, 2.8, 2.9, 2.10, plate 3
James Turrell © plates 5, 6, 7, 8, 9. Plate 5 courtesy of the Principal Financial Group, plates 7 and 8 courtesy of John Beardsley, plate 9 courtesy of Marc Treib.
John Beardsley © page 7, 6.1, 6.2, 6.3, 6.4, 6.5, 6.7, 6.8, 6.9, plates 20, 21, 22
Lance Neckar © 5.1, 5.2, 5.3, 5.4, 5.5, 5.6, 5.7, 5.8, 5.9, 5.10, 5.11, 5.12, plates 18, 19
Marc Treib © 1.1, 1.2, 1.5, 1.6, 1.7, 1.8, 1.9, 1.10, 1.11, plates 1, 2
Metropolitan Museum of Art, Wrightsman Fund © 1.3
Michael Singer © Cover image, 3.1, 3.2, 3.3, 3.4, 3.5, 3.6, 3.7, 3.8, 3.9, 3.10, 3.11, 3.12, plates 10, 11, 12, 13, 14
Raphael Justewicz © 4.4, 4.5
Rebecca Krinke © page 6, 4.1, 4.2, 4.3, 4.6, 4.7, 4.8, 4.9, plates 15, 17
Richard Haag © plate 16

Contributors

John Beardsley is an author and curator whose work has focused on the relationship between art and the landscape. He was one of the first critics to recognize the importance of the land art projects in the 1970s – and brought this work to the public's attention through a show he organized at Washington's Hirshhorn Museum in 1977. Beardsley has written extensively on public and environmental art, including the books *Earthworks and Beyond: Contemporary Art in the Landscape* (Abbeville Press, 1984; third edition, 1998) and *Gardens of Revelation: Environments by Visionary Artists* (Abbeville Press, 1995). Beardsley has organized numerous exhibitions, including "Human/Nature: Art and Landscape in Charleston and the Low Country," at the Spoleto Festival USA in Charleston, South Carolina, in 1997, and "The Quilts of Gee's Bend" for the Museum of Fine Arts, Houston, in 2002. He is a Senior Lecturer in Landscape Architecture at the Harvard Design School where he teaches courses in landscape architectural history, theory, and criticism. He received his A.B. from Harvard University and his Ph.D. from the University of Virginia.

Heinrich Hermann is Principal of Hermann Design Studio in Concord, Massachusetts. The theory and creation of contemplative space is a primary concern of his research and practice. His Ph.D. dissertation in the history and theory of architecture at Harvard University focused on the transcendental dimensions of experience, and strategies employed in architecture and landscape architecture to elicit these responses. Hermann holds Master of Architecture degrees from the Academy of Applied Art in Vienna and Cornell University. He has taught at the Harvard Design School, Rhode Island School of Design, Cranbrook Academy of Art, Washington University in St. Louis, and has practiced in his native Austria and Germany. Recent projects include an Augustinian Garden Memorial for Merrimack College, a nondenominational chapel for Salem Hospital, and a proposal for a long-term Buddhist Retreat Center in a forest in Barre, all in Massachusetts.

Rebecca Krinke is an Associate Professor of Landscape Architecture at the University of Minnesota. Her research and practice is focused on contemplative and commemorative space. Recent projects include: the *Great Island*

Contributors

Memorial Garden, with architect Randall Imai, Cape Cod, Massachusetts (1999), and *Forest Transformation*, a contemplative space she designed for the Minnesota Landscape Arboretum (2003). Krinke is collaborating with artist John Roloff to design the four outdoor courtyards at the addition to Rapson Hall (Steven Holl, architect), on the University of Minnesota campus, with construction underway. She was a primary contributor to the book *Manufactured Sites: Rethinking the Post-Industrial Landscape*, edited by Niall Kirkwood (Spon Press/Taylor and Francis, 2001), which details innovative technologies and progressive practices in reconstructing despoiled landscapes. She has taught at the Harvard Design School and the Rhode Island School of Design, and practiced in Boston.

Lance Neckar, Associate Dean and Professor of Landscape Architecture, University of Minnesota, is a scholar, urban designer, and educator. He has written book chapters on modernist pioneers Christopher Tunnard (*Modern Landscape Architecture: A Critical Review* edited by Marc Treib, The MIT Press, 1993) and Warren Manning (*Midwestern Landscape Architecture*, edited by William H. Tishler, University of Illinois Press, 2000). Neckar has co-authored an introduction to H. W. S. Cleveland's seminal work, *Landscape Architecture, as Applied to the Wants of the West* (University of Massachusetts, 2001). He was co-editor of "The Avant-Garde and the Landscape," a special edition of *Landscape Journal* (10:2, 1991). Neckar has also been engaged in a long-term study of the park and gardens of Castle Howard in Yorkshire, England. His article, "Castle Howard: An Original Landscape Architecture" was published in *Landscape Journal* (19:1). His most recent work on the baroque roots of this sublime landscape will be published in *Baroque Garden Cultures: Emulation, Sublimation, Subversion* (Dumbarton Oaks, 2005).

Michael Singer is an internationally known artist who creates outdoor and indoor sculpture, site-specific art, and public space. His works are part of public collections in the United States and abroad, including the Museum of Modern Art, the Solomon R. Guggenheim Museum, and the Metropolitan Museum of Art in New York and Denmark's Louisiana Museum of Modern Art, among others. Singer has designed many contemplative gardens and retreats, including *Pond Pavilion* (1999), *Woodland Garden* (1990–92), both in Massachusetts, and the *Those Who Survived* memorial in Stuttgart, Germany (1992). In recent years, Singer has been involved in numerous innovative landscape and infrastructure projects in the United States and Europe, often serving as the leader of interdisciplinary design teams. Projects include: Concourse C (1994) within the Denver International Airport, the Phoenix Solid Waste Transfer and Recycling Center (1989–1993), the Alterra Institute for

Environmental Research, Wageningen, Netherlands (1999) and work on several co-generation power facilities in the United States.

Marc Treib is Professor of Architecture at the University of California, Berkeley, a practicing designer, and a frequent contributor to architecture, landscape, and design journals. He has held Fulbright, Guggenheim, and Japan Foundation fellowships, as well as an advanced design fellowship at the American Academy in Rome. Recent publications include: *Noguchi in Paris: The Unesco Garden* (2003), *Thomas Church, Landscape Architect: Designing a Modern California Landscape* (2004, both William Stout Publishers), and *Settings and Stray Paths: Writings on Landscape Architecture* (2005, Routledge). Other publications include: *The Architecture of Landscape, 1940–60*, editor, (2002, University of Pennsylvania Press), *Space Calculated in Seconds: The Philips Pavilion, Le Corbusier and Edgard Varèse* (1996, Princeton University Press), and *Modern Landscape Architecture: A Critical Review*, editor, (1993, The MIT Press).

Preface

This book has its origins in a seemingly straightforward question: What is a contemplative landscape? It's a question that my colleague, architect Randall Imai, and I asked when we were commissioned to design a contemplative landscape for a private residential community on Cape Cod. This opening query soon led to many others: Is a contemplative landscape a place of relaxation, designed to still the mind of thoughts? Is a reductive design vocabulary imperative? Or is it a place that should prompt new insights to emerge – perhaps by providing an intense or unique visual focus? And while our project has been constructed and found to be quite successful by its constituents, it was difficult for us to find research to help us answer our questions on contemplative space. This work inspired a larger series of inquiries that I am continuing to explore: What is the role of contemplative space in a postmodern world? What ideas of nature and culture affect the design or interpretation of contemplative landscapes? Are there any specific aspects of physical design that can be found cross-culturally that contribute to a contemplative realm?

To deepen speculation and develop scholarship and practice in this area, I organized a symposium "Contemporary Landscapes of Contemplation" held October 18 and 19, 2002 at the College of Architecture and Landscape Architecture at the University of Minnesota. The symposium led to the essays by John Beardsley, Heinrich Hermann, Lance Neckar, Michael Singer, Marc Treib, and myself that are collected in this volume. I invited this group of contributors for three key reasons. They all possess a wealth of knowledge and insight on the history of designed landscapes as well as current theory and practice. Second, in addition to their scholarship, many of these contributors are makers of landscapes themselves, primarily Michael Singer, who has built many works of art and design that address the idea of contemplative space. And finally, the depth of experience and thinking this group can bring to the investigation of contemporary landscapes of contemplation is especially important given that this is an underdeveloped area of scholarship.

The essays in this book have a focus on Western landscapes, although the traditional landscapes of Japan are discussed as well. And while

Preface

contemplative space has been a part of virtually all of the world's religious traditions, most authors selected secular settings for discussion, perhaps underscoring life in our contemporary Western world. Marc Treib's essay broadly frames ideas, speculations, and questions into contemplation and contemplative space. In what ways does the designed environment engage and support our attention? His essay ranges from ancient Japan, to the eighteenth century English landscape and landscape painters, to the aesthetics and intentions of the Shakers, to contemporary American and European projects in his response. Heinrich Hermann addresses the transcendent dimension of contemplative space. His essay posits two paradigms for the creation of contemplative landscapes, using the Salk Institute and Woodland Cemetery as case studies. Michael Singer's interview underscores his work and life as an investigation into the human relationship with nature. Singer's art and design challenge fundamental assumptions about contemplative space, as he increasingly seeks out settings with complex social and ecological conditions. Lance Neckar's essay contributes important ideas about the role of language and culture in making landscapes of commemoration and contemplation in contemporary Berlin. How do issues of history, identity, memory, and reflection manifest in the everyday life and form of the city? John Beardsley's essay explores fundamental strategies in the East and West to facilitate contemplation. He elaborates on this discussion to investigate the relationship between contemplative and commemorative space, using two contemporary American projects to probe their similarities and differences. My own essay explores the links between contemplative landscapes and restorative landscapes, with the latter defined as a landscape that provides measurable benefit to human health.

This book is designed to contribute to both scholars of the landscape and those involved with the making of landscapes. Definitions, theories, and case studies of contemplative landscapes are explored. The essays investigate principles and strategies that are guiding the creation of contemplative landscapes and evaluates their effectiveness. This work will appeal to the reader who has an interest in art and design, and those more broadly interested in issues and ideas of contemporary life. The book is seen as a beginning step in the discussion of contemporary contemplative landscapes, and it is hoped that other scholars and designers will be prompted to delve into this typology of space. Insights gained into contemplative space have particular importance to commemorative space and restorative space – but there is also a larger potential for ideas related to contemplation and the landscape to broadly impact and infuse virtually any of the spaces we design.

Acknowledgements

As this project comes to a close, it is a pleasure to give thanks to the many people who helped along the way.

I am indebted to my colleagues at the University of Minnesota, especially Lance Neckar, Associate Dean, for inspiring me to develop a symposium and book on contemplative landscapes, and who provided important assistance on the symposium itself. I am grateful to Tom Fisher, Dean, and John Koepke, Department Head, for their strong interest in and support of the symposium.

Special thanks and acknowledgment to Patrick Nunnally who provided extremely useful responses to my essay in process.

Thanks and deep appreciation to my contributors: Marc Treib, John Beardsley, Michael Singer, Heinrich Hermann, and Lance Neckar. Special thanks to Marc Treib for his thoughts on an early version of my essay, as well as sharing his expertise in symposium organization and publishing. Thanks also to David Abram for his participation in the symposium.

I am grateful to my mentors and colleagues at other institutions, especially George Hargreaves, past Chair, Niall Kirkwood, present Chair, Department of Landscape Architecture, Harvard Design School and Martha Schwartz, Professor, Harvard Design School, for inviting me to teach and write with them. I thank you for changing the course of my career to profoundly stimulating new territories.

I have had the pleasure and privilege to work with many gifted and insightful colleagues in practice. Thanks especially to Randall Imai for inviting me to collaborate on the contemplative and commemorative gardens, opening up new avenues in my art, design, and scholarship.

Thanks to my editor, Caroline Mallinder, at Routledge for her faith in this manuscript. I appreciate the assistance of the entire team at Routledge who haved worked with me on this book, especially Amanda Lastoria for her calm efficiency during the production phase.

Many thanks to James Turrell, Kyung-Lim Lee, Richard Haag, Richard Brown, Candy Ludlow, and Raphael Justewicz for sharing images and/or their experiences with the projects featured in this book.

And deepest thanks to Lee Alnes for his ever-present support.

Rebecca Krinke
September 2004

Introduction
Contemplation, landscapes of contemplation, contemporary

Rebecca Krinke

Contemplation

If we look up the word "contemplation" in Webster's, we find that the first meaning given is simply "to view or consider with continued attention." Are we then involved with contemplation everyday? Or does contemplation imply a special kind of concentration? Robert Thurman, professor of Indo-Tibetan Studies at Columbia University and a Tibetan Buddhist, doesn't see contemplation as a rarified activity. It is his perspective that all of us are already involved in contemplation and that contemplative energy can be focused on anything. Thurman writes:

> Television, modern culture's peculiar contemplative shrine, supplies a contemplative trance to millions of people, for hours on end day after day year in and year out. It is unfortunately a trance in which sensory dissatisfaction is constantly reinforced, anger and violence is imprinted, and confusion and the delusion of materialism is constructed and maintained.[1]

From a Buddhist analysis, Thurman defines contemplation differently: there is "calming contemplation," which focuses on the elimination of thought, benefiting body and mind, and "insight contemplation," which is similar to reflective states, and is considered to contribute more to psychological, intellectual, and spiritual development than calming contemplation. Both of these contemplative techniques require instruction and practice. Thurman concludes, "Thus, when we talk about seeking to increase and intensify contemplative mind in our culture, we may really be talking about methods of transferring contemplative energies from one focus to another."[2]

Webster's synonyms of "reflect" and "ponder" may better define contemplation for some of us since these words intimate that the individual is engaged at a deep level with what they are viewing or considering. Rather than being mindlessly entranced, we are actively involved. We may be seeking an answer, a new insight or understanding. Contemplation indicates a deliberate attention, often implying a concentration on ideas, objects, or places that are somewhat outside our day-to-day thoughts. For example, art is often linked to contemplation: the artist may be seen as being in a contemplative state to create, or the viewer is seen as contemplating the work of art, or art is seen as able to induce a contemplative response. The work of artist Claude Monet illustrates these ideas. Monet contemplated moment-by-moment changes in light, while challenging his entrenched ways of seeing light, and worked to capture this new awareness in paint. The artist Wassily Kandinsky found a Monet painting of haystacks to be revelatory. He wrote of the "unexpected power . . . of the palette, which surpassed all my dreams" and "engraved itself indelibly on the memory."[3] Water in particular was Monet's fascination; he explored the relationship of water, light, and water lilies in hundreds of paintings. He continually redesigned his garden at Giverny to give him different views and understandings of light and reflection, all to benefit his art. Towards the end of his life, Monet's goal was to build a pavilion where his immense water lily canvases would encircle the viewer, creating a contemplative space. Monet is quoted as saying that "nerves tense from work would be relaxed there . . . the room would [offer] the refuge of a peaceable meditation. . . ."[4] Monet's work gives us an example of a reflective type of contemplation, one that affected his art in an ongoing way, and in turn provoked new perceptions in his audience.

Another description of contemplation aligns it with meditation and stress reduction. For more than 20 years, Dr. Jon Kabat-Zinn's pioneering work with patients at the University of Massachusetts Medical Center has introduced the contemplative practices of mindfulness meditation (defined as focused attention on the present moment) and yoga to patients with chronic medical problems. Through this work, his appearances on Bill Moyers' "Healing and the Mind" program on PBS, and his books, he has been very influential in bringing the stress reduction properties of contemplative practices to American mainstream culture. Kabat-Zinn finds "contemplation" or "meditation" to be two terms that are virtually interchangeable. He writes:

> [These terms] refer to methods of disciplining the mind by focusing on a specific object of thought or by completely letting go of all thoughts and emotions, and just simply watching or witnessing whatever arises in consciousness. Such practice usually results in a growing awareness of non-attachment to the contents of our

Introduction

mind, with an increasing ability to exercise choice in how we use our mind. In practical terms, this usually brings about a greater sense of self-mastery, well-being, equanimity and reduced stress.[5]

The beneficial effects for the body and mind through meditation or contemplation have been well documented by research and are exemplified by a calm, relaxed state, including a lowering of blood pressure and a lessening of muscle tension that contributes to physical and psychological health. Other positive effects include: "heightened self-awareness, improved concentration, empathy and perceptual acuity . . . alleviation of many symptoms in the chronically ill, and more effective performance in a broad range of domains from sports and academic test-taking to creativity."[6]

Contemplation is often described as the opposite of action, yet contemplation and action are frequently perceived as paired opposites – with both activities seen as necessary for living a successful life. Robert Durback, a former Trappist monk, finds contemplation to be an activity that deepens our involvement with the world. He writes: "Contemplation is not about escaping to some celestial dream world that offers immunization from concern with the evils in the world around us."[7] Contemplation may start from a definition of "fixed attention of one thing," but it is not a fixed action or goal, instead it is developmental activity. Contemplation moves from "fixed attention" to "identification," which he defines as becoming one with the object one is contemplating, until eventually, "identification deepens, and there is the sense of communion."[8] He finds that contemplation leads to action, and that contemplation sustains action, since it provides a grounding and renewal for the participant. Contemplative life today is also seen as "integrally linked with action on behalf of social justice or ecology."[9] For example, the Center for Action and Contemplation in Albuquerque is located in an economically depressed neighborhood, and participants in the Center's programs combine retreat and contemplation with community volunteer work.

Virtually all of the world's religious belief systems contain a contemplative tradition. In the contemporary postmodern world of myriad voices and visions, the search for meaning has reconnected some with the traditional aspects of a particular religion, while others investigate both ancient and contemporary sources of knowledge and practice. Mary Frolich, professor of Spirituality at Catholic Theological Union in Chicago elaborates:

> [T]oday, many contemplative seekers find themselves without the benefit of . . . a single integral tradition. Meanwhile, we are presented with unprecedented breadth of access to an array of spiritual practices, movements and texts from past and present. . . . [T]hrough written materials, tapes, traveling teachers, and the

Internet, the wisdom and practices of all the world's religions are knocking on our doors.[10]

This ready availability of multiple points of view has inspired many to create new hybrids of meaning, synthesizing elements from more than one tradition into new approaches, or even inventing new practices. For example, the Center for Action and Contemplation is Roman Catholic in orientation, but employs the Zen practice of sitting meditation. While a belief system and its methodologies may be invaluable in developing a contemplative practice, Professor Frolich feels that no special training or experience is mandatory. She writes:

> We can define contemplative experience as awareness – whether fleeting or habitual – of that most foundational, most original depth of being. . . . Because this is our most foundational reality, contemplative experience is potentially available to every human being, at all times and in every circumstance. It can and does "happen" to people without any preparation and while they are engaged in pursuits that are not concerned with seeking it.[11]

We've seen a range of ideas about contemplation – creating a description along a continuum from the everyday activity of fixed attention, to a reflective, sustained attention, to a developmental activity that assists physical and psychological well-being and growth – to an experience of the transcendental that may or may not require special training to experience. These descriptions may prompt us to ask how contemporary designers and artists are defining "contemplation" or "contemplative landscape." Are there any common strategies for supporting a contemplative experience through the designed landscape, especially if we consider the physiological responses to a contemplative practice to be seemingly universal? How do the myriad conceptions of nature and culture affect our understanding and reception of contemplative landscapes? And one may ask, is contemplation or contemplative space really necessary or important in the contemporary world?

Landscapes of contemplation

For landscape architects and architects in particular, the phrase "contemplative landscape" may bring traditional precedents to mind: a Zen temple garden or perhaps a medieval cloister garden. Psychologist Daniel Goleman reflects on these traditions when he writes:

Introduction

While Eastern cultures and the Western mystical and monastic heritage offer ample exemplars of the contemplative mind, they are scarce in lay society in the West. The seeker alone in nature is one archetype, exemplified by Thoreau at Walden Pond; if there is a root text for considering the contemplative mind in American society, it might be Thoreau's *Walden*.[12]

And as I developed this book and earlier symposium, a question I have been asked by several people is: "Wouldn't the wilderness be the most effective contemporary landscape of contemplation?" Perhaps as an outgrowth of reading books such as *Walden* or personal experiences, some see the wilderness as capable of evoking a more potent contemplative response than other settings. And it is true that elements of nature have been seen around the globe and throughout time as having restorative benefits. Until recently this has been essentially an intuitive understanding, but the research of environmental psychologists Rachel and Stephen Kaplan, Roger S. Ulrich, and others has indicated that contact with nature, especially vegetation, has a beneficial effect on physical and psychological health.[13] Ulrich designed several different types of studies that demonstrated that contact with nature produced faster and greater recovery from stress as shown by lower blood pressure, less muscle tension, reduction in anger and an increased feeling of well-being.[14] These are many of the same beneficial effects found through a contemplative practice.

The question of whether wilderness might be the most effective contemporary landscape of contemplation adds another layer to our discussion, because the question implies that untouched nature is more powerful than a designed landscape as a contemplative realm. It also reveals that a retreat from our predominately urban life is seen as restorative. Research has shown that contact with nature is beneficial, but not what settings are the most beneficial. The Kaplans have studied "wilderness experiences" and their research has found that "nearby nature," which they define as everyday places such as backyards, has virtually as much restorative power as the wilderness.[15] These findings may seem counterintuitive, or perhaps reassuring. The effect of exemplary, designed spaces on human health and development is an area ripe for research.

If the idea of the wilderness as a realm of contemplation provides an ongoing myth about our relationship with the earth, what might be some of the other myths that contemporary culture is writing? The Bloedel Reserve's Reflection Garden (page 6) has qualities of beauty and serenity that we may intuitively associate with a contemplative realm, but what about the Landscape Park Duisburg North (page 7), on the site of a former blast furnace near Duisburg, Germany? Is it possible that this park, undergoing remedia-

**Final design,
Reflection Garden,
Bloedel Reserve,
Bainbridge Island,
Washington**
Richard Haag,
1984

Landscape Park Duisburg North, Duisburg, Germany
Latz and Partners, 1991–2000

tion for contaminated soil and water, with portions of it still contaminated, could also be a contemplative space? Is the postindustrial landscape exactly what we should be contemplating? What ideas of "beauty" underlie our ideas about a contemplative landscape? Does the presence of technology undermine a contemplative realm?

Technology also mediates our experience of the contemporary landscape. Thomas de Zengotita, an editor of *Harper's* magazine, posits in his essay, "The Numbing of the American Mind," that we in contemporary American culture have little direct experience of nature, or of anything else anymore: most of our experiences are through some form of media. And if we try to have a direct experience, it isn't really possible because we have become media saturated.

> [A] couple of weeks out in Nature doesn't make it anymore . . . you will virtualize everything you encounter. . . . You won't see wolves, you'll see "wolves." You'll be murmuring to yourself, at some level, "Wow, look, a real wolf, not in a cage, not on TV, I can't believe it. . . ." And you will get restless really fast if that "wolf" doesn't do anything. The kids will start squirming in, like, five minutes; you'll probably need to pretend you're not getting bored for awhile longer.[16]

Do we agree with this assessment? Are there landscapes we could create that could wake us up again to the direct experience of nature? Or is a contemplative practice the way to wake up to direct experience?

Could innovative technology be a key to creating contemporary landscapes of contemplation? *Osmose* is an immersive virtual reality program of translucent trees and terrain created by the artist Char Davies. She was inspired by her scuba diving experiences to create a different kind of user interface for *Osmose* than the typical hand-dependent methods, such as the joystick or data glove. *Osmose* participants wear a harness around their chests to register effects of their breath and balance. (They also wear goggles for real-time visual effects and her program contains localized, interactive sound.) With this hands-free interface, the participants' focus is space, not objects. She writes that her intention is to explore virtual reality's "capacity for refreshing our 'ways of seeing.'"[17] More than 5,000 people have been immersed in *Osmose* since 1995, and many participants report effects very similar to experienced meditators, such as a profound sense of body/mind relaxation, and losing track of time. While watching the *Osmose* participants, it was apparent to observers that most participants move quite rapidly from a state of "doing" to one of "being." After approximately ten minutes, most participants undergo a noticeable change – their gestures and expressions relax and slow – as they are drawn into this new world and their new perceptions. This is in sharp contrast to their initial state of immersion, where their movements are quick, and focused on exploring the virtual landscape as much as possible, similar to how one may explore an actual new setting.[18]

Davies feels *Osmose* is revitalizing human perception, and successful at this because it is a place and experience unlike those of our embedded habits and typical understandings.[19] Davies grew up in the landscapes of rural Canada, which deeply influenced her art, and continues to do so. She feels it was possible for her to create *Osmose* only because of her relationship with the physical world.[20] Her art has created a strangely beautiful new realm where the focus on breathing is deeply relaxing. This makes room for other modes of perception; instead of the mind running on automatic, it begins to pay attention in the present. Davies writes:

> "[P]laces" like *Osmose* may one day be accessible on line as virtual sites of contemplation, so too such sites may signal the demise of traditional places of self-reflection and tranquility. In particular this includes "nature" as we know it. . . .[21]

Do technologies like *Osmose* threaten our connection to the physical world or do they offer possibilities for reconnection? If *Osmose* is an effective contemplative technology, would its more widespread adoption be a positive addition to contemporary life? What might a perceptually refreshing work of landscape architecture look like?

Contemporary

Our contemporary condition is often described as postmodern; a time characterized as the collapse of modernism's optimism, "accompanied by a radical destabilization of much of the normal sense of rootedness in place, tradition, and conviction."[22] Robert Thurman sees the current postmodern situation as one "in which we must oscillate between terminal, doomsday pessimism about our chances of surviving as a species at all, and . . . utopian, optimistic visions about how the entire society must become a contemplative community, in order to survive and thrive."[23] Thurman has come to the conclusion that he "personally consider(s) broad-scale individual development of contemplative insight to be necessary for survival."[24] A recent article in the *New York Times* on the "Wireless Age" also discusses the importance of contemplation as a key to surviving modern life, but notes that "we work hard to avoid being alone in our heads"[25] and many of us cannot imagine disconnecting from the contemporary technology and lifestyle that keeps us always working, talking, and available.

Whether our current condition is seen as a crisis or filled with excitement and opportunity, there seems to be a consensus that contemporary life is quite stressful. Stephen Hatch writes, "Stress in the workplace and home, the breakneck pace and complexity of the 'information age' and a growing lack of connection to the natural world drive many to seek a life of greater silence, peace, and simplicity."[26] It is clear from the numbers of stress reduction programs, yoga and meditation classes now available that increasing numbers of people from virtually all walks of life are being drawn to contemplative practices.

Jon Kabat-Zinn finds a "profound social/cultural revolution" in its beginning stages, a revolution that is driven by "strong inward longing in our society for well-being, meaning, and connectedness."[27] The search for meaning and connection is not something that is talked about much in contemporary design, seemingly verging on the taboo, but the search for meaning is a fundamental human endeavor, and art and design have always been a primary means of exploring and expressing this relationship. Char Davies elaborates: [My work] "explore[s] what it means to be embodied conscious being. That's not New Age. It's not necessarily spiritual. It's about human experience."[28] She concludes, "My goal is to remind myself and others how extraordinary it is to be here."[29]

The idea of contemporary landscapes consciously designed as places of contemplation raises intriguing questions: What values do these spaces reveal? Do these landscapes explore fundamental questions about life, relationships, earth or cosmos? How do these spaces affect us? How could these spaces change us?

The following essays investigate many of the questions raised in this introduction. And while some of the questions I have posed may be virtually unanswerable, each reader is invited to explore their own attitudes and ideas through the different perspectives highlighted by the authors. Drawing upon both scholarship and personal experience, the essays offer very inviting forays into contemporary landscapes of contemplation.

Introduction

Notes

1 Thurman, R. A. F. (1994) "Meditation and Education: Buddhist India, Tibet and Modern America." Online. Available HTTP: <http://www.contemplativemind.org/resources/pubs/thurman.html>.
2 Ibid.
3 A. Forge, "Monet at Giverny," in C. Joyes, *Monet at Giverny*, New York: Mayflower Books, 1975, p. 9.
4 Ibid., p. 12.
5 Kabat-Zinn, J. (1994) "Catalyzing Movement Toward a More Contemplative/Sacred-Appreciating/Non-Dualistic Society." Online. Available HTTP: <http://www.contemplativemind.org/resources/pubs/kabat-zinn.html>.
6 Goleman, D. (1994) "The Contemplative Mind: Reinventing the News." Online. Available HTTP: <http://www.contemplativemind.org/resources/pubs/goleman.html>.
7 R. Durback, "Contemplation: Journey Inward or Journey Outward?" in V. Manss and M. Frolich (eds) *The Lay Contemplative: Testimonies, Perspectives, Resources*, Cincinnati, OH: St. Anthony Messenger Press, 2000, p. 14.
8 Ibid., pp. 15–16.
9 M. Frolich, "A Roman Catholic Theology of the Lay Contemplative" in V. Manss and M. Frolich (eds) *The Lay Contemplative: Testimonies, Perspectives, Resources*, Cincinnati, OH: St. Anthony Messenger Press, 2000, p. 56.
10 M. Frolich, "Lonely Valleys and Strange Islands: Contemplative Conversations With the 'Other'" in V. Manss, and M. Frolich, (eds) *The Lay Contemplative: Testimonies, Perspectives, Resources*, Cincinnati, OH: St. Anthony Messenger Press, 2000, pp. 71–2.
11 Frolich, "A Roman Catholic Theology of the Lay Contemplative," op. cit., pp. 45–6.
12 Goleman, op. cit.
13 For example, see R. S. Ulrich, "Effects of Gardens on Health Outcomes: Theory and Research" in C. C. Marcus and M. Barnes (eds) *Healing Gardens: Therapeutic Benefits and Design Recommendations*, New York: Wiley, 1999 and the Special Issue on Restorative Environments in *Environment and Behavior*, 33, 4, July 2001.
14 R. S. Ulrich and R. Parsons, "Influences of Passive Experiences with Plants on Individual Well Being and Health", in D. Relf (ed.) *The Role of Horticulture in Human Well-Being and Social Development*, Portland, OR: Timber Press, 1992, pp. 99–100.
15 R. Kaplan and S. Kaplan, *The Experience of Nature: A Psychological Perspective*, Cambridge and New York, Cambridge University Press, 1989, p. 195.
16 T. de Zengotita, "The Numbing of the American Mind: Culture as Anesthetic," *Harper's*, April 2002, p. 37.
17 C. Davies, "Changing Space: Virtual Reality as an Arena of Embodied Being" in J. Beckmann (ed.) *The Virtual Dimension: Architecture, Representation, and Crash Culture*, New York: Princeton Architectural Press, 1998, p. 145.
18 Ibid., pp. 146–9.
19 Ibid., p. 145.
20 C. Gigliotti, "Reverie, Osmose and Ephemere: Dr. Carol Gigliotti Interviews Char Davies" in K. Deepwell (ed.) *n. paradoxa, International Feminist Art Journal*, 9 (Eco)Logical: 64–73, 2002. Online. Available HTTP: <http://immersence.com/index.html>.
21 Davies, op. cit., p. 153.
22 Frolich, "Lonely Valleys and Strange Islands: Contemplative Conversations With the 'Other'," op. cit., p. 72.
23 Thurman, op. cit.
24 Ibid.

25 J. Gleick, "Theories of Connectivity," *The New York Times Magazine*, April 22, 2002, p. 112.
26 S. K. Hatch, "The Formation of the Everyday Contemplative" in V. Manss and M. Frolich (eds) *The Lay Contemplative: Testimonies, Perspectives, Resources*, Cincinnati, OH: St. Anthony Messenger Press, 2000, p. 59.
27 Kabat-Zinn, op. cit.
28 Quoted in E. Davis, "Osmose," *Wired Magazine*, 4, 8, August 1996, p. 192.
29 Gigliotti, op. cit.

Attending

Marc Treib

To many Western eyes, a garden of rocks and gravel will immediately trigger associations with Japan and Buddhism (Fig. 1.1). It might even be described as a "Zen garden," and seen as a vehicle to stimulate contemplation: the conscious or unconscious considering of the world at a level far deeper than the normal. These associations are but half truths, however. There really is no singular "Zen garden," nor single form for a landscape intended to provoke contemplation: indeed, to assert that one type of garden serves best for contemplation is somewhat of an anathema to Zen Buddhism. The philosopher and religious scholar Daisetz Suzuki once cited these lines as an essential summation of Zen belief:

> No dependence on letters or words,
> Pointing directly at the Mind in every one of us,
> And seeing into one's Nature, whereby one attains Buddhahood.[1]

Firmly rooted as it has been in the mundane world, antagonistic as it was to the involved rituals of the earlier esoteric sects of Asian Buddhism, and believing that *satori*, or awakening, could strike a person at any moment – how could a vehicle for attaining enlightenment be restricted to any particular landscape form?

But half-truths often make good stories, and there is certainly no denying that many of these gardens – more accurately termed *kare sansui*, or dry landscapes – were constructed as an important constituent of Zen temples throughout Japan, and especially in Kyoto. Is there something in the form and space of these gardens that really *does* incite introspection?[2]

Marc Treib

1.1
Ryoan-ji, Kyoto, Japan, *c.* 1500

To what degree does the ability to concentrate depend on the environment, and to what degree does it lie with and within the individual? Or perhaps a more germane question is to ask at what stage, and in what way, does a designed environment support meditation? For me it concerns *attending*, that is *attending* as a verb related to the noun *attention*. We attend to forces external or internal, or both. If we agree that a landscape can aid or retard attending, perhaps then we can then examine how certain garden forms have done so in the past to suggest how we might do so in the present, or even the future.

Our archetypal dry garden, Ryoan-ji in Kyoto, was renovated about 1500 into more or less the form it retains today (there has been some debate about changes made over the centuries, however). An earthen boundary wall capped by a protective thatched roof encloses a field of raked gravel and fifteen stones of varying sizes and shapes. Some few patches of moss surround certain rocks, effecting a transition of sorts between stone and gravel. The garden is meant to be regarded from a seated position on the temple's veranda, and from anywhere along its length it is impossible to see all the stones at the same time. This staged obscurity heightens the sense of infinity and the feeling of human inadequacy to know all things. Some have interpreted the Ryoan-ji garden as a representation of mountains or islands in a sea, or a mother bear and her cubs swimming across a river. But Zen belief does not really admit direct interpretations – certainly not in garden design – and we would better consider these images as *evocations* rather than *representations*. More critically, the garden serves equally as a vehicle for contemplation in its *making* and *tending* as well as in its viewing. That is, the care and maintenance of the garden are also part of monastic life, and according to doctrine, awakening normally arrives suddenly without restriction to time and place: even, perhaps, while raking gravel in a garden.

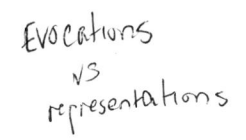

Contemplation implies a higher degree of concentration than that which accompanies perception in normal life. The environment may serve as stimulus, as subject, or as both, but significance ultimately derives from the interaction of people and place. Thus to be contemplative we must direct attention toward or within a setting. But why should rocks and gravel stimulate contemplation more effectively than other environmental manners? If contemplation can take place both within *and* without us, the nature of the environment should not matter to any great degree. But it does, at least to most people. Those with strong meditative powers might not require any physical reinforcement; those of lesser ability, in contrast, will benefit from some external assistance.

Consider a hectic American urban or suburban environment such as the Strip – the quotidian American traffic artery lined with businesses and packed with over-scaled signs competing for our attention. It would be difficult for many people to think profoundly within the aural and visual distraction of such a milieu. First, one would need to discern what validates attuning and what needs to be tuned out. But if the environment itself is visually and aurally "poor" – if there are but a few elements available to attend – the process is considerably simplified (Fig. 1.2). This is why we may close our eyes during a concert or during sex; we allow one sense to advance in presence by *dampening* the influence of the others. The simplification of the dry garden then is much like closing one's eyes; not completely, but in a manner that allows for greater concentration and increased wonder. The dry garden presents few forms or features or relationships between them upon which to attend. A sort of visual exhaustion sets in, although those with advanced powers of observation may discover more than enough interest even within the seemingly blanched field. In time, one may indeed find infinity within the garden's bounded space. Or one may simply close one's eyes and exchange things physical for those metaphysical.

These thoughts raise the issue of meaning in the designed landscape. To my mind, no place is created with meaning, despite any designer's intention to do so. If we can accept that meaning derives from the transaction between the perceiver and the place, significance becomes a *byproduct* of that transaction, individually produced. One need qualify such a strong assertion. I would allow that in a folk or closed society, where literally everyone shares the same culture, religion, morés, and built forms, it *would* be

Marc Treib

1.2
Easter landscape, near Paoli, Pennsylvania, 1982. Attending the everyday landscape

possible for an individual to create a place that is meaningful to others within that shared value system.³ But in our multicultural, multi-temporal, multi-geographic society, it is difficult to believe that we could ever achieve such consensus again. That is not to say that I may not create something which *becomes* meaningful to you – I believe most designers would hope to do so. But in the end that meaning would derive from you, your experience and education, your joys and biases; we would derive coincident meanings from the landscape only rarely.

Psychologists tell us that perception takes place in at least two stages, or so they would like us to believe.⁴ The first is the random type of information processing that allows us to deal with the world as a complex whole. It provides the means by which we are able to drive down the street, reaching our destination without really engaging all the names of streets and stores, and all the people and objects, along the way. The second type of perception is more directed: like when we are specifically looking for a shoemaker. The psychologists qualify this manner as a form of "pattern recognition;" we approach the world with a goal in mind, and we try to match something out there with something inside the head. This focused thinking might also be directed toward contemplation. Although we may concentrate on our breathing or external devices such as mandalas, it appears somewhat as a philosophical contradiction to think that we can *concentrate on contemplation*, since most of the enlightened ones tell us that much of the process depends on our letting go. Perhaps it is only a means to an end that admits these sort of contradictions, like a Zen *koan*.[5]

Transcendental philosophy proposed that nature was the great source of the sublime, a world of percepts so vast and so beautiful that they reflected the Divine Nature of the deity. Landscapes, rendered or constructed, embodied these visions. The rugged mountains, the vast plains, the endless waters of the oceans – all of these stupefied the viewer into silence, causing him or her to fall back in contemplation. It is a romantic notion of course, one shared by German nineteenth-century writers and artists, as well as English garden makers. The paintings of Caspar David Friedrich offer us just this idea of nature: the magnificent landscape subject that strikes speechless the figures before them. In Friedrich's works people attend the landscape as if standing before God: awed yet poised, calm, silent. That fragments of civilizations past are also embedded in many of Friedrich's paintings only underscores the pathetic efforts of human beings to still the effects of time. The Gothic window and the dolmen are ruinous and small before the greatness of nature (Fig. 1.3). We are forced to contemplate Friedrich's images as we might contemplate nature itself and the human position within it. In the nascent United States the tone became more gentle, and in the famous painting *Kindred Spirits* by Asher Durand of 1849, we witness the poet William Cullen Bryant and the painter Thomas Cole set within the New World Wilderness (Fig. 1.4). They appear attuned to nature rather than awed by its extent; the human here is more a part of the wilderness, and more comfortable in the presence of the divine.[6] Communing supersedes contemplation.

The English landscape garden makers of the early eighteenth century also sought a semantic landscape that would inspire the visitor to muse. Early Georgian gardens such as The Leasowes and Chiswick took no chances, using inscriptions and iconic elements rather than relying on vegetal forms alone as bearers of meaning.[7] William Kent's designs for Lord Burlington at Chiswick broadcast intention in an overt manner, offering to garden strollers whiffs of past cultures upon which to reflect (Fig. 1.5). Obelisks smacking of Egypt and her civilization that fell to Roman hands, temples recalling elements of the Pantheon, naïve cottages or elegant neoclassical temples – all of these were destined to make the visitor pause and ponder. Today, many of the elements appear theatrical and overblown, almost as cartoons of meaning that lack the subtlety and true patina of a classical age. But in their time, to their constituency of aristocratic privilege, they were significant and effective in stimulating thought and thinking.[8]

The transcendent has found expression in more recent landscapes as well. The design of the justly celebrated Skogskyrkogården (normally translated as the Woodland Cemetery) in Enskede outside Stockholm, also directs

1.3
Caspar David Friedrich, *Two Men Contemplating the Moon*, circa 1830

1.4
Asher B. Durand, *Kindred Spirits*, 1849

Attending

1.5
Iconic temple and obelisk. Chiswick House, England, early eighteenth century. The photograph was taken during restoration
William Kent (?)

[handwritten margin notes:]
still
silent

can be in
St Patricks
cathedral
and feel
still and
silent

us to attend and deliberate. Completed in 1940 after a design and construction period of a quarter century, the cemetery is a landscape so beautifully conceived, so beautifully composed, and so right in every way, that even for those without the Christian faith, the place reads as sacred. To effect healing the funereal landscape dampens the noise in one's life so that the still small voice may be heard. The Woodland Cemetery speaks stillness, especially in the winter when the land is blanketed with snow and the sun rakes low across the contours (Plate 1). In its silence, even a muted bird call or a distant car horn acquires enormous presence. We visit cemeteries to forget as well as to remember, to attend to people and times past, to enter a sanctified arena whether as a form of homage or to foster bereavement (Plate 2). This particular cemetery relies only lightly on formal symbols, and relatively few of them appear on its gravestones and buildings: the notable exception finds condensed symbolism in the great stone cross set on the lawn, as much an assertion of concentrated energy as a religious icon. But this simple-looking landscape of lawn and birch and pine and earthen contours is far more powerful in its collective than in its individual aspects. If dampening supports attending, then this landscape is a wondrous vehicle for suppressing the undesired.

Much of what has been said to this point may seem rather simple if not simplistic, but I believe these observations bear squarely on the topic of contemplation, at least to some degree. Attending means paying atten-

19

tion. It may be more or less difficult to achieve, like trying to listen to a flute sonata when the driver of an adjacent car has rap music playing so loud that its bass line dents the door of your car. But if one can truly listen to the inner voice, even a complex visual or formal environment should not be an obstacle. Or so I am told.

Historically, contemplation has accompanied withdrawal from the web of normal life, whether to institutions such as monasteries, or to landscapes perceptually reduced to aid the process. Monasteries and convents represent places of retreat. One withdraws from society for a religious or personal ideal; it demands some sacrifice, for example, the relinquishing of worldly possessions, sexual appetite, perhaps even the gift of speech. But through this denial one gains a stronger sense of who one is and why one is present. The results can be potent. One reads of the ecstasy that accompanies truly religious experience. To some, Gianlorenzo Bernini's statue of *Santa Teresa in Ecstasy* appears as an illustration of baroque excess, to others it clearly reveals the conflation of divine and mundane emotion (Fig. 1.6).

1.6
Gianlorenzo Bernini, *Santa Teresa in Ecstasy*, **Santa Maria della Vittoria, Rome, Italy, 1650s**

Attending

The cherub striking the quasi-prostrate saint with the divine presence has been interpreted in more than one way, and some criticism has ventured that the saint's expression is just too corporal and worldly.[10] Perhaps contemplation, too, may lead to a kind of ecstasy, but an ecstasy, one assumes, that accompanies peace.

The Shakers, a popular name for The United Society of Believers in Christ's Second Appearing, were a religious sect that developed in the eastern United States in the later eighteenth century – although the group's central figure, Mother Ann Lee, had been born in England and came to the United States only as an adult.[11] Shaker architecture and furniture appear to represent a rejection of the world's values, with a purposeful simplicity that thwarts distraction and temptation.[12] Their designs are described as highly functional, displaying virtually no cognizance of style (Fig. 1.7). In actual fact, Shaker forms derived from those of "the world" at the time of the sect's origins, as they "gathered in" converts and absorbed their personal holdings. The evolution of their designs was, in some ways, more one of ossification than simplification; fashions and styles moved on, but the Shaker designs did not. Of course they built on these existing prototypes and over the years made them their own, and in that sense there *were* developments: but they were developments that followed a path set obliquely to the commercial market, despite the production of furniture and other items fabricated specifically for sale.

The Shaker environment, however, shares many parallels with other groups who have chosen to retreat from the world. Contemplation

1.7
Attic storage area, centre family dwelling, Pleasant Hill, Kentucky
Micajah Burnett, 1834

always seems to involve the word *retreat*, because it signifies removal from normal attentions in order to reduce distractions and to focus instead on spiritual issues, or more practical topics such as management or economics. But retreat, no matter the subject, implies focus.[13] The form of the Shaker living environment reminded all within that they dwelled there in service, and that they should not be diverted from their project of "Hands to Work and Hearts to God." That the Shakers were a celibate order further complicated the matter since temptation, one presumes, was ever-present. But even today visitors to the Hancock Shaker Village in Massachusetts or the Pleasant Hill community in Kentucky will find it difficult to avoid a sense of reverie and the presence of the devotion felt by the Shaker believers.

There is an assumption here: that reducing the impact of environmental stimuli demands compensation by the individual seeking knowledge, removal, or uplift. Seen in another way, simplification signals contemplation because the story is rendered less obvious. We think of the dry gardens of Japan as contemplative vehicles because they accompanied the rise of the Zen sect and its belief that seated meditation aided the achievement of enlightenment. The contemplative garden was less an invention than a reduction and recasting of existing elements and spatial ideas into a new composite. In Japan, several garden traditions have coexisted at any one time, never just a single type as we might be led to believe by courses in landscape history. The earliest Japanese gardens supported by archaeological evidence – palatial gardens from the eighth century – appear to have been based on natural models, employing streams, ponds, and vegetation to fulfill their makers' intentions.[14] The gardens offered animation and shade, and manifested the passing of the seasons of which the Japanese are so culturally aware. The Buddhist temple compounds of the era, in contrast, relied on courtyards lined with gravel – perhaps raked – framed by buildings and roofed corridors.

By the twelfth century, with some impetus from the teachings of the Jôdo (Pure Land) sect of Buddhism, these traditions evolved into what has been termed the paradise garden. In Pure Land belief, the Amida Buddha waits in his Western Paradise for the enlightenment of all sentient beings; the paradise garden reflects the beauty that awaited. The gardens evidencing this vision were lushly planted and centered on a pond, and although created as religious vehicles they were sensually rich. One also must consider the sources of these temples and gardens which often had origins – like the Shaker examples – in prior villa construction and secular gardens, converted to religious purpose later in life when the patron sensed his or her time was near. Thus the landscape that today is the magnificent moss garden at the temple of Saiho-ji in southwest Kyoto had once been a villa, and then a

Attending

paradise garden, before the arrival of the monk Musô Soseki who reformed the design in closer accord with the tenets of the Rinzai sect of Zen Buddhism in the early fourteenth century (Fig. 1.8). And despite its seeming opposition to the rock and gravel dry gardens, Saiho-ji *is* by all means a garden accepted as a setting for Zen practice.

Musô is normally credited – however apocryphally it might possibly be – with having reconceived the garden as a religious vehicle. The shape of the pond at Saiho-ji, for example, was reworked into a loose rendering of the Japanese character *kokoro*, which signifies heart or spirit. One assumes that Musô dampened at least some of the former plantings, as today the vegetation is restricted to primarily maples with some cryptomeria and pine, and of course mosses, said to number over forty varieties.[15]

Musô also developed the upper area of the garden entered through a roofed gate and a flight of steps. There he created the dry cascade, a composition of boulders the faces of which over time have been claimed by mosses and lichens (Fig. 1.9). The rocks appear so natural, so much the product of hydraulic process, that it is easy to forget that they were composed by human invention, and that flowing water never inundated their surfaces. The realism of the rock groupings stimulates the mind to *imagine* water, however. The net effect matches that of an aqueous presence, and perhaps – being now a human creation – the process conjures a

1.8
Saiho-ji, Kyoto, Japan. Mosses subsume all surfaces except the water of the pond
Musô Soseki, attributed, *c.* 1338

1.9
Saiho-ji, Kyoto, Japan. The dry cascade
Musô Soseki, attributed, c. 1338

"hyper-presence." This engagement represents another instance where the lack of an external subject induces greater engagement by the individual. This may or may not have been Musô's intention; of course we do not know for sure. But one poem by Musô reads:

>   A high mountain
>   soars without
>   a grain of dust
>   a waterfall
>   plunges without
>   a drop of water
>   Once or twice
>   on an evening of moonlight
>   in the wind
>   this man here
>   has been happy
>   playing the game that suited him.[16]

Some say the rocks were created as seats *from* which to contemplate the scene; others claim they *were* the subjects of contemplation in and of themselves. As in Zen itself, there may have been an intention, but there certainly was no conclusion. We are left with another unanswered question, like one posed by the French poet Paul Claudel: "Is it nothing, that Nothingness which delivers us from everything?"[17]

Zen informed to a large degree what we call in English the tea ceremony (in Japanese it is more closely translated as "hot water for tea"). With beginnings in the midst of political chaos near the start of the sixteenth century – after almost a century of civil unrest – the tea ceremony offered a ritual retreat from the cares and complexities of the mundane world. But it also represented an advance into a realm of much higher aesthetic and spiritual pursuits. In more urban settings, a small garden called the *roji* or "dewy path" often connected the street with the tea house; on larger plots the tea house and garden together comprised a subunit of the greater landscape. In both cases the *roji* functioned primarily as a transitional zone to calm the guests, and prepare them for tea. The tea garden reintroduced the figure into the landscape after its many years of sitting on the veranda, and in that sense the tea garden was more physically engaging than the dry garden – but it served another purpose as well.

The afternoon and evening hours preferred for the ceremony meant that the clay soils used for pathways might be damp, dark, slippery, and somewhat hazardous to negotiate. To mitigate these problems, garden makers introduced stepping stones and lanterns, both of which would become hallmarks of the stroll gardens of the seventeenth century (Fig. 1.10). But in the tiny tea world the stepping stones served haptic and spiritual purposes as well as functional ones. A body wrapped tightly in kimono could comfortably traverse a distance of only about one foot at a time, thus requiring great care in walking and negotiating the path. One looked down for surety and to avoid catastrophe. By using rough stones or smooth stones, long stones or short stones, stones in proximity or stones widely spaced, the garden-maker modulated movement through the garden and the sequential revelation of views. Small distances could be made to seem large, and the care necessitated by the placement of the stones focused the mind on the immediate task – already one step, so to speak, towards the world of tea.

Within the tea house restraint prevailed. Natural materials predominated, normally in an environment based almost entirely upon the rectilinear grid of the *tatami*. The singular exception to this orthogonal ordering was the *tokobashira*, or central post, whose irregular shape had been nurtured from early in its growing life. Colors within the tea house were muted, and the filtered light through the rice paper *shoji* shone soft and milky. The *tokonoma*, or ceremonial alcove, presented the primary aesthetic objects: perhaps a hanging scroll and flower arrangement that reflected both the season and the refinement of the host.

One of the early and defining tea masters, Sen no Rikyu, ventured that the tea ceremony was nothing more than boiling water, making tea, and

**1.10
Shokin-tei, Katsura Villa, Kyoto, Japan, seventeenth century. The stepping stones direct movement from the boat landing into the tea house**

drinking it. Perhaps in the early years it was just that, although the world of tea was always accompanied by heightened aesthetic invention and a re-seeing of the quotidian. The architectural forms for tea were adapted and sophisticated from the simplicity of folk houses and agricultural structures; the rustic tea house at first appeared familiar, but in fact everything was incredibly refined and rarified. But in its totality of effect, with its earthen wall planes disappearing into soft shadows, and the bubbling of the boiling water or the rustling of kimono sleeves as its principal sounds, the tea house was truly a prosthetic for contemplation.[18]

Today, in a more secular age, the art museum represents one of our leading reflective environments, where the museum's "white box" contains objects – often set in wondrous isolation – that require attentive scrutiny to reveal their "meaning." In some ways the gallery functions as a tea house writ large, although few recent museum buildings could be characterized by any form of restraint. One enters the museum willingly, and therefore enters to consider its contents as significant and more valuable than those that exist beyond its walls. The museum frames contemplation, and like the dry gardens of the Zen sect, modern curatorial techniques have set the object in isolation, reducing the interference between the viewer and the object viewed. Framing and aesthetic dampening should make it easier to experience the significance of the object, even if it be a prosaic object like a urinal, labeled a "fountain" as an aid for shifting the viewer's preconceived associations.

The museum also raises the question of appropriate behavior and whether the stimulus lies encoded in the environment, or derived from prior learning. We have all witnessed children running up and down the aisles of churches, being shushed by their parents – in essence, being instructed in how to behave in certain spaces. If this instruction is to be effective we need to ensure that a church appears as a church, and that a museum may demand behavior befitting a religious structure. At times, the museum also instructs us with Do Not Touch signs and other cautions that utilize more overt coding. In most cases the museum walls set off the artwork to be considered, using the environmental matrix to constrain our focus on the object. Other works of art, however, function in just the opposite way, directing us to all that surrounds them as they display their own particularities.

Walter De Maria's *Lightning Field*, set in the high New Mexican desert near Quemado, was completed in 1977. Until I visited the work some years ago I had always conceived the content of the piece – and had even taught it that way – as concerning the superimposition of a geometric order upon the irregularity of a natural terrain. The field of stainless steel poles, the tops of which form a single plane, measures one mile by one kilometer, the two systems of measurement by which the developed world has been objectively described. Having spent considerable time in New Mexico, I was well aware of the sudden thunderstorms that frequent late summer afternoons and the possibility of lightning strikes (Plate 4). But my visit was in late autumn and neither storm nor lightning troubled the mostly clear skies. The power of the semantic dimension, however, was omnipresent nonetheless, and the *thought* of lightning was constant, even though none was to be seen.

To visit *The Lightning Field* is a somewhat involved process: you are taken to the site in mid-afternoon, remain on the land over night, and are retrieved about noon the following day. De Maria reworked an old rancher's cabin on the site into a place of rather sophisticated rusticity. It sleeps about six people. When our group arrived one Halloween afternoon the site was muddy from days of rain; the air was still mild. Negotiating *The Lightning Field* was difficult as shoes stuck to the mud as if it were some sort of earthen epoxy. But one perseveres in rare opportunities such as these. The first pole was astounding. It was beautifully proportioned, beautifully fabricated, perfectly erect, with a taper at its top that recalled the form of a javelin. In point of fact, these tapered tips seem to hold the light even after the sun sets below the horizon.

I then proceed to the next pole. "Hmmm," I thought, "it looks a lot like the first one. It is beautiful though." By pole number three I was rapidly losing interest in the form that poles of stainless steel can take. In fact, I discovered that there were only really three views by which to see the work: looking squarely on a row of poles; the classical perspective between two rows, and a view outside the field – but at that point all sense of depth is gone and you are essentially seeing the work in elevation. Instead of fixating on the poles I began to notice how the chamisa and other plants grew at the base of the poles and across the plain, the locus of the sun shifted noticeably, and how the light and the chromatic tones changed in relation to the position of the body – in effect creating human eclipses by choice. Clouds moved and the light diminished; the sun in the sky fell towards the horizon and what had been the brights were now the shadows. The colors mutated from blues and grays to yellows and reds, then soft pinks, and ultimately that pale blue zone just above the horizon, caused by the shadow of the Earth on the rose sky of sunset.

We visited the field by moonlight as well; it was cold, with temperatures rapidly dropping below freezing. And when we rose early for the requisite sunrise viewing the ground was frozen solid, making walking considerably easier. Some of the experience of the prior afternoon was repeated, only this time in reverse order. But other observations were new: for example, that De Maria had found a site bounded completely by mesas, however distant. What I learned from my visit – much to my surprise I might add – was that despite any specific intentions by its maker, *The Lightning Field* also functioned as a contemplative vehicle; not so much for addressing art or human creation, but for attending the land, its vegetation, and the light that fills its atmosphere. Here, the artwork intrudes on human consciousness as an instrument that dampens formal interest through repetition, and coerces us instead to look at, and then consider, other things.

Certain art works support transforming perception into contemplation, and here the work of James Turrell is particularly relevant.[19] Turrell's interior installations involve light and duration: Immediate perceptions change over time, continually evolving until a sort of mature state of revelation emerges. Entering these rooms from the exterior the eyes see only complete darkness. As the minutes pass, at times agonizingly slowly, the iris dilates and the eyes begin to discern differences in light patterns and eventually distinguish form. In several series of works the artist operates at the threshold of perception, where the level of illumination is so low that light seems to exist in crystals. At first perception the barely-discernible rectangles of his Space-Division series appear as painted shapes on solid surfaces, and they hover as such in our perception (Plate 5). In fact, the rectangle is an aperture in the plane that separates the room we occupy from a second space behind it. In some variants it is illuminated only by the light gathered from the front room in which we stand. It is difficult to distinguish two from three dimensions and we are forced to question our vision, or as Robert Irwin phased it, we perceive ourselves perceiving.[20] "When you reduce light and the pupil opens," says Turrell, "feeling comes out of the eye as a sensuous act."[21] In addition, the works instigate a sort of contemplation of perception in which we question how we interact with a world that we normally take without question. Or as Edmund Burke offered in his classic eighteenth-century tract on the sublime:

> [A]ll edifices calculated to produce an idea of the sublime, ought rather to be dark and gloomy, and this for two reasons: the first is, that darkness itself on other occasions is known by experience to have a greater effect on the passions than light. The second is that to make an object very striking, we should make it as different as possible from the objects with which we have been immediately conversant.[22]

Turrell's grand masterwork, the *Roden Crater Project*, assembles a number of perceptual situations including a grand entrance tunnel, "sky-seeing spaces," and the crater of the extinct volcano itself (Plates 6, 7, 8, 9). Here the great cinder bowl has been reshaped so that four visitors at a time may lie on their backs and experience an exaggerated sense of the dome of the sky – an effect known to pilots as celestial vaulting. Turrell explored this theme in small works such as the *Celestial Vaulting* at Kijkduin in The Hague from 1996. But while this piece relates in nature to the experience of the crater, it can not complete with it in scale. The *Roden Crater Project* is an incredible gesture that at once positions the body in the great sweep of the American high desert, and within a grand celestial percept. Should we read it as a contemplative vehicle or as a perceptual psychology experiment elevated to the status of art work?

On a smaller scale, but still powerful in effect, James Turrell has created a series of pieces known as "Spaces that See." At the Israel Museum in Jerusalem, for example, he dug into one of the terraces of the sculpture garden designed by Isamu Noguchi to fabricate a space square in plan and in its opening to the sky. Key here, as it was for the earlier Space-Division pieces, was forming the roof edge to an angle so acute that no edge surface reflected any light that might distinguish the plane of the ceiling from the plane of the sky. Under certain conditions, the sky is pulled taut and flat across the opening; in other lights it seems to become a dome, the impression broken only by the passing of a cloud or airplane.

The 2001 installation *Knight Rise* at the Scottsdale Museum of Art utilizes an ellipse rather than a square, softening further the distinctions between the enclosing surfaces and the ceiling that caps them. Its effectiveness outdoes the square rooms, particularly in the later afternoon, as the sun retreats and the sky darkens. Here we can see the difficulty in perceiving – even for the photographic film – the distinction between ceiling and sky, as the relationships shift from white and blue to yellow and black – a sky that seems far blacker than it does when seen without Turrell's frame. This dampening garners attending, and the result is a feeling of something far beyond the room. "An excited calm," says Turrell, "is a little bit of an expression of the sublime."[23]

These works as a group provoke our consciousness of perception, perhaps even to contemplate how and why we perceive, and what value it might have to the way we construct or interact with the world. You don't "get" a Turrell work immediately. It demands time. You must be willing to invest the time, as to achieve any sort of awakening you must spend time in meditation. Almost every artwork demands such attention to some degree, but rarely is there so little tangible payoff unless you devote the time to perceive. That, and its ultimate aesthetic rewards, are what grant Turrell's packaging of light such power, at least as I see it (so to speak).

Despite any of the vehicles discussed above, we could speculate that contemplation is essentially an interior process independent of any particular setting. The conditions might be those of a bus, a busy street, a concert, a baseball game, a storm, or a painting: the *what* of the particular environment is less critical than *how* we attend. Ultimately the vehicles we use are only the means to the end, although they may provide us with some very beautiful means along the way. Some of them, like *The Lightning Field*, may support our thinking about the existence of nature, even if we never get to thinking about the nature of existence. This distinction may suggest that contemplation occupies at least two levels: the first removes us from the quotidian, the second turns consciousness above the everyday or within the individual.

Great buildings, like Peter Zumthor's superb baths at Vals in Switzerland, heighten the senses as a means to reach the mind. Here water and wall surfaces prod the haptic dimension; light teases the eyes with its abundance and absence, its sources from above or laterally from the mountainside (Fig. 1.11). Under these conditions, which appear in sum almost as those of an aqueous temple, the normal duality of mind and body is somewhat effaced, as the stone-veneered wall planes and soft internal illumination dampen external stimuli while the baths literally dampen the body. Dampening and heightening, retreat and advance – as discussed above – all contribute to making environments conducive to contemplation, although there are certainly no guarantees that they will be equally potent for everyone. Again, one questions the degree to which the setting provides the basis for mediation and to what degree that pensive state derives from the individual him or herself. If the mind is right, all environments, interior or exterior, may serve as effective contemplative environments.

Film critic Pauline Kael said of one film that "the extreme of [its] banality allow[s] us to catch a glimpse of the sublime."[24] John Cage phrased it somewhat differently: "The music never stops, we just stop listening." We might take that as a clue. The German photographer Thomas Struth contributes to our understanding when he tells us about a series of pictures he calls *Paradise*:

> The photographs taken in the jungles of Australia, Japan, and China, as well as in the California woods, contain a wealth of information which makes it almost impossible, especially in large formats, to isolate single forms. One can spend a lot of time in front of these pictures and remain helpless in terms of knowing how to deal with them. There is no sociocultural context to be read or discovered, unlike in photographs of people in front of paintings in museums. Standing in front of the façade of the cathedral in Milan, one experiences oneself as a human being defined by specific social and historical conditions. The jungle pictures, on the other hand, emphasize the self.[25]

Which returns us to the nature of contemplation, perhaps again cast as an existential exercise. [26]

There are numerous stories of Zen masters and Zen practice that have come down to us, many of which are highly provocative in themselves. Some take the form of *koans*, or conundrums, by which seeming oppositions can be transcended – perhaps. But other simple vignettes also provoke thought. Here is one. It concerns a learned abbot named Shinkan, who had returned to Japan after years of study in China. He was frequently sought after to answer questions, but he normally refused. "One day a fifty-year-old student of enlightenment," the story begins, "said to Shinkan: 'I have studied the Tendai school of thought since I was a little boy, but one thing in it

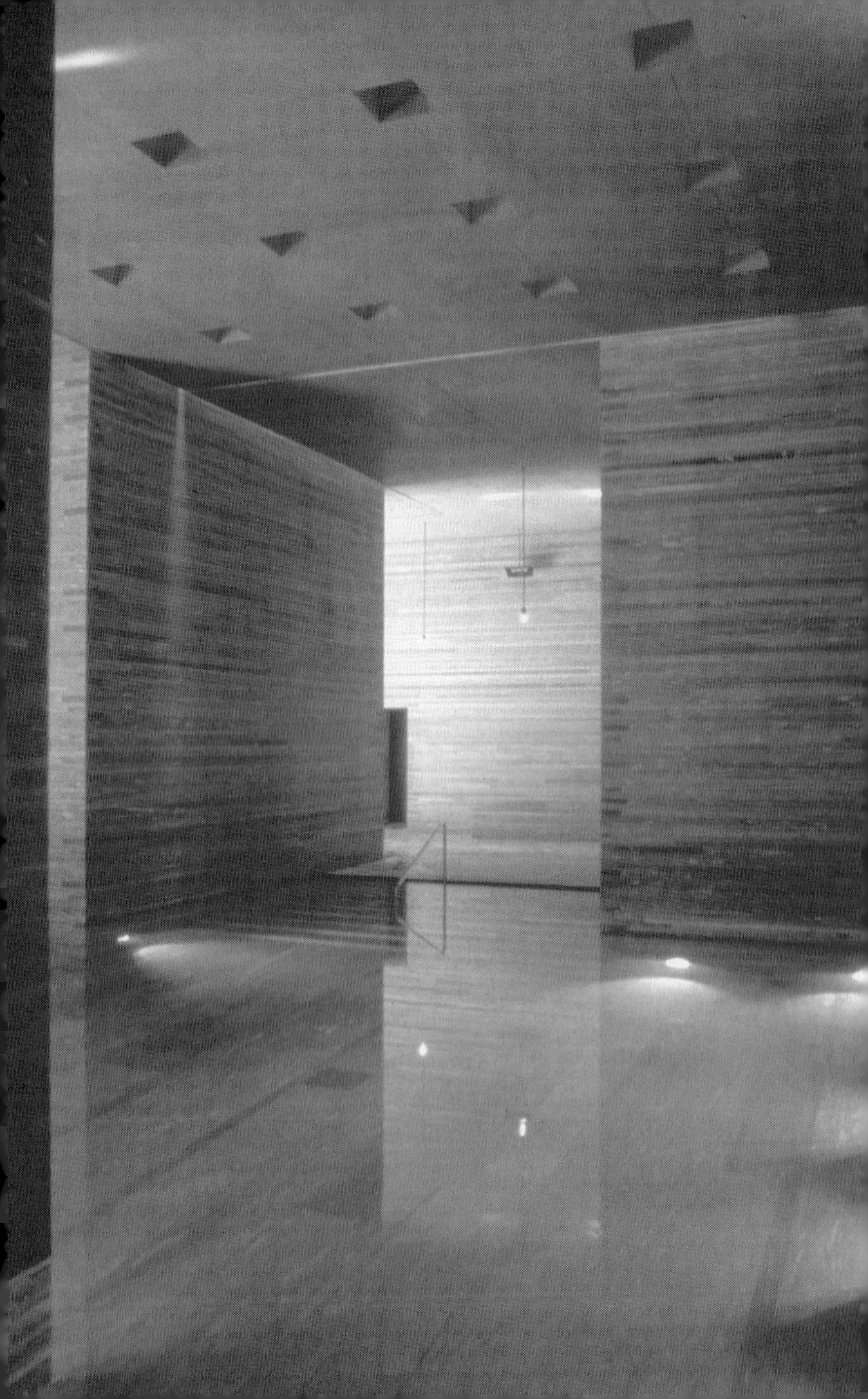

Attending

I cannot understand. Tendai claims that even the grass and trees will become enlightened. To me this seems very strange.'

'Of what use is it to discuss how grass and trees become enlightened?' asked Shinkan. 'The question is how you yourself can become so. Did you ever consider that?'

'I never thought of it in that way,' marveled the old man.

'Then go home and think it over,' finished Shinkan."[27]

Notes

1 Daisetz Suzuki, *Zen and Japanese Buddhism*, Tokyo: Japan Travel Bureau, 1970, p. 19.
2 According to art historian Arthur Fallico, in order to stimulate our response, the artwork must consider the nature of that response. Fallico writes that:

> I am unable to respond to just any thing. I must be capable of enacting the very stimulus to which I can respond. The thing is already, not *any* thing, but a very special kind of thing, as well as a particular thing, to which I have already accorded, by my very posture in purposing, the power to help me speak and to guide me in forming my very own words in speaking.

Arturo B. Fallico, *Art & Existentialism*, Englewood Cliffs, NJ: Prentice-Hall, 1962, p. 144.

3 Marc Treib, "Must Landscapes Mean?: Approaches to Significance in Recent Landscape Design," *Landscape Journal*, 14, 1, Spring, 1995, pp. 46–62.
4 See Ulrich Neisser, *Cognition and Reality: Principles and Implications of Cognitive Psychology*, San Francisco, CA: W. H. Freeman, 1976.
5 I must admit that I'm not a very spiritual type, so perhaps I am the wrong person to even address the topic – although my skepticism does provide me with some critical distance.
6 See Ella Forshay and Barbara Novak, *Intimate Friends: Thomas Cole, Asher B. Durand, William Cullen Bryant*, New York: The New York Historical Society, 2000.
7 See Kimberly Rorschach, *The Early Georgian Landscape Garden*, New Haven, CT: Yale Center for British Art, 1983, and John Dixon Hunt, *William Kent, Landscape Garden Designer*, London: A. Zwemmer, 1987. Hunt cautions against attributing the various elements of the Chiswick garden to Kent:

> Kent's involvement, then, at Chiswick is undeniable but still rather hazy as regards both dates and contributions. . . . Yet we must also recall that Kent's contribution to the main section of the gardens in the 1730s was the Italianate exedra, with its opening through a possibly Palladio-inspired screen of trees to the orangery garden . . . and perhaps the theatrical disposition of the Orangery . . . as well as the re-erection of the Inigo Jones gateway.
>
> (p. 70)

8 Burke's composition of the beautiful and the sublime, and the somewhat later addition of the picturesque, took place in England, where many have argued the true terror of the sublime and the real roughness of the picturesque never really existed, hence its creation in literature and its celebration in paintings by Claude and Salvador Rosa. See Edmund Burke, *A Philosophical Enquiry into the Origin and Our Ideas of the Sublime and Beautiful*, 1757, reprint Oxford: Oxford University Press, 1990. Barbara Novak, in her admirable study *Nature and Culture*, traces the changes in picturesque theory when it reappears in the United States. The great mountain ranges of the Rockies, the Adirondaks, the Smokeys, were truly sublime sights, matched in their grandeur by the terror of the great storms that swept across

1.11
Thermal baths, Vals, Switzerland
Peter Zumthor, 1996

their peaks and through their gorges. American picturesque theory was never quite the same, never quite as awe-ful as it was in England. But the Transcendentalists did think hard about the divine presence in the landscape, and its role in making us think about life and our place within it. Barbara Novak, *Nature and Culture: American Landscape and Painting 1825–1875*, New York: Oxford University Press, 1980.

9 The sculpture, which dates from the 1650s, is found in the church of Santa Maria della Vittoria in Rome.

10 Bernini created a sculptured picture of Teresa's Ecstasy, which was itself originally a mental picture as well as a powerful physical phenomenon. The "truth" of the vision is consequently conveyed on more than one level: ideally we enter the chapel, observe the *Ecstasy* – removed, white, mysteriously illuminated, but also very solid and realistic - and ultimately participate in a religious experience of our own, aided by the mystic concretion hovering before our eyes.

Howard Hibbard, *Bernini*, Harmondsworth: Penguin Books, 1965, p. 138. Hibbard provides a detailed discussion of the statue and its architectural setting on pp.128–39.

11 See Marguerite Fellows Melcher, *The Shaker Adventure*, Cleveland, OH: The Press of Case Western Reserve, 1968; and Edward Deming Andrews, *The People Called Shakers*, 1953, reprint, New York: Dover Publications, 1963.

12 On Shaker furniture see Edward Deming Andrews and Faith Andrews, *Shaker Furniture: The Craftsmanship of an American Communal Sect*, 1937, New York: Dover Publications, 1964; Edward Deming Andrews and Faith Andrews, *Religion in Wood: A Book of Shaker Furniture*, Bloomington, IN: Indiana University Press, 1966; and John Shea, *The American Shakers and their Furniture*, New York: Van Nostrand Reinhold, 1971.

13 I'd prefer to think of an *advance* toward contemplation rather than a *retreat*, but language isn't with me on this one.

14 For an overview of the history of Japanese gardens see Lorraine Kuck, *The World of the Japanese Garden*, Tokyo: Weatherhill, 1968; Teiji Itoh, *The Japanese Garden*, New Haven, CT: Yale University Press, 1972; Günther Nitschke, *Japanese Gardens*, Cologne: Benedikt Taschen, 1992; and Marc Treib and Ron Herman, *A Guide to the Gardens of Kyoto*, Revised edition, Tokyo: Kodansha International, 2003.

15 Although its official name is Saiho-ji, the garden is commonly referred to as Kokedera, or the "Moss Temple."

16 Musô Soseki, translated by W. S. Merwin and Sôiku Shigematsu, *Sun at Midnight: Poems and Sermons*, San Francisco, CA: North Point Press, 1989, p. 32.

17 Claudel served in the French diplomatic corps in Japan in the 1920s. Quoted in Fallico, op. cit. p. 32.

18 This was the genius of our ancestors, that by cutting off the light from this empty space they imparted to the world of shadows that formed there a quality of mystery and depth superior to that of any wall planting or ornament. The technique seems simple, but was by no means so simply achieved. We can imagine with little difficulty what extraordinary pains were taken with each invisible detail – the placement of the window in the shelving recess, the depth of the crossbeam, the height of the threshold. But for me the most exquisite touch is the pale white glow of the shoji in the study bay; I need only pause before it and I forget the passage of time.

Jun'ichiro Tanizaki, translated by Thomas J. Harper and Edward G. Seidensticker, *In Praise of Shadows*, New Haven, CT: Leete's Island Books, 1977, pp. 20–21. See also Okakura Kakuzo, *The Book of Tea*, 1906, Rutland, VT: Charles Tuttle, 1956. In describing the tea room Okakura writes:

> It is an Abode of Fancy inasmuch as it is an ephemeral structure built to house a poetic impulse. It is an Abode of Vacancy inasmuch as it is devoid of ornamentation except for what may be placed in it to satisfy some aesthetic need of the moment. It is an Abode of the Unsymmetrical inasmuch as it is consecrated to the worship of the Imperfect, purposely leaving some thing unfinished for the play of the imagination to complete.
>
> (pp. 54–5)

19 Among the numerous books about James Turrell's work are Peter Noever, (ed.), *James Turrell: The Other Horizon*, Vienna: MAK, and Ostfildern-Ruit, Germany: Cantz Verlag, 1999; Richard Andrews, (ed.), *James Turrell: Sensing Space*, Seattle, WA: Henry Art Gallery, University of Washington, 1992; and *James Turrell: Spirit and Light*, Houston, TX: Contemporary Arts Museum, 1998.

20 On Irwin's thinking and work see Robert Irwin, *Being and Circumstance: Notes Towards a Conditional Art*, Larkspur, CA: Lapis Press, 1985, and Lawrence Weschler, *Seeing is Forgetting the Name of The Thing One Sees*, Berkeley, CA: University of California Press, 1982.

21 James Turrell in an interview with Jim Lennox, in Claudia Giannini, (ed.), *James Turrell: Into the Light*, Pittsburgh: The Mattress Factory, 2003, p. 47.

22 Burke, op. cit., p. 74.

23 Ibid, p. 45.

24 Pauline Kael, quoted in Annette Michelson, "Eco and Narcissus," *Artforum*, March 2002, p. 128.

25 Thomas Struth, "Thomas Struth talks about his 'Paradise Series,'" *Artforum*, May 2002, p. 151.

26 In *Art & Existentialism*, Arturo B. Fallico writes:

> [T]he inspection of the object must lead back to the intending observer whose thought about it defines the object he is observing. It necessarily follows that the description of an object must disclose something about the subject, even something of his very condition of being.
>
> (p. 8)

27 Paul Reps, compiler, *Zen Flesh, Zen Bones*, New York: Doubleday, not dated, pp. 42–43.

On the transcendent in landscapes of contemplation

Heinrich Hermann

Introduction

For as long as humans have designed their world, they have produced some exceptional environments that stand out by not merely meeting physical/utilitarian needs, but by addressing the plane of higher human aspirations – the emotional, intellectual, and spiritual levels. These exemplary works have profoundly inspired the human spirit by effectively fostering individual and communal contemplation. The twentieth century too produced exemplary works that have encouraged what Emerson has called "an original relation to the universe."[1] Both as a practicing architect and a teacher of design, I have long been interested in whether masterful works of the near and far past could yield insights (including underlying principles, strategies and devices) that might enable creative individuals to design works for today that can similarly move and spiritually enrich people. In the course of my research of representative works from many periods of history spanning Western, Eastern, and "primitive" cultures, and of the human response to these works, I came to realize that an environment's contemplation-inducing, poetic/spiritual dimension is ultimately its capacity for making a visitor/user's concerns of day-to-day reality recede temporarily into the background in favor of an openness to contemplative beholding. The ensuing processes of contemplation effectively cause one to step outside one's typical frames of reference of time, space and self, and can lead to a greater feeling of being in the present and partaking in a greater harmony of all being. In that, they are comparable to the early stages of using mind-stilling techniques from meditative traditions, such as a mantra, or tying one's attention to the breath, all of which are intended to "trigger" the mind into entering a meditative state.

A growing body of research indicates that the ability to enter a meditative state and to reach the heightened awareness resulting from it is an integral part of the human make-up, even though it is dormant in most persons. This is confirmed by a comparison of mystical paths of the East and West and of other meditative traditions throughout history,[2] including contemporary, de-spiritualized clinical versions, such as Dr. Herbert Benson's "Relaxation Response", or biofeedback.[3] Medical studies during recent decades scientifically demonstrated for the first time the beneficial physiological changes and measurable health benefits resulting from the use of mind-stilling techniques[4] and studies are increasingly establishing direct correlation between health and happiness. Research on the "psychophysical immune system" suggests that our psychological well-being directly influences our physical health: each emotion actually has a different chemical fingerprint and there is communication between emotions and the immune system, via neuropeptides. This research indicates a "wisdom of the body" which registers and immediately responds to stimuli before the brain can consciously grasp a situation.[5]

All of the meditative/contemplative traditions employ what I call "trigger devices" (breath, mantra, etc.) and I began to recognize a parallel to the spiritually charged spaces I was interested in. I found that these spaces' capacity for eliciting emotive/spiritual responses was traceable to a comparable presence of "trigger strategies and devices" that I will discuss in detail in this essay. Similarly, important human rituals and commemorative human activities rely on related strategies to affect us cognitively/emotionally.[6]

All the environments I studied in this investigation had the capacity for inducing silence in receptive visitors. The importance of silence has been explored in meditative traditions of all historic periods and geographic regions over thousands of years.[7] In all of these traditions there are general steps recommended to induce and maintain a meditative state.[8] Aside from the critically important mind-set of the individual,[9] silence is part of the favorable "outer" conditions sought or recommended. Silence here is to be understood not only in the acoustic sense, but as the absence of all distracting sensual stimuli. The absence of overly distracting sensual stimulation is of great importance since meditation aims at "disconnecting" the brain from sensory impulses, freeing it for inner perception and communion.

37

Contemplation and reflection are cousins of meditation. While they are not carried out with the single-mindedness and "one-pointedness"[9] a which characterize meditation, they too depend on and benefit from an environment that may contain a suitable level of supportive stimuli, while shielding one from distracting or otherwise adverse stimulation. From the role silence plays in meditation, one may conclude that it naturally fosters contemplative beholding by freeing the mind's capacity for being fully present to what is at hand.

I propose that this silence-inducing capacity could be interpreted as a visceral, unmediated response to certain stimuli encountered within the environments that absorb one's undivided attention – while being perceived as peaceful and soothing. This perspective borrows from the emerging medical notion of "a wisdom of the body." Another perspective borrows from the medically demonstrable psycho-physiological changes that occur during the initial stages of using a mind-stilling technique, where beneficial psychical and physiological responses are triggered by certain stimuli within the environments. In both interpretations a *tabula rasa* and silence are induced, and become foundations for contemplative beholding. Memory plays an important role in both interpretations: memories of soothing, peaceful states within one's current life experience – ready to be triggered – and memories of fundamental life situations of the collective human past. The potential for eliciting a contemplative response is available to environments both religious and secular in function.

I have identified three paradigms for how a contemplative state may be elicited by an environment, and illustrated each through an exemplary masterwork of the twentieth century. Each case study has been analyzed in terms of its strategies for inducing contemplation. The paradigms are illustrated by three environments (each with characteristics of sanctuary) where conscious awareness of spatial and temporal frames of existence is induced in human beings, along with the potential for an expanded understanding of the self. Respectively, they move from the "natural" to the "created sanctuary," as described by Gerardus van der Leeuw (and cover both ends of the continuum of the architecture-nature dialogue): the all "natural" versus the all "human created," and the middle ground in the form of the well blended "natural/created" sanctuary.

In paradigm I, a perceptual linkage between the human and the cosmos is facilitated through a balanced "natural/created" sanctuary. As a model, I used the Salk Institute for Biological Studies in La Jolla, California by Louis I. Kahn (design and construction from 1959–65). In this setting, two parallel laboratory wings separated by a courtyard (the created, finite part) frame a slice of the coastline, the vast ocean and the cosmic panorama (the natural world of seemingly infinite expanse). Contemplation is induced through the juxtaposition of human life (finite, fragile, yet mentally capable of boundlessness) and nature, with its serene beauty, vast scale, and occasional awe-inspiring force defiant of human control. Both nature and architecture form the frame and context for the perception and experience of the other.

In paradigm II, strategically inward-oriented built space is shaped into a "created" sanctuary. The Monastery-Church of Sainte-Marie de la Tourette near Lyon, France by Le Corbusier (design and construction from 1953–60) was my model. Contemplation is induced – beyond the religious program – through the inward orientation of the space, the allusion to human ritual activity, the use of the built environment as a datum for reflecting the cyclical nature of time, and the absence of any distracting visual, acoustic or symbolic stimuli.

In paradigm III, archetypal cultural symbols are employed, in a "natural" sanctuary, exemplified by the Woodland Cemetery in Stockholm, Sweden by Gunnar Asplund and Sigurd Lewerentz (design and construction 1915–40). Contemplation is triggered by external stimuli that invoke memories of essential life situations of the individual and collective human past. Archetypal design elements such as: forest sanctuary, thresholds, open air altars, sacred mountain, and *axis mundi*, speak directly, across distances of time and space, to the human understanding of the temporality and continuity of life, and our essential link to the natural world.

The contemplative state triggered in an encounter depends both on one's degree of receptivity to the spiritual/poetic realms and on the depth and duration of one's experience in these realms.[10] Each paradigm describes an environment that may enable a visitor (to varying degrees) to transcend, gradually (not necessarily sequentially), one's perception of the finiteness of space, the finite time-frame of one's life span, and the tendency to center on one's own self.

In keeping with this book's focus on the contemplative landscape, I will discuss insights only from the Salk Institute and the Woodland Cemetery and the corresponding paradigms I and III. As a conclusion, I offer a reflection on ways of "imbuing" landscapes with a transcendent dimension – so they truly can become landscapes of contemplation.

At the seam between the finite and the infinite: Louis I. Kahn's Salk Institute

A famous story recounts the opening of a newly completed tea room and garden by the Japanese tea master Rikyu. The invited guests came with great expectations, due both to Rikyu's famed ingenuity and the setting overlooking the Pacific Ocean. Upon arrival, the guests were astonished to find the anticipated ocean views blocked by densely planted trees. The mystery was lifted only after they proceeded over the stepping stones to the water basin for the ritual cleansing prior to entering the tea room. As the guests bent over to lift a dipper full of water, they were granted an unexpectedly memorable experience: during that humble bow, they saw both the dipper full of water in their hand, and through a small opening in the vegetation, a perfect view of the vast ocean. In a profound inner reorientation they realized the similarity between the dipper of water relative to the unfathomable sea and their own smallness relative to the universe.

The story of Rikyu's sixteenth-century tea garden demonstrates one of the most inspiring potentials of design: to disclose perceivable links between a human being's spatially and temporally finite existence on earth and the unfathomable vast context of the universe beyond. Perceiving this interrelation can invoke a contemplative state that may, depending on the length and depth of the experience, lead one toward transcending one's customary notions of the finiteness of space, the finite time frame of one's life span, and one's focus on the self. In Rikyu's garden, that experience results from the carefully orchestrated, precise alignment of a visitor, during the ritual cleansing preceding the tea ceremony, with the (only then available) "glimpse of infinity" – the view of the sea.

The biological research laboratory that Louis I. Kahn built four centuries later for Jonas Salk (who invented the first effective polio vaccine) in La Jolla, California, is also on a site overlooking the Pacific Ocean.[11] This project suggests a strong inner relationship to the work of the Japanese master, across time, space and cultures. This affinity is due not to similarities in form, style, or ritual, but is rather rooted in the fact that both environments have similarly transcended the utilitarian/functional level of the task at hand (in Kahn's case to design a biological research laboratory and the "finiteness" of this respective setting) and to facilitate a feeling of connection between visitors and the cosmos. While Salk, who was deeply concerned with overcoming the split between modern science and the humanities, did not explicitly ask Kahn for a contemplative space (although he discussed with him organizational ideas observed in the monastery of San Francesco in Assissi), he was drawn to Kahn as a kindred spirit that could meet the challenge of creating a place that would both excel in science and foster exchanges with cultural figures. (He wanted the setting to be worthy of entertaining Picasso.)[12] As the design evolved, a balance was achieved between the need for places to foster concentrated thinking in solitude, and the need to foster interaction.

On the Transcendent

Experiencing the Institute

Approach

The nearly 100,000 square feet Salk Institute (this is its original form preceding the mid-1990s expansion) is located on 27 acres of the Torrey Pines Mesa half an hour north of San Diego. Kahn divided the campus into three parallel zones: the main parking lot, a grove of eucalyptus and olive trees, and the Institute itself, consisting principally of two east–west oriented laboratory wings linked by an open courtyard. For the purposes of our discussion, I will focus primarily on the courtyard.[13]

After parking, one passes through one of five openings in a waist-high concrete wall and enters a tranquil eucalyptus and olive grove, thus leaving behind the world of the highway. Surrounded by shade, bird song and various fragrances, one meanders gently upward along one of several paths, all converging near the main entrance where a flight of four travertine steps takes one to an iron-gated, travertine-paved, elevated landing anchored by two halves of a geometrically planted orange grove (Fig. 2.1). Here, visitors pause in astonishment as they glimpse the courtyard for the first time.

The courtyard

This threshold marks the beginning of a realm distinctly outside one's usual references. Five travertine steps lead down to an austere, yet intimate,

2.1
Salk Institute, near La Jolla, California. The access path and grove leads to the entrance to the courtyard – at the far right of the photo
Louis Kahn, 1959–65

travertine-paved courtyard of 85 × 31 yards that is flanked on its north and south by four story high structures (Fig. 2.2.). After a glance around, one's mind is powerfully pulled out to the Pacific Ocean where a limitless sky seems to rise and vault back over the courtyard. One's mind gradually returns to the courtyard to observe in greater detail what it finds. As one steps down, a low travertine bench extends nearly across the courtyard's entire width. While the courtyard appears completely open, the bench allows only one's eyes to roam freely through the courtyard and beyond, while forcing the body to turn either left or right. Before turning to enter the courtyard however, one's attention is captivated by a square travertine fountain, where a narrow water channel emerges; called the "River of Life," (Fig. 2.2, 2.3. and Plate 3) it runs axially toward the ocean and, surprisingly, seems to feed the ocean – a parallel to Rikyu's dipper full of water and the vast sea in the distance. The plaza's carefully proportioned travertine paving has narrow bands moving toward the ocean (the central one split apart to frame the water channel) and rectangular transversal slabs filling the resulting fields. Narrow open joints allow the water to drain quickly following the frequent rainfalls. Upon finally entering the courtyard itself from either corner, one is richly rewarded by an experience of the perfectly symmetrical space in dynamic perspective – ever-changing as one's body moves. Evoking a quality of silent presence, the architectural wings seem to observe the gentle murmuring of the rivulet of water in the center.

2.2
Salk Institute, near La Jolla, California. Courtyard with "River of Life" fountain in the foreground
Louis Kahn, 1959–65

2.3
Salk Institute, near La Jolla, California. The courtyard's "River of Life" fountain
Louis Kahn, 1959–65

The laboratory complex

Upon entering the courtyard, the Institute's organization begins to unfold. Five towers face each other laterally across the courtyard. Forming four-story high porticos of scientists' studies, their ground floor has passages aligned like arcades (interrupted by the gaps between the towers), while their second and fourth levels (which are offset from the laboratory levels) contain studies. An open portico occupies the third floor of each tower (aligned with a laboratory level) for chance encounters amongst Salk's peripatetic scientists, for whose use Kahn provided slate chalkboards on the walls. Each study has lateral views across the courtyard – through windows in teak panels – but also direct ocean views through triangular niches that protrude into the courtyard. Pairs of 45° angled (toward the ocean) wall "fins" stand rhythmically on either side of the courtyard and support the triangular niches. They resemble theater props, and the ones toward the land are always wider. The resulting rhythm of staggered pairs of concrete walls and the resulting volumes cause a sense of pulsating motion toward the horizon. While they allow free lateral movement into the courtyard from both sides, they imply a movement toward the horizon with their ocean-facing angle.

Lateral staircases connect each tower with the laboratory zone and flank two-story deep sunken courtyards – providing sufficient air and light to the lowest lab level in addition to the two above ground. The laboratories themselves are glazed from floor to ceiling on all sides. The complex interplay of all these elements across the central courtyard and up to the sky provides for deeply satisfying, ever enticing visual/spatial experiences.

Design strategies for transcending finiteness

Transcendence of the utilitarian approach to a research environment
An extraordinary journey has taken one from an asphalt parking lot off the highway through a lush grove and green lawn, to an entry threshold of immaculate travertine to the culmination of the journey in an oasis of silence – a special if not sacred realm where the focus of attention is the wordless dialogue between oneself, the finiteness of the courtyard and the seeming infinity of the sky above and ocean beyond. One inevitably wonders what gives this environment its overwhelming capacity for eliciting a contemplative response.

In contrast to many design projects that understand a building program in narrow, functional/utilitarian terms and see little value in making one's surroundings uplifting, the Salk Institute was from the outset conceived in much broader terms. Jonas Salk was a uniquely enlightened client who desired for his intended laboratory complex nothing less than the reintegration of the sciences and humanities, where an active cultural program could enrich the work of the scientists and encounters with cultural figures would be fostered. For Kahn, providing a laboratory complex that worked well would have meant nothing had he not been able to carry the project far towards the realm of the immeasurable.

Transcending space through perceivable links between human and cosmos

The experience of Rikyu's tea garden may be considered as poetically/spiritually deeply moving. And if one considers the entire surface of the earth as a similar potential zone of intersection between the physically and temporally finite human existence with the seeming infinity of the cosmos, then one senses hidden latently in every building task the possibility of disclosing phenomenally perceivable links between human and cosmic realms. Like Rikyu's garden, the Salk Institute masterfully demonstrates a capacity for disclosing this poetry.

One's feeling of interconnectedness with the cosmos at the Salk rests principally on three components. First, the finite receptacle of the courtyard is the vehicle for the viewer to understand the seeming infinity and significance of the ocean and the cosmic panorama. Second, the courtyard seems to function as an auditorium, and the framed portion of the ocean and the sky are the corresponding "cosmic stage" on which atmospheric dramas are continuously performed. Third, expanses of space and the passage of time are multifariously registered through the movements of the sun, moon, stars, the magical sunsets, thunder and lightning and other phenomena, both agitated and serene (Plate 3).

The courtyard's strategic, partly introverted, configuration of a canyon-like view corridor excludes all distracting visual and acoustical stimuli, so one's attention is free to perceive the cosmic panorama in its daily and seasonal unfolding. The courtyard's alignment with the rising and setting sun intimately connects any person at the Salk with solar and lunar movement, registered dramatically through the passage of light and shadows along the concrete walls and paved surfaces. The ocean's vastness seems to be fed by the smallness of the water channel, the symbolic "spinal cord" of the complex. The water channel seems to merge with the sky and thus to dematerialize the travertine floor, revealing an unexpectedly cosmic depth hidden in the stone's solidity.

To privilege the courtyard as the place from which to experience the cosmic panorama and avoiding a feeling of emotional numbness resulting from overexposure, longitudinal views towards the ocean are blocked

2.4
Salk Institute, near La Jolla, California. Upper level arcade, showing blocked longitudinal views
-Louis Kahn, 1959–65

on all major circulation paths, on all levels (Fig. 2.4). The view from the courtyard to the ocean is perspectively amplified by the pairs of 45° angled walls, which also channel lateral movement from the labs to the courtyard and from the longitudinal paths towards the center.

Transcending time

The openness of the courtyard allows one to observe the movement of the sun across the sky directly. It is a subtle mechanism for registering the passage of time via constantly moving shadows cast by the angled side walls onto the travertine floor. The entire complex interacts with light – receiving, reflecting, registering it, and casting shadows – making one acutely aware of the passage of time and its cyclical nature.

"Arresting" time
The courtyard's absence of distracting visual and acoustical stimuli quickly puts one's mind at ease, shedding extraneous thoughts and mundane concerns. One's mind is "arrested" through a concentrated, contemplative attention on this experience. In his book *Reverie and Cosmos*, the philosopher Gaston Bachelard speaks about the human relation to the world via the capacities of perception and comprehension opened up through reverie:

> When a dreamer of reveries has swept aside all "preoccupations" which were encumbering his everyday life . . . that dreamer feels a being opening within him. Suddenly such a dreamer is a *world dreamer*. He opens himself to the world, and the world opens itself to him. . . . Time is suspended. . . . The World is so majestic that nothing any longer happens there; the World reposes in its tranquility.[14]

Bachelard could have described the inner reactions of someone experiencing the Salk Institute for the first time. The strong impact of being there may cause one to contemplate fundamentally the nature of one's interrelatedness with the world and one's fellow human beings. Deeply absorbed in reflection, one may even forget, for a while, who one is, and the narrower world of the day-to-day, in which one's life is also anchored, beholding, as one does, the wider context of one's existence. In Bachelard's words: "[C]osmic reverie causes us to inhabit a world. It gives the dreamer the impression of a home . . . in the imagined universe."[15] In addition to hearing the sounds of the fountain, viewing the ocean and the sky may unlock deeper levels of consciousness: "There is still water at the bottom of all memory" which "integrates all things, the universe and its dreamer. In this union, the soul meditates."[16]

Resisting time, eluding time, contemporaneity and timelessness
Protecting its fortress-like interior with its other-worldly focus on time and space (especially via transcending expanses of ocean and sky), the Salk Institute "resists" the influences of time. Kahn actively pursued a duality of the contemporary and the timeless in his work through exploring what is possible at a given time (the very activity of biological research and its mission to stay at the cutting edge of biological science render it perpetually contemporaneous or ahead of its time) and simultaneously linking his work with deep-seated memories of millennia past (Ancient Egypt and Rome, medieval Islam, the Enlightenment period), expressive of what he often called "origins." Kahn wrote, "The reason for man's living is to express. And art is his medium. . . . Man's works belong to eternity. Not men as living things; they go but their works remain."[17]

The courtyard's archaic character, the rhetoric of the materials employed, their scale, and the degree of abstraction in the volumes and overall form, remove the Salk Institute from easy classification and categorization. While the sophistication of the poured-in-place concrete and its glass and steel place it firmly within the twentieth century, the complex's "outside of regular time" quality defies its belonging to any historic period. The building does not reveal its purpose or whether it is a public or hermetic structure. It evokes both memories of ancient architecture and inklings of future ages.

Transcending the focus on one's own self

From a general contemplation of time and space – as triggered by the courtyard – it is but a short leap to picturing how someone else has stood in the same spot where you are standing, with the same thoughts and feelings, years before, or how years from now numberless others will stand there with identical reactions. This would be true for lay people and scientists alike, whose knowledge of their own disciplines illustrates how they are standing on the shoulders of giants before them. Such chains of reflection may lead one to a ritual beholding of one's own selfhood and humanity, to comprehending one's integrally partaking in all of humankind, of the past, present and future, and recognizing the nobility of serving the common good of all – one's "larger self."

The individual, the collective, and the world
The philosopher Israel Scheffler sheds light on the cognitive processes that occur during one's relating to the world which Gaston Bachelard had reflected on via reverie. Scheffler describes the capacity of repeated performances of a rite to influence the mind of a performer, his concepts and sensibilities, via his contact with the symbolized properties.[18] While the beholding of self and

Heinrich Hermann

an individual relation to the world, as previously described, constitute rites in Scheffler's use of the word – his comments on the mind-influencing capacity of rituals should hold true for the chains of cognition during active sensing of one's embeddedness within the wider cosmos as well – which, especially through repetition, become ritual in character. He writes:

> [T]he performers of past ritual [performances] constitute a body of actors to which present performers relate themselves through reenactment and, hence, indirectly to one another. The community thus defined bears not only common bonds to the past but also common orientations in the present and outlooks for the future. Thus, an organization of time, as well as of the space occupied by a historical community, is facilitated. . . .[19]

Awareness of the cosmic frame of one's existence also makes one recognize one's place within the human chain and the shared existential condition across time and space. The theoretical interchangeability of what is "auditorium" and what is "stage" in this "cosmic theater," of beholding and being beheld, probably adds to the described chain of reflections. A person standing in the courtyard and beholding the cosmic panorama is in the auditorium, beholding the cosmic stage. If the person is religious, he or she will likely enjoy the thought of being watched by God, and feel like an actor on stage. The courtyard actually functions as an auditorium for persons in the northern and southern laboratory wings who can behold what occurs there. Conversely, the transparent glazing around the laboratories renders these simultaneously a stage when viewed from the auditorium of the courtyard.

Transcending physical reality to reveal its latent spiritual dimension
One of Kahn's goals for the Salk Institute (as is true of his later works) was for it to disclose another reality, which he alluded to as the "immeasurable". He expressed his deep belief in the immeasurable – the transcendent nature of architecture – in his writings as well as lectures, such as the one given in 1969 in Zürich, which he ended by telling the following story:

> There was a Priestess who was going through her garden in spring, and of course it was a glorious day. As she went through her garden, observing everything, and came to the threshold of her house, and there she stopped in admiration – standing at the threshold, looking within. And her servant-in-waiting came over to her, saying "Mistress, Mistress. Look without, and see the

wonders that God has created." And the mistress said, "Yes, yes, but look within and see God." In other words, what man has made is the very, very manifestation of God.[20]

The Salk Institute is among the rare works that, through their way of making us look without, induce us into contemplatively seeing within.

Nature and archetypal symbols: Asplund and Lewerentz's Woodland Cemetery in Stockholm

In the presence of nature a wild delight runs through the man, in spite of real sorrows. . . . In the woods, is perpetual youth. . . . In the Woods, we return to reason and faith. There I feel that nothing can befal me in life, – no disgrace, no calamity . . . which nature cannot repair. Standing on the bare ground – my head bathed by the blithe air, and uplifted into infinite space – all mean egotism vanishes. I become a transparent eye-ball. I am nothing. I see all. The currents of the Universal Being circulate through me; I am part or particle of God.[21]

Ralph Waldo Emerson

Emerson here speaks of the tremendous regenerative power that nature holds for the receptive human spirit, of nature's healing effect and capacity for awakening slumbering memories of the very inner human core, which transcends the narrow, habit-bound focus on day-to-day reality, and finds respite in far loftier planes. The Woodland Cemetery, named for the pine forest in which it was built, is not nature in a virgin state as were Emerson's woods, but is a "natural" sanctuary nonetheless, and elicits reactions similar to those described by the transcendentalist-philosopher from Concord.

The Woodland Cemetery came into being through altering an existing forest landscape surrounded by agricultural land. Carefully selected and interrelated design elements were inserted within it, to arrive at a symbolically charged, nearly all "natural" landscape. These elements serve not only pragmatic utilitarian functions, but also transcendence-inducing, spirit-uplifting ones. Beyond primarily accommodating funeral rites and serving as a burial ground for the greater Stockholm community, the cemetery's landscape and the process of perceiving its elements has a specific kind of impact on a person's mental state. The cemetery can induce fundamental reflections on the temporality and meaning of one's existence; on humanity's proper place within nature and its interrelation to other life forms; on humankind as

Heinrich Hermann

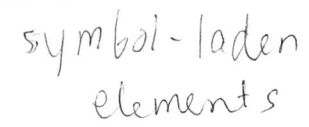

a continuous chain; on one's interrelation to fellow human beings of the past, present and future (both known and unknown); and on the human spirit's embeddedness within the much larger frame of existence, the cosmos.

The most important contributors to the cemetery's capacity for spiritual transcendence are its symbol-laden elements, such as the Meditation Grove, the open-air altar with its associated ceremonial plaza, the Monument Hall, and the forest tombs, all of which generate rich associations for a visitor. These elements were deliberately selected and their interrelation finely honed in the evolution of the design. I shall focus on the most important physical and symbolic features one perceives while walking through the landscape, on how the cemetery's built forms and the landscape complement one another, and how meanings are embodied and a contemplative state is elicited in visitors.

The Woodland Cemetery resulted from a 1915 international design competition to expand an existing cemetery south of Stockholm, won by the team of Gunnar Asplund and Sigurd Lewerentz. The competition followed a period of gradual removal of control over burials exerted earlier on by the Lutheran Church, and marked the search for a fitting new form of secularized burial form.[22] Asplund and Lewerentz's genius lay in utilizing the latent spiritual character of the existing landscape and amplifying it by making the forest the principal resting place. They proposed to sensitively insert the needed buildings and road network, and included several primary armatures facilitating orientation. Their proposal was enthusiastically received and subsequently realized between roughly 1918 and 1940.

Experiencing the cemetery

Located six kilometers south of Stockholm's center in the suburb of Enskede, the 90-hectare cemetery is easily reachable from anywhere within the city. Its western edge borders a major north-south thoroughfare and it is served by a subway stop at its northwestern corner. While people approaching by car often enter at a western gate along the thoroughfare, large numbers come by subway and enter from the north via a gate along the cemetery's principal access road that separates it from the older cemetery.

Approach
A tree-lined street cuts through the surrounding land, held back on both sides by massive retaining walls clad in ashlar stone. This wall prevents views into the cemetery, except for a large semi-circular forecourt directly across the narrow entrance to the old cemetery. Before following the entry drive south into the cemetery, one sees a Doric entablature on four columns protruding from the ashlar wall, revealing a recessed fieldstone wall over which water trickles. It evokes perhaps tears of bereavement or Orpheus' songs of

mourning for Eurydice that had once caused even stones to shed tears. This fountain symbolically marks the beginning of a special, sacred realm.

The Central Clearing: a void of natural and created nature
As a pedestrian, one has time to take in the quiet panorama of the clearing – this first place of repose (Plate 1). Several primary features emerge from this gently ascending, large open lawn. A path of rough flagstones set into the lawn leads to a low wall (demarcating a columbarium, a walled urn-garden), and uphill to the massive granite cross on the horizon (the Way of the Cross). Behind this, one sees the front of a large columnar hall facing the clearing (Monument Hall). In the distance, a flight of stairs leads up a ridge, crowned by a square shaped grove of trees (the Meditation Grove), surrounded by the access road. Beyond the cross, a silhouette of dense treetops announces the presence of a forest on lower ground. Within the clearing's perfect equilibrium one recognizes a structure of movement indicators (the Way of the Cross, the access road winding to the right, and the stairs leading to the Meditation Grove), in dialogue with points of stasis (the small plaza near the entrance, Monument Hall, and the Meditation Grove). One perceives an interweaving of architectural and natural features, exemplified by the "rational" shapes of the columbarium wall, the columnar porch of Monument Hall, the cross, and the architectural, geometric formation of nature – the perfect square of 12 weeping elm trees at the Meditation Grove, the line of linden trees along the columbarium wall, and the blending of architecture and nature found in the steps cut into the Meditation Grove hill – and finally the "rational" act of keeping the "natural" central clearing free of trees or tombs (Fig. 2.5).

The clearing's scale renders human beings small, without dwarfing them, but paradoxically also makes them feel welcome and at home. Instinctively one senses it to be a space of repose that should be occupied not physically but through one's mind. Without having yet actually seen a single grave, one recognizes this void as the symbolic heart of the cemetery. Ever since approaching it one has felt a spreading "inner silence" that slowly creates a peaceful, reflective mood before moving onward.

The Way of the Cross
The Way of the Cross strongly entices one forward. It is the principal pedestrian access path to the chapels of the cremation complex (Fig. 2.6). To de-emphasize the cross's specific Christian connotations (it was added in a later phase), Asplund abstracted it enough to symbolize a more universal anthropomorphic image. Facing the main entrance, the cross stands stoically as a forceful symbolic marker within the lawn. Its outstretched "arms" mark the east-west plane that separates the columbarium from the precinct of the

1 Entry Threshold	7 Lily Pond
2 Central Clearing	8 Catafalque
3 Way of the Cross	9 Meditation Grove
4 Columbarium	10 Cremation Chapels
5 The Cross	11 Way of Seven Wells
6 Monument Hall	

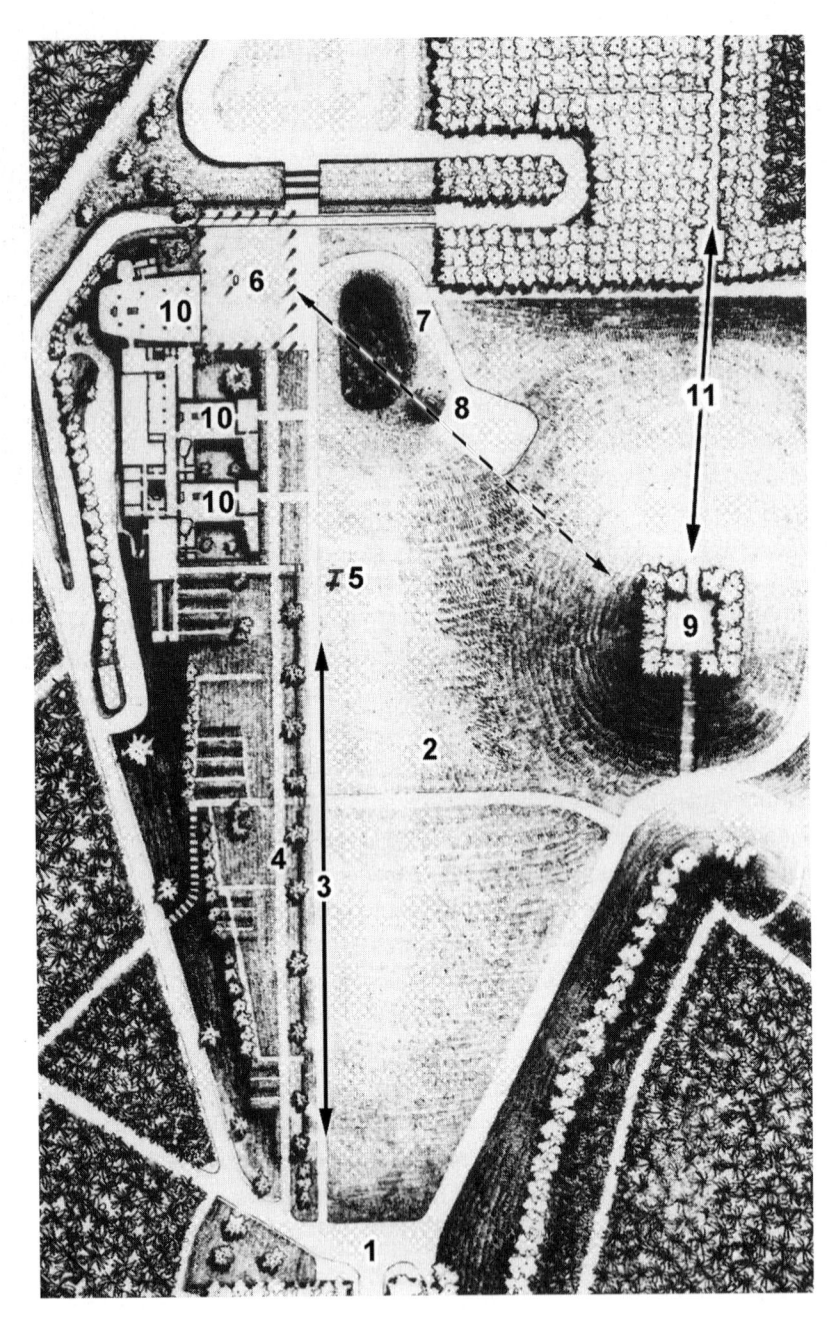

2.5
Woodland Cemetery, Enskede, Sweden. Entry landscape showing axial relationships between paths, Monument Hall, Lily Pond, Catafalque, and Meditation Grove
Gunnar Asplund and Sigurd Lewerentz, 1915–1940

**2.6
Woodland
Cemetery,
Enskede, Sweden.
The Way of the
Cross, with the
columbarium to
the left**
Gunnar Asplund
and Sigurd
Lewerentz,
1915–1940

three cremation chapels (and the large porch-like Monument Hall), while its "torso" reaches high and visually interconnects earth and sky, bridging them across the horizon line. Symbolically, the two arms of the cross also point respectively to the skyward meditation grove and the earthward columbarium, and to sunrise and sunset. The path's north-south orientation on the eastern side of the large clearing provides exposure to sunshine from late morning to sunset and offers a solemn, uplifting experience. Laid out as a distinct place just north of the cremation chapels, the columbarium is enclosed by low walls that contain a series of taller, east-west-oriented urn walls arranged in parallel groups of three or four. The spaces between these walls are narrow and intimate, but in visiting an urn-grave one simultaneously perceives the vastness of the central clearing, visible just across the low wall and the Way of the Cross.

The crematorium complex, including the Chapels of Faith, Hope, and the Holy Cross, and Monument Hall
When Asplund was awarded the commission in 1935 to build a large chapel (to accommodate 300 people) and two smaller ones (for 100 persons each), each capable of accommodating up to five ceremonies a day, he placed the complex on the eastern side of the large clearing (as previously planned with Lewerentz) and utilized the slope to insert a service level for all cremation functions underneath and beyond the chapels.

The Way of the Cross effectively culminates at Monument Hall which abuts the Chapel of the Holy Cross, the largest chapel. One passes first through a garden court north of Monument Hall, and enters the chapel from the north through a waiting room; after a funeral service, mourners leave it axially in a westerly direction, onto the porch of Monument Hall. The western façades of the Chapels of Hope and Faith to the north of it consist of a rhythmic alternation of solids and voids (waiting rooms and recessed entry courts), with taller chapels rising behind. Each chapel is entered on its northwestern corner through the waiting room (with an enclosed garden beyond) and exited through large doors in the western walls into the entry court and clearing beyond.

2.7
Woodland Cemetery, Enskede, Sweden. View from Monument Hall to Meditation Grove, with the Lily Pond and the Catafalque in between
Gunnar Asplund and Sigurd Lewerentz, 1915–1940

The open-air catafalque, the ceremonial plaza and the lily pond
To further intensify the dynamic interplay between the two main elements of the clearing – Monument Hall and the Meditation Grove – (Fig. 2.7), Asplund and Lewerentz introduced three more components: an open-air stone catafalque for use in large public funerary services, a ceremonial plaza to accommodate the community during such services, and a sizeable lily pond. These are closer to Monument Hall but aligned in a north-westerly direction so that the sky-oriented Meditation Grove forms a powerful physical and symbolic backdrop. The stone catafalque holds the coffin of a prominent citizen during open-air funerals. It is raised on an earthen circular plinth and

On the Transcendent

accentuated vertically by six candelabras arranged around it in an honor guard-like formation. Its northeast-southwest orientation causes it to be seen from nearly all positions on angle, always pointing to both Monument Hall and the Meditation Grove. The flagstones of the ceremonial plaza are discreetly blended into the lawn with its gentle incline. The lily pond amplifies the feeling of silence exuded by other elements of the clearing and, through its reflective property, interlocks earth and sky. From many angles, the pond appears to magically dematerialize the surroundings.

The meditation grove

From the central clearing, a knoll gently rises, crowned by the Meditation Grove. It was carved from the gravel ridge to the right of the cemetery's main entrance, a decision that also allowed vehicles along a loop road in the western portion of the cemetery. Its steepest slope is on its northern side – which one sees from the entrance. On the crematorium side, it slopes down gently toward the cross and Monument Hall. Visitors are led to the Grove by seven flights of granite stairs – noticeable as one enters the cemetery (Fig. 2.8). A seven-foot wide gravel path leading into the forest crosses it along its north-south direction. The stairs are unique in that they compensate for the climber's growing weariness as they ascend to the grove. The steps both decrease in height and increase in depth, and the landings become larger

2.8
Woodland Cemetery, Enskede, Sweden. Stairs to the Meditation Grove
Gunnar Asplund and Sigurd Lewerentz, 1915–1940

as one nears the top, thus making them appreciably gentle to climb. Ascending these stairs takes one even further from the everyday world. The upward-looking vista conveys a strong feeling of moving to a higher spiritual plane.

The Meditation Grove is framed by a waist-high, three-foot deep ashlar wall with two openings: the northern one opens onto the stairs, and the southern one opens onto the path to the forest. This walled space is surrounded by another square formed by the trunks of 12 mature weeping elms which, through the central opening created by their four trunks on either side, align a visitor with the four cardinal directions. The pattern of concentric squares continues inside the space: the path from the stairs here becomes a seven-foot wide gravel ring where inward-facing wooden benches are set against the wall. This in turn surrounds a smaller square of lawn with a water well in its center. Far removed from the activities within the cemetery, this grove orients one both physically and spiritually. It turns one's mind inward to silence, and up toward the sky. On the hill's southern side, the Way of Seven Wells, another seven-foot wide gravel path, gently slopes down toward the forest, which, when viewed from above, looks like a green canyon where the path cuts through.

The Way of Seven Wells
A footpath leads from the Meditation Grove through the forest to Lewerentz's Resurrection Chapel. The path takes its name from the seven wells (water symbolizing the renewal of life) originally intended to punctuate the path – beginning with the one in the Meditation Grove – although this is the only well that was built. After entering the tall forest through a row of weeping birches, the straight path descends imperceptibly to the Chapel of Resurrection, where it ascends again, framed by tall spruces on either side.

The forest and the forest tombs
At the southern edge of the central clearing, Asplund and Lewerentz planted an expansive grove of birches in a square grid fronted by a row of weeping birches as an airy transition from the bright open field of a clearly human-made order to the lush, dense and nearly untouched forest beyond. The grove of tall birches is kept free of graves. Upon entering the forest on the Way of Seven Wells, one notices the first tombstones among the tall pine trees. They are mostly thin slabs, many with rounded tops, simply set in the ground. The ground here is a continuous blanket of surprisingly lush, green lawn (Fig. 2.9 and Plate 2). The forest contains sections, perhaps comparable to city blocks, where small paths are used during funeral ceremonies. But for visitors to reach a tomb, one simply walks across the lawn.

On the Transcendent

2.9
Woodland Cemetery, Enskede, Sweden. The forest tombs
Gunnar Asplund and Sigurd Lewerentz, 1915–1940

Throughout the cemetery, one notices that most tombstones face east, toward the rising sun (of renewal?) while visitors standing in front of them are facing the setting sun (of life departed). One cannot help but recognize the apparent desire to maintain the fundamental human ties to the cosmic cycles with its important implications for the living. The eastern orientation of the tombstones causes one to experience a curious phenomenon. When moving aimlessly through the forest – as one walks either north or south – one faces only the stones' narrow sides and hence barely notices them. What little one sees of them echoes and amplifies the vertical thrust of the trees. Moving east or west, on the other hand, makes one confront the faces of the stones or their backs in their full size, and some sections of the cemetery appear crowded from that angle.

The first burial section one encounters when entering the woods is one of the oldest, with tombstones dating from the early 1920s. Many stones have aged so much that it is difficult to read names and one realizes that, in comparison to younger sections nearby, the deceased here have by and large been forgotten by society. While family members tend the newer graves and bring flowers, the barren, aged stones in the older areas act more powerfully as archetypal symbols. In this setting one cannot help but recognize that the deceased have long ago returned to the earth and have even potentially fed the life of nearby trees. One may begin to imagine oneself buried here and being observed by someone else, perhaps a century from now, summoning a recognition of the interconnectedness of all human life. These forest tombs bring forth not just an intellectual, rational response that one might have in any burial ground, but a palpable emotional reaction.

Woodland Chapel, children's cemetery and willow grove
The Woodland Chapel by Gunnar Asplund was the first chapel to be constructed in the cemetery. He enclosed the site of dense old pines with a massive, gray-plastered wall and, deep within this precinct, built the chapel facing east. It is a hybrid building that blends classical temple architecture with the typical Swedish forest church with its steep, dark slate roof. Passing through a gate niche, one sees the catafalque and altar on axis straight ahead but is completely surprised by the space's expansion upward to a light-filled dome and a translucent ocular pouring forth light.

Outside the domed interior, a path leads down several steps to a rectangular area depressed into the earth extending in a southerly direction, which serves as the children's cemetery. After it traverses the lower field, this path takes one into the adjoining forest and culminates in a low, round earth platform surrounded by lacy, miniature willows, a second meditation grove in which to find solitude in nature.

Chapel of the Resurrection
Designed by Sigurd Lewerentz as the second chapel, the Chapel of the Resurrection forms a major orientation point within the cemetery as the culmination of the Way of Seven Wells, and from which it is experientially inseparable. Built in a neoclassical style with refined materials and proportions, it choreographs one's experience of the funeral ceremony in a way that subtly differs psychologically from Asplund's Woodland Chapel. Here one enters from the north through the monumental portico, becomes oriented toward the catafalque and altar in an easterly direction, but leaves afterwards not the way one entered, but through a gate underneath the organ loft in the western wall and emerging in the "light-filled world of the living" facing a long rectangular clearing depressed in the earth.

The memorial ground
At the top of the entry drive, one can turn back north on a paved road that ascends to a ridge overlooking the entry drive. Here Lewerentz was asked to make his last contribution to the cemetery in form of a Memorial Ground. New regulations permitted the disposal of ashes without urns or permanent markers. His proposal created a sensitive frame for this new burial rite by utilizing inherent properties of the ridge's landscape. Leaving the forest's heather and blueberry cover intact for the informal strewing of ashes, he also

created a small clearing of lawn for urn-less burial of ashes near the southern tip of the ridge, opposite the Meditation Grove. Stone areas with a trickle of water are inset along the pedestrian route up the ridge, serving as a place for memorial flowers.

Design strategies for transcending finiteness
My analysis of Woodland Cemetery will focus on the strategies and devices involved in triggering memories, reflection, and contemplation. Key to this is the rich interplay of the design components along the main entry sequence (including the large clearing's "haven of silence"), the sequences leading to Resurrection Chapel and Woodland Chapel respectively, and the forest tombs throughout the cemetery. Not only do these features orient visitors physically, but they can also cause a profound inner reorientation. Several of these elements have a strong capacity to generate narrative due to their reference to fundamental human life situations that resonate universally, such as the Meditation Grove (offering silence and a feeling of being removed from the world) or the catafalque (which one can read as a sacrificial altar evoking memories of ancient texts). All of these elements work together to trigger associations, and awaken memories of one's own experiences and others pertaining to the larger social body. Eventually, they elicit empathy for others' lives (past, present and future) and reflection on one's own. Notwithstanding its more somber aspects, the cemetery is a surprisingly uplifting, even happy environment that attracts one as such. The architects sought to render the cemetery both as a place for encountering nature, and to draw upon nature's ability to soothe and comfort through its silence – an important factor in the contemplative aura that attracts one to this setting.

Orienting the individual within a larger order
One's orientation within this cemetery always occurs on two levels. Clues from the environment are needed to discern one's physical location within the vast cemetery grounds. An inner reorientation is also necessitated. The cemetery evokes transcendent concerns such as coming to terms with the temporality of human existence, feelings of bereavement (should one have lost a loved one), and ultimately with the meaning of one's own existence. This allows one to tap inner wellsprings of insight and renewal that can reconcile and strengthen one before leaving the cemetery. Many design decisions were made to assist this process, allowing us to extract general principles for creating a contemplative realm.

The necessity for transcending confinements of program
For a work to be not just a mute, quantitatively sufficient solution for utilitarian needs, but instead a purveyor of complex meanings capable of eliciting

subtle and lofty responses, the architects needed to reformulate the given task, perhaps initially even completely subordinate the functional requirements to their desired psychological, symbolic vision for the work. Asplund and Lewerentz accordingly appear to have avoided being guided solely by contemporary Christian funeral practices, but also avoided the then stifling influence of the Lutheran denomination that predominates in Sweden. Instead, they thought universally, and drew upon ideas of death and dying throughout the West, including classical Greek and Roman examples and especially the Nordic pre-Christian pagan past. While their final design employed many symbolic elements that still held specific significance for the Protestant population, they used most of them in universalized ways so as to transcend religious specificity. Due to that universalized character, the cemetery can affect individuals who have no religious beliefs in ways similarly to those who do. By far the most important deviation from the initial programmatic functions was the eventual creation of the void of the large clearing, a "space of absence." It is a free offering to the human spirit that is not utilitarian in economy-driven functional terms, but highly important, and indeed unforgettable in psychological-experiential terms. Therefore, the original task of designing an expansion to an existing cemetery had to be rethought to include the psychological agenda of creating a landscape of remembrance, reflection and transcendence – of poetically/spiritually addressing the fundamental human condition. The distinct topographic features of the site's rugged terrain served as a good starting point for implementing various association-generating components.

Preparing the land
Asplund and Lewerentz first contained the land, as a walled, inward-oriented, silent oasis within the larger urban environment of southern Stockholm, and then rendered it "gentle" through earth movement. Where necessary, they made the forest (i.e. nature) the principal resting place for the deceased, by leveling the pine forest's floor, clearing it of undergrowth, and smoothing over the gravel excavation pits, rendering it soothing and peaceful. They created a large clearing as the heart of the cemetery, and elevated it above the site's periphery, creating a physical void where key elements of the cemetery emerge. With the contrast between these elements and the void mutually amplifying their significance, a distinct threshold is created between the secular, day-to-day reality and this set aside, spiritualized realm.

In the overall site strategy, the architects subordinated notions of symmetry to an overall dominant asymmetry. Asymmetry is more suitable for achieving an almost natural sanctuary while it also creates the continuous surprise from changing vistas and the constant, subtle reorientation of visitors as they move through the cemetery.

Establishing/anchoring symbolically charged elements within the land
The Woodland Cemetery's intended subtle, multilayered impact on a visitor stems from the complex interplay of its various components and their ability to evoke memories (both personal and more general ones), elicit recognition, and induce contemplation. Among the strategies the architects used for triggering such associations were:

1. Selectively insert, build up, distribute, anchor, or use throughout the site elements with strong connotations (some with archetypal characteristics) that focus on life and death, mourning, nature, and the continuity of the collective human family, such as: the large clearing (a paradise garden in the sense of a peaceful, tranquil open-air abode), the Meditation Grove (sacred mountain, also burial mound), the stairs to the Grove (Jacob's Ladder, levels of spiritual advancement), the Way of Seven Wells (pilgrimage path), the catafalque (open-air altar), the lily pond (mirror to the sky), the forest and individual groves (sacred grove), the meditation circle in the forest near the children's cemetery (forest clearing), or Monument Hall (collective meeting hall) – all of which serve, together with the network of paths, the large clearing, and the topographic differences, as the fundamental armature for one's orientation within the cemetery;
2. Establish hierarchical relationships by using the clearing's void as both center of gravity and field in which to plug peripheral elements, recognizing the clearing as the principal zone through which to orient oneself;
3. Render some of these elements as signs (important way-finding devices) within the cemetery, the cross for example, which facilitate one's orientation and establishes broader structures of symbolic interrelations.

Enhancing orientation through linkages and transitions
So that the cemetery would gradually reveal itself to a visitor as much more than just a sequence of otherwise isolated, unrelated elements, the architects used a variety of linking devices:

1. Meaningful interrelations were created between the richly symbol-laden elements via a strategic path and road network, which emphasizes preferred sequences among a great number of possibilities. While the paths and elements are of primary importance to the choreographing of a visitor's experience, they also fundamentally facilitate one's orientation within the site.

2. Transitions were carefully worked-out between different conditions, such as between architecture and landscape, leading to the blurring of their boundaries, for example, in the Way of the Cross's paving blending with the lawn, at the forecourts of the Chapels of Faith and Hope with their low dividing walls and gates which are both part of the chapels and the central clearing, and the Monument Hall piers and the trees of the Meditation Grove which both separate and connect inside and outside.

3. Vegetation was used in architectural, geometric formations, for example, in the grid layout of the birch grove between the large clearing and the forest southwest of Monument Hall. Architectural elements were used in an analogous way to the geometric use of vegetation, exemplified by Monument Hall piers and their relationship to the square form of the Meditation Grove's tree trunks. The architectural use of a natural element was also often employed, for example at the straight edge of the pond which is "willed" to be parallel to Monument Hall's porch and thus echoes it, and through the geometric relationship between earth and sky, especially in the Meditation Grove and the atrium-like opening in the roof of Monument Hall.

4. Linkages and transitions were made between more and less "sacred" zones. The Meditation Grove is physically above the cemetery's other parts, privileging the Way of the Cross over other paths; the columbarium and Woodland Chapel are enclosed with a wall (versus unwalled precincts); graveyards, such as the children's cemetery or the area west of the Resurrection Chapel, are depressed into the earth (versus less distinct burial areas), and an axial approach guides one to the main entries of Resurrection and Woodland Chapels.

5. Physical and visual interrelations were carefully worked-out, and often achieved through framing – sometimes through vegetation (as in the canyon-like approach to the Resurrection Chapel along the Way of the Seven Wells) – and sometimes through architectural forms (as in the view of the main clearing at the entry drive). Connecting devices were employed, such as the columbarium wall that links the main entry area with the cremation chapels. Amplifying devices such as the Way of the Cross, the columbarium wall, and the line of linden trees inside, mutually support the forward momentum of each, and together exert a powerful upward pull on the visitor.

Accommodating collective rituals of death
The central purpose of the Woodland Cemetery is to accommodate the rites of final passage, the outer way in which society acknowledges and celebrates the end of individual lives. With five chapels of differing sizes, three used for cremations, the cemetery accommodates the final rites of up to five funerals simultaneously. Every morning, the funeral services scheduled for that day are posted at the entrance. All chapels are oriented to the east, and in four of them one exits at the end of a service on a different route from how one entered. All release one into "the world of the living" in bright areas facing west. This can be felt especially strongly in the chapels of the cremation complex where the floors incline slightly down toward the catafalque near the eastern wall. Upon leaving one rises toward the light, and one may sense how correspondingly, space for thinking and feeling opens up within oneself.

The outdoor spaces associated with the crematorium, including the courtyards adjacent to the chapels, serve the needs of funeral rituals indirectly by accommodating waiting individuals or groups of mourners and help to accommodate differing degrees of formality and informality. The occasional city-wide farewell to an important public figure is served by the open-air catafalque and its associated ceremonial plaza. The cemetery's ample size and its topography enable persons not directly participating in the rite of passage to partake from a distance without feeling they are transgressing.

Accommodating solitude, assisting the turn inward
While funeral rituals are the primary acts through which society marks the return of a deceased person "back to the earth", coming to terms with the loss of a loved one, or a beloved citizen, cannot be accommodated simply by these rites. Complete mourning requires inner processes for the bereaved individuals. It is for bereaved persons needing to come to terms with life's sad aspects that the landscape of the Woodland Cemetery addresses itself above all. Solitude is especially beneficial to the bereaved, but often appreciated by everyone experiencing it within the cemetery.

Places specifically intended to provide experiences of solitude and turning inward are the Meditation Grove, the clearing of the Memorial Ground, and the small circular meditation platform near the children's burial area. And one can experience solitude walking through the grounds as a silent observer, able to stop anywhere, any time. Even when surrounded by others, one may still feel free to follow one's own thoughts and feelings as if alone. This is perhaps due to the generally considerate manner of visitors, who tend to maintain a quiet and respectful mood.

Devices specifically chosen by the architects to foster a sense of solitude include:

1. The vastness of scale in the forest and the central clearing's seemingly endless expanses of space create a sense of openness and solitude and render one a silent observer, a seemingly invisible guest.
2. The outward funneling effect of the clearing contributes to an opening up of oneself upon entering the cemetery. The architects employed foci for one's attention – design elements that invite one to shut out the world – in part accentuated by abstraction (i.e. reducing them to their unadorned, essential characteristics), such as the Meditation Grove (which distances one from the world in several senses), and the catafalque, scaled for one human body.
3. Buildings have a muteness of expression. For example, the overall design and detailing of the cremation chapels contributes to a sense of solitude in a peculiar way. While their size, proportion, and warm-colored marble cladding, enhanced with a rich play of light and shadow, render them intimate spaces that invite one to rest – their degree of abstraction and a relative absence of familiar scale also render them mute and deferential to the much more engaging Monument Hall.
4. The reflective properties of the pond prompt one to turn one's mind toward the sky, and contrast the sky's vastness with one's own insignificance and aloneness.
5. Elements that generally symbolize death and the final human transition create a sense of solitude. For example, mournfulness is manifested in such plants as weeping elms or weeping birches.
6. Tombs – the archetypal elements that bring one into contact not only with the memory of the person resting there – but also inevitably bring thoughts of one's own mortality. This may serve to strip one of protective shields and lay one bare to reflective, detached scrutiny.

Transcending the finiteness of space

The transcendence-inducing dimensions of the cemetery are not easily compartmentalized into separate categories, since "to transcend" means to go beyond ordinary perceptions, enable one to "see" beyond the surface of a given reality, and to lose one's customary attachment to time and space, even to lose any sense of time, place and space and one's own self (for the duration of the transcendent experience). What is important then is not the specific kind of transcendence, but simply the transcendent state itself and how it can inspire and enrich. This experience is especially noticeable when one finds oneself returning to ordinary dimensions of reality.

What follows is based on the premise that transcendence-inducing contemplative states, in which one is temporarily freed from ordinary ways of perceiving reality, can be triggered in a variety of ways that captivate one's mind enough to replace the focus on ordinary reality, encompassing all of one's ordinary ways of perceiving, feeling and thinking, including the dimensions of space, time, and sense of oneself. To transcend space means to transcend time, and also to recognize the limiting aspects of focusing on oneself, and vice versa. Moreover, the environment impacts one not through any one isolated aspect, but through a complex interplay of many components. Nonetheless, I will categorize types of transcending experiences: of space, time, and the self, and how these experiences are particularly promoted by features or qualities present at Woodland Cemetery.

Revealing larger and smaller senses of space
After only a short while one senses that Woodland Cemetery has a mysteriously paradoxical quality: while one develops a sense of great familiarity with the setting, the richness of the ever-changing experience renders it perhaps ultimately unknowable. There are surprises built into it, such as ascents to "the unknown," or one's anticipations at bends of the roads and turns of the paths, with their corresponding concealing and revealing. One begins to relate to space through the specific part of the cemetery one is in – small or large – that often provide glimpses to other parts, offering other ideas of scale, as in sensing the clearing's vastness from the columbarium's intimacy (Fig. 2.10). There are spaces of anticipation, where one is led to a destination which one can only guess at ahead of time, such as the footpath from the columbarium, leading across the clearing and disappearing beyond the Meditation Grove's knoll, or when ascending the stairs to the Meditation Grove. There are also spaces of personal intimacy, exemplified through a "one-on-one dialogue" at a loved one's tomb, during which all other space might seem to cease existing.

Cosmic linkages through architecture and nature and symbolic references to infinity
While the cemetery is embedded within the larger context of Stockholm, aspects of it make one reflect on the vastly larger cosmic context of a seemingly infinite universe, through devices such as:

1. Skyward-oriented spaces (the Meditation Grove, the small meditation clearing south of the children's cemetery, the roof opening in Monument Hall, and the sky-reflecting lily pond). In addition, the

Heinrich Hermann

entire central clearing lays itself bare to the cosmic vault so that one experiences reminders of the relative impotence of humankind in the face of much larger forces.

2. Sunrise-oriented spaces or elements, exemplified by the five chapels that are loosely oriented eastward, and most tombstones face the rising sun.
3. Through symbolically skyward-oriented spaces or elements (the domed sanctuary of Woodland Chapel with its reference to the cosmic vault, the "cosmic marker" of the large stone cross) one becomes acutely aware of the cemetery's relations to the cosmos.

2.10
Woodland Cemetery, Enskede, Sweden. View from the columbarium to the Meditation Grove
Gunnar Asplund and Sigurd Lewerentz, 1915–1940

The cemetery as microcosm of life

In the course of funeral rituals, one begins to reflect on how the community of mourners mirrors society at large, with its smaller and larger units. One may be prompted to reflect further on the state of society "as it is" in contrast to what it "should" or "could" be, and pose the questions, "What is it truly that remains of one's life?" and "What is the highest purpose that one is born for, and how can one manifest it?" (Even if not believing in any such cause or reason.) The cemetery reflects, in frozen and "equalized" form, the urban society of Stockholm. Regardless of their interaction in life, the remains of a great many deceased citizens are now resting side by side peacefully, and silently remind visitors of their own past futures and future pasts.

For visitors holding religious beliefs, the cemetery is a forceful reminder of their own latent ideal humanity (which their beliefs call upon them to strive to fulfill). The cemetery may also serve to remind them of how they should ideally interact as a community of believers, and how they should make renewed efforts toward those ideals upon leaving.

Transcending the finite time frame of human life span

As repositories of the dead, cemeteries forcefully remind one of the limits to life's duration. Equally forcefully, they attest to the continuity of the larger human family. They manifest two fundamentally different relations to time: the limited linear span of individual life, and the cyclical frame of the perennially renewed human race. In addition, Woodland Cemetery allows one to experience several other time frames that may lead one to question and transcend one's ordinary relation to time and subtly change how one understands one's own existence.

Revealing linear and cyclical time

The cemetery allows one to sense both the linear and cyclical nature of time, and its different ways of unfolding, partly based on phenomenal experiences, partly through trains of thought and feelings triggered by the symbol-laden environment. The plain function of the cemetery (a burial ground and history book of the city, from its dedication to today) reveals a linearity of time (also revealed in the aging of the tomb stones – primary records – of which many from the 1920s are now barely legible).

Transcendence of time may be prompted by highlighting the cyclical nature of time. Light and shadows are crucial for they essentially contribute to one's way of experiencing both the buildings and nature. The passage of the sun along its daily, monthly, and seasonal cycles – crossing over vegetation, architecture, and modulated topography make palpable the passing of hours, days, and seasons – while the warmth of the sun and its life-giving force may help one overcome bereavement. Seasonally specific tactile sensations such as walking over fallen chestnuts in October on the Way of the Cross, or over colored autumn leaves cause comparisons of life spent, then renewed. Winter changes the appearance of the cemetery a great deal, but the short days and low sun angle are partly compensated by the snow's reflections. In winter, the bright openness of the central clearing is psychologically needed more than ever.

Arresting, eluding, resisting time

The massive stone walls around the entire cemetery suggest they protect a realm under a spell, frozen in time, an interior oasis of silence that is carved out from the ordinary world and not polluted by it. The cemetery's function as a repository of the remains of the deceased renders it as a realm beyond ordinary space and time.

Time may stand still in other instances, as when gazing at the lily pond and suddenly finding oneself engrossed by the reflected sky, all else suspended. The symbolic properties of certain elements may cause the same reaction, as when observing the Meditation Grove from a distance, or the catafalque, or when suddenly feeling intense silence, primarily in spaces intentionally created for such responses (such as the Meditation Grove). For a mourner, the small tomb of a loved one may be respite from the larger world, a microcosm of arrested time within which communion with the loved one continues, while otherwise ordinary time continues.

In encountering the cemetery, one's habit-structured mind-set of daily life experience is radically interrupted by this so very different environment, notably marked by the sheer dimensions of the clearing, and the seeming depth of the forest, which initially take one's breath away and seemingly freeze one in time (albeit briefly). The cemetery's silence, resulting from the careful control of the type, nature, and amount of stimuli, induces one to listen outward and inward. The setting invites one's eyes to wander along journeys of discovery, inducing one to be lost in thought and contemplation. The archaic character of elements such as the catafalque recalls ancient sacrificial rites, and while the cremation complex's architectural language locates it firmly within the twentieth century, its weathered sandstone-like marble evokes memories of ancient Egypt, setting it outside a specific time.

Transcending the narrow focus on one's self

The cemetery contributes to triggering transcendence of one's narrow focus on the self, chiefly through its capacity to elicit empathy. It uses collective acts of funerary rites to foster one's sense of being an integral part of a community; public funeral rituals offer self-affirmation as a community, such as in the larger ceremonies for prominent citizens; and private acts of mourning around countless possible foci of attention (beginning with a particular tomb, or grave); foster compassion for grief suffered by others, feeling others' pain, "stepping into other selves" and the recognition that the other and oneself are part of a socially and spiritually larger self. The cemetery powerfully induces a sense of connection between oneself, the deceased, and the mourners as hypothetical other versions of one's self – other humans subject to the same struggles, experiences, and capacity for joy and sorrow.

Summary

The Woodland Cemetery owes its transcendence-inducing dimension to specific ways of establishing complex relational systems on many overlapping levels within a given environment, all centered around a plan to accommodate Stockholm's need for an additional cemetery for funeral rites and as a dignified place to remember the dead. In addition, the city planners wanted to express, in the spirit of the early twentieth century, the independence of funerals from the Lutheran Church that had dominated until then.

The cemetery's transcendent, uplifting character depended at the very beginning of its conception on an act of transcendence by the architects who radically questioned funeral practices of their time and expanded their frames of reference to a universal scale, including both pre-Christian traditions and Western classical antiquity. To spiritually affect visitors, the cemetery depends to a large extent on facilitating a reorientation upon entering the grounds, accomplished through the vast openness or void of the large clearing, which creates a sense of loftier planes (places), while at the same time orienting them physically. The clearing stimulates reflection on one's attitudes toward death and its implications, and the actuality of life and its beautiful possibilities. Only after that preparatory experience do visitors proceed to the specific location they came for.

The Woodland Cemetery demonstrates how architecture and landscape, in tandem, can set aside a fraction of the world – a clearing – to which it welcomes us as human beings and renews within us the memory of a fuller measure of our own humanity.

Conclusion

This essay has illustrated two paradigms for how an environment can elicit a contemplative response. Woodland Cemetery was explicitly a contemplative/spiritual work, while the Salk Institute was implicitly understood as such by both its client and architect.

I have shown that contemplative environments not only provide the pleasure of experiencing beautiful, soothing places, but can have an even more profound impact, leaving a person inspired and enriched by the encounter. Why then are there so few environments capable of moving the human spirit and fostering contemplation? At least in part this is due to the unfamiliarity among designers with underlying principles that can render a work inspirational by triggering insights of subtle or deep meaning within the activating viewer/user. I'd like to close by referring to only a few insights from my research on how latent possibilities abound, and how countless design tasks could be transformed, if only one had eyes to see and a mind-set to respond to universal conditions and themes.

Every work offers *some* contemplative opportunities if a designer chooses to pursue them. The paradigms I proposed can be translated into design in countless ways because their underlying principles are universally present:

- In our age, the exposure to vast amounts of sensory stimuli is so common that most persons only know deep silence in their sleep. Environments that minimize detrimental stimuli may offer outer "silence" that can slow the mind to corresponding inner "silence" that is beneficial to contemplation. As the example from biofeedback showed, the ability to enter a meditative state is part of the human psycho-biological make-up. Entering such a state has measurable benefits for our health and well-being. Contemplative environments can help us to enter a related state and affect us in multiple, positive ways.
- The vast expanse of the universe – the wider context of our existence – surrounds us everywhere on earth, but our awareness of it is numbed by a myriad of thoughts and information. Stilling the mind to be "fully present" requires design ingenuity, although opportunities abound (even in as subtle a way as revealing light moving along a wall).
- We all share in memories of fundamental life situations, both of our individual lives and the collective human past. In humanity's highest efforts and aspirations at comprehending the meaning of existence, a vast storehouse of symbolic meanings has been created that is still available to us. From this storehouse, relevant parts may be selected to make our environments conveyers of archetypal stories that we "re-tell" in the new design encounter. The primary life-sustaining symbols are very likely the sun and water.
- The dialogue between the human-made and the natural is an ever-present opportunity, even if an environment becomes all human-made and the natural is abstracted to nothing more than the poetry of light and shadows.

Needed then are the will to create environments charged with poetic/spiritual, contemplation-inducing qualities and the will to educate and persuade clients of their desirability; knowledge of basic principles and strategies that can enable environments to elicit a contemplative response; keen perception and vision that identifies salient features within a site and functions within a program as opportunities; the vision to transform a program so it can offer opportunities for lifting the design beyond its utilitarian dimension; artistic ability to translate opportunities into inspiring built reality; and great stamina, infectious enthusiasm and persistent persuasion to help everyone involved realize the work at its highest potential.

Notes

1. Emerson, R. W., "Nature," in Spiller, R. E. and Ferguson, A. R. (eds), *Nature, Addresses, and Lectures*, [using text of 1836 edition of *Nature*, Boston: James Munroe & Co], (1979), Cambridge, MA, and London: Belknap Press of Harvard University Press, p. 7.
2. On meditation see e.g. Goleman, Daniel, *The Meditative Mind: The Varieties of Meditative Experience* (Los Angeles, CA: Jeremy P. Tarcher, 1988), or the issue on "Meditation," *Journal of Dharma*, II, 2, April 1977.
3. Typically assigned tasks in biofeedback include reducing muscle tensions, lowering the pulse rate, and lowering the body temperature (all in response to the graphic and acoustic "biofeedback" given by a TV monitor). In the experience of the Biofeedback Unit of Harvard's Health Services, there is an apparently universal latent ability to achieve results, but it typically takes six months of consistent practice for a novice to do so, using any kind of meditation system. (From notes taken during a session with Ellen Haley, director, December 2, 1988.)
4. e.g. in Wallace, Robert Keith, and Herbert Benson, "The Physiology of Meditation," in *Scientific American* (February 1972), pp. 84–90.
5. Olness, Karen, "Self-Regulation and Conditioning," in Bill Moyers, *Healing and the Mind* (New York: Doubleday, 1993), pp. 71–85; or Pert, Candace, "The Chemical Communicators," in ibid., pp. 177–93.
6. Scheffler, Israel, *In Praise of the Cognitive Emotions* (New York and London: Routledge, 1991).
7. Meditation understood as effort undertaken toward genuine inner perception of the nature of reality and to commune with the Divine.
8. See e.g. Goleman, D. op. cit., or the issue on "Meditation," *Journal of Dharma*, op. cit.
9. In yoga meditation is so called because of the concentration of the individual on the point between the eyebrows, the seat of the "spiritual, third eye."
10. This presupposes the ability of entering into a contemplative state (see endnote 3), triggered by aspects of the work. Each individual cannot respond equally or with equal intensity, however, due to *differing degrees of receptivity* - as pointed out by Nelson Goodman with respect to art: "*The work of art is apprehended through the feelings as well as through the senses. Emotional numbness disables here as definitely if not as completely as blindness or deafness*" [my italics]. See Goodman, N., *Languages of Art* (1976), Indianapolis, IN: Hackett, p. 248.
11. For a short history of the commission's evolution and how the Mexican architect Luis Barragan inspired Kahn to make the courtyard a plaza with "not one leaf, nor plant, nor one flower" in it, see Friedman, D. S., "Salk Institute for Biological Studies," in Brownlee, D. B. and De Long, D. G., Louis I Kahn: *In the Realm of Architecture* (1991), New York: Rizzoli, pp. 434–9.
12. Recounted by Brownlee in ibid., p. 5.
13. The courtyard is open to the public during regular working hours.
14. Bachelard, G., *The Poetics of Reverie: Childhood, Language, and the Cosmos* (1971), Boston MA: Beacon Press, p. 173.
15. Ibid., p. 177.
16. Ibid., p. 196.
17. Latour, A. (ed.), *Louis I. Kahn: Writings, Lectures, Interviews* (1991), New York: Rizzoli International, p. 208.
18. Scheffler, I. op. cit., p. 62.
19. Ibid., p. 68.
20. From "Silence and Light," reprinted in Latour, op. cit., p. 246.

Heinrich Hermann

21 In Spiller, and Ferguson, op. cit., p. 10.
22 For the cemetery's history and its design evolution see especially Constant, C. (1994) *The Woodland Cemetery: Toward a Spiritual Landscape*, Stockholm: Byggförlaget, and sections in Ahlin, J. (1987) *Sigurd Lewerentz, Architect 1885–1975*, Cambridge, MA and London: MIT Press.

Map of memory, an interview

Michael Singer with Rebecca Krinke

Introduction

Michael Singer's presentation (titled "Map of Memory"), given at the "Contemporary Landscapes of Contemplation" symposium, University of Minnesota, October 18, 2002 was used as a framework for this essay. The presentation was videotaped. This essay also incorporates an interview, that was taped with Michael Singer by Rebecca Krinke, held at his studio in Vermont on January 4, 2004. The essay/interview was transcribed and drafted by Krinke and edited collaboratively by Singer and Krinke for clarity and length. This process to create this contribution by Michael Singer for this book was decided upon mutually by Singer and Krinke in the planning stages of the symposium.

Culture and nature

Since the 1970s, Michael Singer's art has been engaged with a series of questions that explore the human relationship with nature. Contemplation is a key concept in Singer's work, and one that functions on several levels for him. Originally from New York City, Singer's home has been rural Vermont for over 25 years. The woods, including a nearby beaver bog, were his studio for five years. The sculptures that he constructed there in the early 1970s consisted primarily of fallen trees found on the site and then rearranged, investigating the theme of balance. The art world did not see these works, and galleries did not sponsor them. This was artwork as a contemplative and investigative practice, a full engagement of self with site. When Singer was working in the beaver bog, rather than reading art journals, his interest was *Sierra*, *Audobon*, and other environmental texts. The ecological consciousness that was being born in the 1970s was a powerful inspiration to him, one that related to his own artistic sensibilities.

These early investigations led Singer to other remote sites, where he continued to explore "what it means to be a human being interacting in a natural world."[1] In the saltwater marshes of Long Island, he began his critically acclaimed and well-known *Ritual Series*: sculptures made of reeds, bamboo and wood, embodying qualities of fragility, balance, and strength. The works have a mysterious presence, as they seem to allude to both artifact and structure. These objects are created for either interior gallery spaces, or temporary outdoor exhibitions. Curator Diane Waldman wrote of Singer's *Ritual Series* work, "These magical enclosures evoke ritualistic associations and encompass a universe that is part nature, part myth."[2] Singer still works on a body of sculpture and drawings that he names *Ritual Series*.

In the mid 1970s, just as scientists received permission to study the fragile ecosystem of the Florida Everglades, he as an artist, asked for and received permission to create ephemeral works of art as part of his research. In this primordial setting, Singer explored a feeling or quality of awe; his art was focused on seeing qualities *of* the landscape rather than making something *in* the landscape.[3] The process of art and ritual informed his experience in selecting a site, spending time in the site, and (as with his earlier investigations in the woods), the resulting temporary structures and photographs.

From his work in natural environments, Singer's art increasingly began to engage the public realm through indoor and outdoor shows and invitations to create temporary works of public art. Three early exhibitions: Harriman State Park (1975), Nassau County Museum (1976), both in New York State, and Dayton, Ohio (1979) provided Singer with opportunities to share the results of his solitary investigations. He created ephemeral sculptures of wood, bamboo, and phragmites, carefully sited in ponds and rivers, exploring ideas of object and space, light and time. He also choreographed experiences for the visitor. For example, in the Dayton project, to access his sculpture of bamboo and phragmites, delicately set within a stand of cottonwoods in a tributary of the Miami River, he loaned sets of waders to visitors in order for them to experience the art and the floodplain ecosystem first hand. From the very beginnings of his career, Singer's work has been shown in major museums and exhibitions, including: *Ten Young Artists: Theodoron Award Exhibition* (1971), *Michael Singer*, a one person show (1984), and *The*

Guggenheim International (1985), all at the Solomon R. Guggenheim Museum, New York; *Primitivism in 20th Century Art*, Museum of Modern Art, New York, (1986), as well as exhibitions at the Hirshhorn Museum of Art, Washington D.C., the Whitney Museum, New York, and *Documenta*, among others.

Interview –
Michael Singer and Rebecca Krinke

RK *Can you tell me about how you came to Vermont from New York, and about its impact on you and your work?*

MS I was very fortunate having my work chosen for the *Ten Young Artists: Theodoron Award Exhibition* at the Guggenheim in New York (Fig. 3.1). It was a wonderful opportunity and it was also kind of scary to me because I wondered what that kind of success was going to mean in terms of what I believed it meant to be an artist. I was 25 years old, and I wondered if I was going to use this extraordinary opportunity as a way to set up my career? Or was I going to use it as a way to get deeper into the exploration of questions I was asking at that time as an artist? It seemed to me that one way to understand this better would be to leave the city, to leave the environment where all the issues of the contemporary art world were happening and go somewhere where it didn't really matter. My sister had a ski house in southern Vermont, and I rented a small farmhouse in the area for very little money. It had no central heat, just a wood burning stove. It was a 200-year-old farmhouse; it hadn't been modernized. And I was a city person. I didn't have a clue about how to do this, but the whole thing became very exciting to me – in terms of leaving this New York art world which viewed itself as the center of the universe – and asking, "What happens if I remove myself from that and enter a place where there are other issues, a natural environment, natural systems at work? And what would I do?" It completely – on many levels – pulled the rug out from the support and securities I came to know in New York.

    Of course, the Guggenheim show was encouraging to me. First of all, it gave me some income in order to make this move, and it also gave me an emotional support for leaving what could have been a source of security. I used this opportunity to go out and explore. It was a platform to stand on and move from. It was a conscious decision to put myself in the natural environment, which I knew very little about, but that I was very interested in understanding. Also, in the late sixties

3.1
Installation view, Ten Young Artists: Theodoron Awards Exhibition, Solomon R. Guggenheim Museum
Michael Singer, 1971

and early seventies, the idea of the environment and ecology begins to come into the culture. And there is talk of interconnection between species and ecological systems, and between humans and the natural systems they effect. One of the first things I experienced when I came to Vermont was a beaver bog. A neighbor took me for walk, and the whole sense of what beavers did in their environment and the whole larger sense of interconnection really hit home. I learned that Native Americans used the clearings made by beavers. The silted soils were so rich in nutrients that the bogs became perfect planting fields. These kinds of systems were something I wanted to learn more about. I got very interested in human interactions with nature and looking more at native cultures. Western cultures seem to be looking at nature from a place of opposites, from dichotomy, civilized versus natural. I learned that at Lake Titicaca in Peru, the native culture was focused on reeds, for example. They build their houses, boats and floating islands using the reeds that grow there. They even eat from parts of the reeds. I was much more interested in reading books and journals that dealt with other cultures and their interactions with nature than I was in reading *Artforum* or about the issues that were specific at that time to the art world.

Map of Memory, an Interview

RK   *Was this due to moving to Vermont? Or was this a continuation of something begun earlier?*

MS   Nature always provided me a certain solace and a sense of connectedness, and at those times in my life when I find things very disturbing, I find myself going to nature for a kind of healing, a seeking out. Living in New York, surrounded by an artificial, built environment, offered a certain amount, but moving to Vermont reconnected me to something I felt was missing. It helped me remember something I think is forgotten in our contemporary culture. However, it was a difficult transition because there was a certain degree of isolation as well.

RK   *You went to Cornell, which has a landscape not totally dissimilar to Vermont. In art school, were your pieces similar to what led you to the Guggenheim? Were you working in a natural environment and/or with natural materials?*

MS   In art school, I was a painter. So I never did sculpture there.

RK   *Was nature an inspiration to your painting?*

MS   Yes, I was definitely involved with landscape. I love Cézanne's landscapes. I love Van Gogh and his landscapes. I copied these works and I made these artists my mythical mentors. I wanted to paint like them, see like them, and I loved going out into the landscape. I didn't actually start making sculpture until I got out of college.

RK   *What shifted you from painting to sculpture?*

MS   Well, that's a big question. I was considered an accomplished painter in school, a good painting student. I learned how to do it, how to get the approval of teachers. I had a certain facile ability with paint. And yet there was a moment when I had the sense that creating an illusion on a two-dimensional plane was less interesting to me than being connected to the real world. Partially this was inspired by my leaving Cornell for a term to study with Allan Kaprow, who was the originator of "Happenings". He had done a "Happening" at Cornell that completely opened up my thinking about what art could be, and I knew I needed to know more about this. I got permission to go and study with him at the State University of New York at Stony Brook. He was a brilliant teacher, actually an art historian. And I was like a fly on the wall watching him and his interactions. Through him, I met Marcel Duchamp and Joseph Cornell; they were Allan's good friends. From the way Allan and these extraordinary artists were looking at our world – I was suddenly thrust into seeing potentials and possibilities that had created, and were continuing to create, tremendous change in the culture and

Michael Singer

in my perceptions. The experience opened my thinking about the role of art, traditional notions of art. Time and risk and investigation were central to their work, and this was expressed in many different ways. It became much more exciting to get involved with performance and creating space and place through real materials and situations than to be in a studio working on a flat two-dimensional plane, capturing a moment, stopping time through art. So I literally just stopped. I don't paint now but I do draw, although I didn't draw for several years. One of the first things I did when I came to Vermont was to get involved going out into the woods.

RK To the beaver bog?

MS Even before the work in the beaver bog, I used to take walks in the Vermont woods and find what I called "situations". For example, where a tree had been windblown over, I would attach a "come-along" [a gripping device for pulling heavy items] and pull the trees into positions, one on top of another until there was a fulcrum, and a balanced situation (Fig. 3.2). That carried over from the work I showed at the Guggenheim. These pieces dealt with very heavy materials being put into balance so that a light touch could move them. They were minimal in their sensibilities – about boundaries and edges.

RK *Did you work only with what you found in this period? Or did you bring other materials outdoors?*

MS No, I insisted at the time to only use what I found at the site. In fact, if I cut the trees I did it in a way that would result in jagged edges that I would touch up with paint. I thought if someone ever passed this spot, they should have no idea that a human activity took place. I wanted to create something that was a mystery, something that someone would not know was human made, and yet someone could have made. I didn't want to leave my imprint on the site. Even when I was working in the snow, I would cover my tracks, so I could come back the next day and find this very fresh and new situation.

RK *So this activity of exploring and arranging; this went on about five years. Did you have any idea it would go on this long? Did you have a plan or strategy?*

MS No, no plan, and no sense of where it was going. And I don't think anyone ever saw it. I didn't take people to see it.

RK *Was it a kind of contemplative act for you?*

MS Completely; and it was very educational.

Map of Memory, an Interview

3.2
Situation Balance II, Wilmington, Vermont
Michael Singer, 1971

RK   *You mentioned that you studied with a tai chi master in New York; was your process or work related to tai chi in any way?*

MS   I was doing tai chi at this time and it was very important to me. Tai chi is very much about shifting weight in your body, feeling that shift in energy and how it affects different parts of your body. I was interested in balance in my sculpture as well as performance.

Michael Singer

I choreographed pieces where people were on seesaw-like constructions, and to complicate it, just by shifting their arm or their weight one way or another, the whole thing moved. It was an unexpected event that could not be controlled. If one person moved slightly everyone else was affected. Years later I observed wood storks in the Everglades, very large birds that roost together in slender small trees. When one lands, all the other birds have to adjust to the shifting branches and stresses.

During those five years, I worked alone in these natural environments, in the woods in Vermont but also in the Everglades and in saltwater marshes. I grew up on Long Island so I was familiar with saltwater marshes and the plants that grew there – phragmities – a reed-like plant. This plant connected to my interest in the native Peruvian culture I talked about earlier. I was interested in wrapping the reeds, and creating these tapering bundles, bringing these bundles into natural environments, studying them basically for how light affected them, how wind might affect them, and how the place itself was affected by my intervention. These site-specific situations became an apparatus, helping me understand more about the place. So, this educated me; got me into exploring either a beaver bog or a special site in the woods, or in the Everglades, or a saltwater marsh. This work got me *into* those areas and they got me to be *with* those areas, and helped me uncover an important question: What could a human role in the natural environment be? And I think this was a question that many people were asking from different professions at that time. And my colleagues, other artists at the time, artists like Robert Smithson and Michael Heizer, found different answers to this question. Their answers were disturbing to me – that the human role of an artist in the environment was to manipulate it. I believe that this manipulation actually created damage to the environments they worked in. They worked on their concepts in studios in Manhattan, went out and built these concepts into impressive and delicate outdoor sites, and then, through photographs, transferred their graphic image, their art, back to the art world, reflecting the current issues and dialogues of that world. My process came directly from my experience and understanding of the intricate nature of the special places I chose to explore. I was using the ritual and process of my work to learn about places, to guide my understanding of what a human being might do in natural places.

RK *The activity of doing that for five years must have changed you a lot?*

MS Tremendously.

Map of Memory, an Interview

RK Would you want to say anything more about that? Because it seems like a very contemplative, meditative, artistic, educational process of layered actions . . .

MS It was. During that time, I lived in Vermont, but I also still had a wonderful loft in New York, and I would go back and forth. I [had been] and was still involved with dance/performance, and in my space in Manhattan, I was experimenting with how to translate what I was learning in the natural environment into an indoor space (Fig. 3.3). How could my understanding of natural places be expressed through an interior piece of work placed in a built environment? I also started drawing at that time, and drawing from a totally different perspective than when I was in school. I became very interested in making my own drawing tools. And I started drawing from a very different point of view, not so much from the point of view of nature as subject, but nature as process. I was interested in exploring how to draw the growth of a tree. What is that? How do you draw the movement of stars through the night as you wake up and they've changed their position in the sky? How do you draw the changes that bring about the phases of the moon? Those questions, mysteries and issues of science and physics were very interesting to me. How could I take those things that I believe are very powerful and poetic – how could I take some of those actual scientific statements about relativity, string theory, and actually draw them? That was my impulse for drawing.

3.3
First Gate Ritual Series 10/78, **Collection Museum of Modern Art, New York**
Michael Singer, 1978

81

Michael Singer

RK *You mention that things shifted socially for you – instead of spending much time with other visual artists – you were spending time with different kinds of people?*

MS I was more interested in people working with the environment, and people studying and affecting social issues, but especially nature issues. But as for the art world itself – I just disappeared. It wasn't the place where I found inspiration.

RK *Were you nervous about how/when/if you were going to re-enter?*

MS Well, again, the 1971 show at the Guggenheim helped me get grants to keep me going. And I had maintained contact with the curator Diane Waldman. Diane was someone I could show my work to, and really to me, this time was a period of research, and in my mind the product was my learning, not an art object. She was very encouraging to that quest, that journey. However, at a certain point, she asked me if I would be interested in showing the results of this research, and five years had gone by, and I said that yes, I was. A few galleries were recommended and one specific one, Sperone Westwater and Fischer was most interested, and I had a show consisting of photographs, drawings, and I did a piece in the gallery. And the piece was specifically related to that gallery space and the size of that room. I was very fortunate; the show was very well received. What was so interesting to me, is that it was also an appropriate moment, I think, for the art world to encounter someone who was not only responding to an inner dialogue of the art world. I was looking outside that world, and I think there were several other artists who were too. In a certain way, this propelled me right back to Vermont, and the success of that situation allowed me to buy property and create the studio I'm in now. Before that I had been renting, and my studio was the woods. I eventually gave up my Manhattan studio in the early eighties.

RK *What would you say is the pivotal piece or the pivotal point, between working in the woods, and creating temporary pieces, and your work that creates more permanent, occupiable places?*

MS The pivotal piece is *Ritual Series 5–79* (Plate 10). In 1976, I began to get commissions to do things like the Dayton, Ohio Project and Nassau County Museum projects. These were very beautiful, very seductive visually, affected by light, structure, and reflections. Nassau Museum is connected with Nassau County Park and I proposed an outdoor piece. I chose an overgrown pond because it gave me the opportunity to create a trail around it. I became very excited by making the trail and carving out the points of view that people would have – and then

Map of Memory, an Interview

the structures I placed in the pond became a point of focus for framing and experiencing the view (Fig. 3.4). The view gave the context. I was more excited about the whole experience of this place and how it set the mood for what I built on the pond. This was a public situation and was well received. Water, reflection, and garden-like walkways around a pond in such a beautiful setting – all of this made me somewhat uncomfortable about the seductive quality of the site.

Soon after this work at Nassau County, I wanted to give myself a different challenge. I looked for a new landscape. I chose a dark hemlock and spruce forest on my land in Vermont. There was no water, no reflective light, just the darkness and stillness of the woods. I began my work by breaking off the dead lower branches of the trees in the immediate area. Doing this opened a space in the woods. I collected and brought all the accumulated branches together. I thought the first thing a human being would desire and need is a level space in these woods. I began building a platform by carefully putting down layers of the branches. Once I had the platform I felt it needed protective sides. I figured out how to stack the branches vertically until low walls surrounded three sides. I realized that I've built a human place, this is clearly a human intervention: it's rectilinear and level, it's made from natural materials. There's no mystery how it was made. After studying this for a time I decided to place a sculptural structure into it, as if I'd been working there. It becomes a room in nature. Please remember that I spent many years working in natural environments from 1972 on – during those years I felt a need to be very cautious about making any

3.4
**First Gate Ritual Series,
Nassau Country Museum,
New York**
Michael Singer,
1976

changes to the given nature and qualities of a site – and then suddenly, I feel as if I have earned my right to intervene, to make changes, from a place of respect. The earlier works, which are so ephemeral and light, were transformed here in this woodland piece (Plate 10). The act of doing this work in the woods began a shift in my life and psyche. I was becoming more connected to issues that were less about transient moments, and more about exploring earth time, geologic time.

Private and public

Michael Singer has received numerous commissions from private clients and public entities for permanent works of art that include gardens, memorials, buildings, as well as objects. These commissions reveal that Singer is continuing to question fundamental assumptions: about art, the role of an artist, and our relationship to natural systems. In the Grand Rapids Riverwalk Floodwall project, for the City of Grand Rapids, Michigan, (1988–1995), Singer collaborated with engineers and city planners to engage the natural and cultural history of a river edge site in the central city. His project created a functional and sculptural floodwall, including river access and native plantings, as an alternative to an Army Corps of Engineers sheer concrete floodwall that would have destroyed the old cottonwoods along the bank. This project became a precedent for further development of the river edge in this city. Singer created interior and exterior gardens for the Becton Dickinson Corporation, in Franklin Lakes, New Jersey (1986). He reveals his view of the power of art to arrest our attention, and facilitate shifts in perception, when he said of the building's interior atriums, "If I put an object in here – it's over – it just becomes part of everyday life."[4] He created instead a series of lushly planted, layered gardens, where most of the garden is below grade. The garden cannot be taken in with a single glance; and with the interaction between water, plants, stone, and natural light, the visitor is rewarded with an environment constantly in flux to contemplate and discover.

Singer has received commissions from several individuals to create private places to facilitate contemplation, both indoors and outdoors, including *Pavilion and Garden*, Vermont, 1982–92. Here, over several years, Singer worked to create a retreat, accessible only from a path through the fields, on a 20-acre rural site. He designed a pond, reshaped the land and reestablished native plants, as well as designing the pavilion and its furnishings. The pavilion consists of a 14 × 20 foot room that extends over the pond edge (Plate 11). Other meditative retreats include: *Contemplative Garden and Shelter*, La Jolla, California (1990), *Pond Pavilion*, Worcester, Massachusetts (1999), and the J. Parker Huber House, Brattleboro, Vermont

(1998), selected as a "Record House" and published in *Architectural Record* in 1999. In all of these projects, Singer was the art/design lead and collaborated with consulting designers and builders.

Public gardens and memorials that have explored the idea of contemplation have also been key components of Singer's work, including *Woodland Garden* at Wellesley College, Wellesley, Massachusetts (1990–92) where he collaborated with architect Michael McKinnell to create a unique work of public art – a genre that is oftentimes thought of as having an urban context. The Wellesley campus has wooded areas with views of Lake Waban, and the selected site is along a pathway that winds through this area that is used by the local as well as the campus community. *Woodland Garden* is a place of repose defined by two-foot tall stone walls – setting up thresholds and boundaries that refer to the long tradition in New England where farmers stacked stones along property lines. The space appears simple at first glance, then grows in complexity as one discovers a space four feet below ground to contemplate, offering the visitor unexpected vignettes of nature and an unusual view of the forest.

For the *A Place to Remember Those Who Survived* memorial in Stuttgart, Germany (1992), the city commissioned him to design a one-acre garden within a larger city park, a garden that became a space for remembrance and reflection. Singer selected a derelict site where two small streams converge, ringed by an old apple orchard slated for removal. In the process of exploring this chosen location, large amounts of overgrown rubble from the bombing of the city in World War II were found on the site. This was the impetus for the space addressing a larger memorial function. *A Place to Remember Those Who Survived* engages the natural water systems on site along with creating a new constructed layer of wells, runnels, and pools (Fig. 3.5). Mystery and silence are explored through the water: moving water is concealed and still water is revealed. Singer describes that the "sound of water masks the sound of the profane world."[5] Looking closely into the water, a complex and enigmatic world of form is revealed below the water level. There are two distinct spaces in the garden, one in shade and one in light. The apple orchard was restored as part of Singer's work. A strong sense of time and transformation are present in the garden, facilitating memory and healing (Fig. 3.6).

Singer engages the body in unconventional ways and in unconventional places to wake us up to the experience of having/being a body and the power of the moment. The process of walking to and through his projects is an integral part of the work. His works engage all of the senses, for example, our sense of smell at the Concourse C project (1994) within the Denver International Airport (Plate 13). By impregnating manure on the pieces he fabricated in Vermont, Singer describes that he "took a zone, made it

Michael Singer

**3.5
A Place to Remember Those Who Survived, Memorial Garden, Stuttgart, Germany. Two streams join at the first well, flowing into a trough cut into the stone walkway**
Michael Singer, 1992

smell, made it wet, and made it grow – and gave life that you don't get in places like an airport."[6] All of these gardens and pavilions begin to reveal Singer's strategies for contemplative spaces; he describes his sculptures and environments as an "apparatus to make you more aware of the world, not of the art."[7]

Interview –
Michael Singer and Rebecca Krinke

RK   *Did you study or look at any traditions such as the Japanese garden? Has this been a part of your research?*

MS   Oh yes, very much. In that period (the eighties) and it still is. I'm interested in looking beyond our culture where subtlety and a sense of discovery prompted me to look deeper, where there are words and concepts for human and natural interactions. The relationship to nature is not dichotomous. Our culture tends to deliver what we want in an

Map of Memory, an Interview

3.6
***A Place to Remember Those Who Survived,* Memorial Garden, Stuttgart, Germany. View from the woodland to the open area, apple orchard, and surrounding park**
Michael Singer, 1992

immediate way, presented to us right up front, at the moment, and we also, as artists, are reflecting the zeitgeist. So certainly Eastern cultures, indigenous cultures, the traditional Japanese arts, landscapes, and architecture, that are about a continuum, are extraordinary for me. I received a grant to go to Japan in the early eighties from the National Endowment [for the Arts] to study bamboo. This was a great way to see Japan, with a translator and being able to go everywhere. I went back a couple of years later as part of a conference, the Hakone Conference, addressing cross-cultural influences, Americans who had been influenced by Japanese culture and Japanese who had been influenced by American culture. There were musicians, writers, filmmakers, performers, and visual artists. Many Americans and Westerners will look at my work and say, "You're obviously so influenced by Japanese culture" and I'd say, "Yes, it's certainly something I look at, and have an affinity towards." But when I showed my work to the Japanese, they didn't see the connection, the affinity. This notion was really funny to them; they questioned what Japanese would go off in the middle

3.7
***Pond Pavilion*, Ecotarium, Worcester, Massachusetts**
Michael Singer, 1999

of nowhere to a beaver bog to go make something that no one would ever see? I mean it was just not part of their cultural mentality or their landscape. They saw my work and process as more representative of American culture because of our abundant open space, wilderness areas, and remote places that we can go to. Our attitude towards individualism and solitude in natural environments is specific, and not similar to someone who is Japanese. One thing they did connect my work with – in the earlier pieces like the reeds and bamboo in Dayton – was Japanese flower arranging, which I found very interesting. They connected the sense of time, beauty, and loss of these earlier pieces to the beautiful and ephemeral nature of a flower arrangement.

RK   *Are there other places, experiences, or people that have been particularly inspirational to you? How about Carlo Scarpa?*

MS   It was interesting working with the architect Michael McKinnell. He – Kallmann McKinnell and Wood – did the building for Becton Dickinson (Fig. 3.8). I had a wonderful experience doing that, so I asked him to collaborate with me on the Wellesley project. It was nice to choose my collaborator, and especially for an artist to choose the architect since it's usually the other way around. This was the late eighties, and it was Michael who introduced me to Scarpa. He said, " You ought to take a look at this fellow – you've got a lot in common." And I looked, and I was just blown away. When I look at Scarpa, I see, for example, that a built element doesn't just get lifted up, it has to demonstrate getting lifted. His work describes a process of becoming. Yes, I can see that I've used very similar strategies in my work that predates my seeing Scarpa's, as well as work after that.

RK   *At the Wellesley project, what's interesting about your selected site is that it says that a contemplative space can have a dialogue with the campus, and not be completely hidden in the woods. Was this a part of your decision-making?*

MS   I was given an opportunity to choose any site on the campus to do a piece, so I spent time exploring and thinking about site selection. The campus is an Olmsted design, sited on Lake Waban, and there are many special places. Nature is a solace and comfort to me, and the idea at Wellesley was to provide a place where students could leave their everyday world of college tensions behind. I wanted to honor the pathway around Lake Waban, and these woods. I think to take that walk around the lake is a way to decompress, but I also wanted to make a place to walk to, and a place to stop, a possible destination to facilitate contemplation or reflection (Fig. 3.9). I like this site because

3.8
Interior atria gardens, Becton Dickinson Corporation, Franklin Lakes, New Jersey
Michael Singer, 1986

Map of Memory, an Interview

3.9
***Woodland Garden,
Wellesley College,
Wellesley,
Massachusetts***
Michael Singer with
Michael McKinnell,
1990–1992

it is a site on this pathway where students can see through the woods, and across the pond to the campus buildings, to see where they were coming from and to know they could gain another perspective from this vantage. We planted over 100 trees and added ferns and blueberries, an intensification of nature, a respect of nature. We didn't take out the dead trees; they provide habitat. Something I found quite interesting was a professor who noted that the other end of the campus contains the Hunnewell Arboretum and Garden – which is a famous Jeffersonian garden, representing the thinking of that era – and the juxaposition of this new garden, built in the early nineties, reflects the interest and need today to respect and enjoy the beauty of the indigenous rather than the exotic.

RK *Is doesn't feel unsafe going there, does it?*

MS No, although the question was raised because it is in the woods. Many people use the woods and this is a very special place for students.

RK *To a certain extent your project "gives them the woods", as there was no destination there before.*

MS I hope so. And when they get there, there's a sense of discovery because this place they find could just be an old stone wall in the woods. It's not until you get close and look into it and below it, and start to see that there are layers to the space and even places revealed with smaller gardens and moss (Fig. 3.10). There is a sequence of discovery. You might walk by the site if you didn't know something was there. We treated the sculpture wall so that moss would grow; a process that takes time. The maintenance person at the museum knows to let the decay occur, to let the plants grow, not to interfere with change. Time is part of this garden and sculpture, and it was built to reveal change.

RK *I would like to spend hours there. Do you spend time sitting in your pieces?*

MS Sometimes I do.

RK *And you get responses back from people?*

MS Definitely. I've gotten wonderful feedback from the Wellesley project. When people have found out about my involvement, they've said, "Oh, you did that project – I love that – it was a special place for me during my years at Wellesley!" and that's very nice. And what has always been most rewarding is hearing comments from people who have no experience with art specifically, or who find art baffling. And, really, unless they have some kind of initiation into it, art is baffling for most people. When people see something which is clearly outside the realm of their everyday experience, and they come away with a very positive experience, this is very rewarding. Probably the nicest thing I ever heard anyone say – I had a show at a gallery in New York, and as I was coming in, two young people were coming out – and they said, "Boy, that was worth the subway ride!" And to me, anything that can be worth a subway ride is a great compliment.

(Laughter.)

You asked me earlier about places, experiences, or people that have been inspirational to me, and a very important opportrunity for me in the late eighties was MIT. Some of the teachers at MIT saw my work – indoor sculpture – at the Louisiana Museum in Denmark, and they sent me a letter asking if I would be interested in teaching architecture at the school. This changed my life – working with these people. The students I worked with at MIT were graduate students in architecture. I taught there for a couple years – a graduate design class – I was known as the teacher who took notes on what the students were saying. I was learning architectural language, process, and issues. I was very interested and curious: What is the architectural creative process, and how is it different than the visual arts? That was an open question for me for many years, until I actually began doing architectural design

Map of Memory, an Interview

3.10
Woodland Garden,
**Wellesley College,
Wellesley,
Massachusetts.
Detail of moss
garden within the
larger structure**
Michael Singer with
Michael McKinnell.,
1990–1992

93

Michael Singer

and landscape architecture, and dealing with human scale and function. The key issues that are different – and it's funny and obvious when I say it now, but it wasn't obvious to me for years – are that the design professions are given a client's program to design to, and artists create their own program. It isn't an external impetus. And I'm not saying this makes one field better than another. I think exciting architecture is when the architect brings forward issues that they have been researching and working with over time into the prescribed program of a specific place; you really can't just react to a program, you need your own themes, ideas, and issues. I got a real kick out of teaching design and architecture, and likewise I get a kick out of teaching in the visual arts where I can challenge students about their personal program and vision, being open to other professions and approaches, and the challenges of letting go, even for a moment, of their personal expression and its agenda.

RK   *Some of your former students of architecture at MIT asked you to work with them on the Alterra Institute project in the Netherlands; did they want you to take the lead role?*

MS   No, we worked collaboratively as a team to enter a competition, and won. We talked about what the landscape strategy could be for this place, and felt the landscape itself could create the meaning for why this building is there rather than the other way around, which is what most architecture does. We were all interested in what to do with the landscape aesthetically, in meaning, and also, how can it function? A sustainable practice strategy – which is a starting point for me – became key to how we looked at the building and landscape being interconnected, and meaning of place flowed from there.

RK   *Was the project better because of all the people?*

MS   Oh, absolutely. Today all of my work is collaborative except for the personal sculpture I do – very private pieces that can be identified as signature work. The projects I'm working on are a collaborative, integrated design process, where professionals respectfully challenge each other. It's so much richer to be challenged, and so much better for the project.

RK   *You've talked about your work, from the beginning, as having an affinity with indigenous traditions that touch the land in a minimal way. Was that a formative idea for your ideas of sustainability? In other words, when you hear the term sustainability – although this term is everywhere now – do you feel that this idea has always been a part of you?*

MS   The first encounter that I had with that thinking, and I don't think the word "sustainable" was in the culture yet, was when I was chosen to do a public art project for Long Wharf in New Haven, Connecticut. I was chosen because I said that I would not make a piece of art. This was 1988 and rather revolutionary. I said that I would work with the site and meaning of the waterfront. They said they were looking for a "signature piece" – that was the term they used. The other artists being considered were Claes Oldenburg, Richard Serra, and a few others. I was on their short list, and I asked them why they were asking me, because at that time my outdoor work was in natural environments. They said they were curious about the approach I might take because at one time, the New Haven waterfront was a natural environment, containing wetlands. Today this site is a mile long in-fill of land. It had become a truck rest stop off the highway even though it wasn't designated as that. It was a "no person land" and the communities were very concerned, asking, "What is this place?" I was asking the same thing, saying that before you can define anything about putting a piece of art here, we need to know what this place is. I won the competition, which was extraordinary. I said that what I will do with the proposal money is a conceptual plan for the site that would first define the site. I was proposing to do an urban plan, as an artist. I'd never done this before and didn't have a clue. So the first thing I did was call people and ask them what I should be doing. I realized I needed to put together a team. I needed historians to tell me about the history of this place, and I needed a cultural anthropologist to tell me about it from a different perspective. I needed someone to tell me about the environmental conditions of the place, and that was Paul Mankiewicz and Bill Kinsinger who worked with John Todd, who started the Gaia foundation and now leads Ocean Arks. These were science and engineering thinkers who were really far out there in the late 1980s, way ahead of their time, folks who worked with natural systems as functioning cleansers.

Bill and Paul came to the site, looked at it, talked with me, and said, "This harbor is basically a dead body of water. It's dying from hypoxia – caused by the presence of too much nitrogen in the water." This was a very depressing story in the sense of how unhealthy the site really was. And I asked, "Is there anything we could do with this mile of waterfront that could affect this place in a positive way?" And they said that what needed to be done to address this hypoxia issue was to recreate the wetlands that had been systematically destroyed over many years. And suddenly it all began to make sense. My historian, Meg Ostrum, tells me about the past 400 years of human intervention on

Michael Singer

the site – the waterfront used to be a mile away – a mile west toward downtown – so the waterfront today is a story of 400 years of continuous filling of the harbor. The fill begins from the silting of two rivers that converge at the harbor, silting through years of agricultural development, followed by 200 years of slowly building Long Wharf until it went a mile out into the water to create a deep-water site. The building of I-95 and development fills in even more wetlands in the 1940s and 1950s. Fill is the actor, and human intervention is the theme of this extraordinary story. I realized what meanings and messages this place could take on at this moment in the process of change.

This is where your question about sustainability enters my work – suddenly I'm realizing that my work, the decisions and creative moves – might actually restore or repair an environment that has suffered this extraordinary amount of degradation. As humans, we will always intervene in the landscape. How about an intervention that repairs, an intervention that informs people about how we can repair, and about the past, and a landscape that promotes active positive decisions for the future? We defined Long Wharf as a public site that educates people; art that recreates habitat and that helped to restore the systems of this place. It has recreational components, educational components, etc., etc. This became part of the master plan that the city is slowly working with. My work on Long Wharf was pivotal to my thinking. It led me to ask questions everywhere and to bring creative problem solvers from many professions to the table. For a public art project in Grand Rapids, I was invited as one of several artists to choose a site in this city, and I chose to work with the river. They were basically going to destroy all the native vegetation and old cottonwood trees for a flood control project, yet the only place that really needed flood control was a small section – 300 feet – and so instead of clear cutting everything, trees could be saved, and money could be saved, too.

Another very important person for me, and who is key to my sensing the importance of natural systems and the beauty of the indigenous is the landscape architect A. E. Bye. In the early eighties, one of my friends Michael Van Valkenburgh, was teaching landscape architecture at Harvard. I said to Michael what's needed is a show and a book about great landscape architecture being done in this country, because artists are basically doing landscape architecture and have no idea what the roots of the profession are. I suggested he choose the great landscape architects – who you'd want people to know about – then let's work together to create an exhibition and a book. It was a great experience for both of us to work together from our points of view, and with Alan Ward as photographer. The book and exhibition was called *Built Landscapes of the Northeast* and it became an important book and show, bringing five important designers to our attention, including Beatrix Farrand and Fletcher Steele, who were deceased, but in the early eighties people outside the profession didn't know who they were. I went with Michael and we interviewed James Rose, who was nearing the end of his life and A. E. Bye and Dan Kiley. I photographed the Kiley and Bye projects with Alan and went to the Beatrix Farrand designed garden at the Rockefeller estate in Maine. This was before the garden was open to the public.

It was so wonderful to see these opposites: Dan Kiley and A. E. Bye – who was this wonderful man, and his work was so refreshing in this realm. Bye was so affirming of my sensibilities. I think he is the step between landscape architecture and sustainability for me. Bye seemed to be saying, "Pay attention to what is right around us, and what is right outside your door, the beauty of the indigenous." I can make the extension from A. E. Bye to John Todd and Ocean Arks. I could see the interconnections of water treatment systems, natural systems infrastructure, a sensitivity to place, and how these issues connected to my sensibilities and aesthetic. I began to imagine what my role could be with engineers and designers of these systems, and how I could try to make their systems beautiful, understandable, and related to communities.

Complexity and contemplation

Michael Singer's work continues to have a dialogue between his private studio work and public art/design projects that increasingly work with complex cultural and ecological conditions. Several of these projects are infrastructure projects – projects that require buildings or functions that many may consider generic or repulsive, such as sewage treatment and garbage disposal. Singer's work continues to challenge assumptions about what is mundane and what is wondrous, and what may be worthy of our contemplation.

At the Concourse C project (1994) within the Denver International Airport (Plate 13), Singer created a completely out of context place: a rich, tactile, scented environment to combat the generic airport experience. The garden is visible from the floor above and the floor below, built between the two trafficked levels of the airport concourse. Like one of the traditional Zen gardens, there is no physical access to this garden for visitors, rather it evokes mysteries of wildness, time, decay, and habitat – including birds that came inside during construction of the building, and who have found a home here.

Michael Singer

Singer and artist Linnea Glatt were commissioned as a team by the Phoenix Arts Commission and the Department of Public Works to provide the architectural and landscape architectural concept design for the Phoenix Solid Waste Transfer and Recycling Center (1989–1993). This 25-acre, 18 million dollar facility transfers and recycles garbage (Fig. 3.11). Singer's and Glatt's design invites public involvement in an infrastructure facility that would normally be closed to the public. They created an amphitheater in the center of the building where school groups and others can learn about the processes that take place on site. Concepts of renewal and transformation were integral to all aspects of the building and landscape design, exemplified by the project's recycling of water and creation of habitat. The project was hailed by Herbert Muschamp, architecture critic of *The New York Times*, as one of the eight most important buildings of 1993.[8]

At the Alterra Institute for Environmental Research, Wageningen, Netherlands (1999) Singer collaborated on the design of the exterior and interior gardens for its new headquarters, working closely with the architects and engineers on this state of the art green building. Within this office environment, Singer asked the question, "Why should contemplative space be outside of our everyday experience?"[9] and answered it by creating indoor and outdoor gardens that are not only compellingly beautiful places, visible from the offices, but settings of ecological stewardship (Plate 12). Underscoring the site and building as an integrated system, Singer observes that

3.11
Solid Waste Transfer and Recycling Center, Phoenix, Arizona
Michael Singer with Linnea Glatt, 1989–1993

the bioswales (depressions that collect stormwater for cleansing) they designed for the parking lot are beautiful. He continues, asking, "We are in the middle of a paved world – why aren't we questioning these kinds of places?"[10] The interior and exterior gardens function as the "lungs and kidneys" of the building – cleaning air and graywater and providing climate control without air conditioning. Water is first diverted to an outdoor constructed wetland and pond, and then it is piped into the first atrium pool where toxins are absorbed, and to a second atrium pool for its final cleansing. The water then drips into a cistern for storage and recycling in the building's irrigation system. The design also provides research and experimentation sites within the gardens, some used by environmental scientists working within the building. Singer notes that the project uses off the shelf materials, and was relatively low budget, yet it is a key project worldwide for sustainable design.[11]

Singer has worked on several power plants, including the AES Cogeneration Facility, in Londonderry, New Hampshire, (2000), the largest power plant in New England, and the Trans Gas Energy Cogeneration Power Plant, in Greenpoint, New York City (2002), an eight-acre urban power plant in a Brooklyn neighborhood (Plate 14). Here the whole facility is designed to be a positive force in the community: it will capture stormwater, capture waste heat, and provide photovoltaic greenhouses to grow native plant material to replant wetlands in indigenous areas. Singer's work is asking critical questions about large-scale infrastructure projects – how they can be a part of the community and provide a potent contemplative experience – and his work with these facilities demonstrates that they can be brought into greater balance with the natural world as he seeks again to wake us up from seeing the world in conventional ways.

Just as working in a beaver bog for five years was an unconventional response to the art world, so too is his work on infrastructure and planning projects. Singer's ability to ask questions and challenge assumptions gives us new possibilities for the human connection with the earth.

Michael Singer and Rebecca Krinke interview

RK *All the different settings you've worked with: private, public, campus, corporate . . . Do you hope for different messages to different visitors? Do we need different kinds of "contemplations" for different settings? Do public settings have a different potency because you may be able to affect passersby instead of just an individual who has commissioned you?*

Michael Singer

MS   I've come to realize more about this role because I've been able to work on places like The New England Science Center, now called the Ecotarium, where the mission is to educate, and they have an environment of 60 acres. I've learned how important it is to invite people to understand what they're looking at. And demonstrate how they can adapt the strategies they are looking at, learning about, to their own environments. I think public space has a responsibility to educate and to encourage the visitor to bring ideas into their own environment. Interpreting has come up more recently for me.

RK   *It seems as if ideas of contemplation are often linked to ideas of beauty and simplicity – and contemplation is often thought of as being removed from the everyday – but it seems that you are creating projects that redefine beauty and contemplation, and are creating these places in very complex situations.*

MS   Why should you not be in a contemplative space when you're treating your water? What is it that we're contemplating? What is our role in repairing or regenerating the world around us?

RK   *There's been a strong feeling that we've degraded the planet, with questions being raised about what else we can do. Some of the spaces that speak to healing seem to be quite powerful for people because otherwise, why would you have people coming to the Phoenix Waste Transfer Station?*

MS   We have to be careful not to overwhelm people with the problems we are facing. I think it's a responsibility to offer alternatives, not just deliver the bad news. I really do believe we can actively address the issues. The Phoenix project helps people understand the problem and it offers solutions. It provides something so unexpected, a dump that is beautiful.

RK   *In the past that project would have been completely hidden, and instead it says – maybe it's best we do look at it – and can it be looked at in a beautiful architectural and sculptural way?*

MS   Yes, and if you are going to bring people into the spaces (Fig. 3.12) – what are the strategies to inform them? I often think surprise works well.

RK   *Would you want to say anything more about contemplation and waste?*

MS   Surprise leads to learning and then on to contemplation, contemplating what is concealed from us. There is also the land itself. The Waste Transfer Station is right next to a landfill that's now closed, but the landfill is a major landform in Phoenix, you can see it from downtown. It's six

Map of Memory, an Interview

3.12
Solid Waste Transfer and Recycling Center, Phoenix, Arizona. Public amphitheatre with views into the recycling building
Michael Singer with Linnea Glatt, 1989–1993

stories high and it's a mile long. It was filled within 25 years and that's a statement in itself . . . You know, "My God, what are we doing?" That's a revealing fact. The closed landfill is already a monument. So Linnea and I didn't really look at this project in terms of "we want to send a specific message". I think you have to be careful because specific messages are often changing messages; we're finding out different things. For instance, today when we're looking at that landfill, we can understand that people are doing all kinds of study, and finding out that the landfill is actually a resource of energy and material. It could be mined someday. That's a turnaround from our belief that a landfill can only be a useless, toxic, hellish place. So really what our purpose was, in the design of this project, and in looking at it from this perspective of change – was to develop strategies to get people to look, to think, to contemplate – to question their own assumptions. Period. To be in a place that is obviously very different than any place in their normal experience. It has points of view that reveal the city or reveal the natural landscape, so you're looking at natural systems and you're looking at built systems from the building. We want people to make connections, but not tell them to experience it. We wanted to be careful not to make something that is a fixed statement. We wanted to create an experience and have the visitor raise questions, to really be compelled to look into that facility. You don't have to say very much because you're seeing human beings inside of this place picking, grabbing, sorting, and working with the garbage of your community. It's a very powerful experience, and raises a lot of important questions.

RK *Do you define contemplation or contemplative landscape?*

MS No. Should I give you a reason why? Just like you would not define what is a piece of art and what is not, I think there's a potential for any situation to be contemplative, even the bathroom at the nature center that I'm working on. We realized the potential of that restroom to provide an enormous amount of information to visitors about natural systems conservation. Now who would – even just a few years ago – have thought of doing any kind of exhibit in a restroom? So I think you have to be very open to the potentials of where contemplation can take place, and what it is you're contemplating.

RK *Traditionally, out of religious worldviews came outdoor settings for contemplation. And now in our secular society, in our postmodern world, I've been thinking, "Where are those places now?" Do we need those places that help us think about our relationship to larger forces, the cosmos, spirit?*

MS I think that no matter what period of time, cultures and individuals have sought out and will always seek places of contemplation – places that allow them to reflect on all sorts of things – sometimes specifically spiritual, but also about relationships, about systems, even mundane issues in their lives. People seek out a place where they can be contemplative, where they can contemplate those ideas. I think the idea of contemplation is very broad and not specific to sacred space, although sacred space is often a place where people would want to go – even though for most in contemporary American life – it's not. You may ask someone, "Where do you go when things are just too heavy?" And they may say to Starbucks, to one of their big comfortable chairs, even shopping, or that they listen to music . . .

RK *Maybe finding contemplative space through sound or through a virtual setting is particularly valid for contemporary life. Is there a role for designed landscapes?*

MS Yes, there is a role, and speaking from my own work, I seek to provide an experience – whether it's from my personal sculpture, or if it's from a building, a room, a landscape, whether it's part of a power plant – my goal is to really give people a place where they can reconnect to something that is recognizable. Someone once said to me – and this was a wonderful complement – that my work had gotten them to remember things they had forgotten, helped them remember to remember.

RK *What were they referring to? Did they elaborate?*

MS I think they were referring to the sense of being human. What are we as human beings? Where do we fit in the longer and bigger scheme of things? What role does time and transformation, and concepts like that, play in the bigger human experience?

RK *It seems as if sacred space used to try, and perhaps still tries to answer or acknowledge those questions, and those big questions don't go away.*

MS Certainly one of the goals of my work – whether it's accomplished or not – is to address those big questions. I'm less interested in being connected to issues that are "of the moment" or current in style. I'm interested in a bigger picture than that. My work provides something for me personally as well: the process of doing the work and the result of that research, the learning, and whatever the product is that results, which is then something that I can experience which raises questions and issues for me too.

RK *In a way, your work seems to have grown in complexity, yet it still has these ongoing ideas about the earth, and the human interventions in the earth. What are the other ways or possibilities for our interaction with the earth?*

MS That is also one of the goals of my work, to help me or the viewer to understand the connection between humans and natural environments and built environments and to recogize new interactions between them. And how do we evaluate that connection? How do we enhance that connection? How do we improve the connection? That sits pretty much at the top of the list for me. And then questioning the assumptions we have about these connections and where we are. Do we draw the line at certain places? Why should we draw the line at a sewage treatment plant? Do we say a place like that doesn't exist? Of course it exists – we made it. And power facilities, or any of the infrastructure projects I'm working on, all of these things are there to support our living. They sustain us. I think the culture needs to better understand the connection we have to those places. Why they are there and how they function or don't function. How they can be improved and actually be interconnected. There are synergies that are possible. Creating a place where you contemplate the interconnectedness of all life is definitely at the top of the list for me too.

RK That's important because it starts to point the way to new paradigms. You are getting asked to work on all sorts of hybrid projects with hybrid teams of people addressing reclamation, infrastructure, etc. I'm curious – do you have a feeling about the kinds of projects you really want to be doing or get even more involved with? You did mention that you'd like to get more involved with your studio work.

MS My personal studio work is a place that is very private and feeds issues and questions that get addressed in projects that are taking on issues in the real world. I personally find I need more time with that private investigation, but I am very excited about the projects that I am working on right now. For example, I'm working with the Brattleboro Food Co-op, and when I look at the idea of a food co-op – what is it really? What is a community? What nurtures a community? These questions are very exciting to be involved with. Is a food store just a store or is it the heart of the community in every respect? And especially if it's a local co-operative instead of the local chain supermarket, which is a corporate entity. Working with people to look at how these systems interconnect is very exciting to me. Working with power plants is very exciting to me too because a power plant has very useful waste, heat and graywater, and it has the potential to be something in the community that no one has imagined. It has qualities both positive and negative; we all need the power, but it can be so much more than that, not only in its visual qualities, but in its programming and as an amenity. I would like to create spaces or places or pieces that encourage people to contemplate how to regenerate our systems, how to actually affect the health of our social and natural environment, how to set in motion a healing process.

RK That's very interesting to me since many people have said to me that the most contemplative landscape is untouched nature. And that can be a very powerful contemplation but it doesn't always put the human into the equation and that seems to be a potent part of your discussion.

MS   I'm actually working on very potent landscape: the "100 Mile View" overlook here in Vermont, where the project is to site a natural history museum. What we realized is that the view of course is the draw. It's an extraordinary site to be building on and people already stop to do exactly that – to get that point of view of powerful untouched nature – and what we decided to do in our role in this as designers, is to interpret this place. The whole team is working on how to get people looking *into* that landscape not *at* that landscape. Into. How to raise the issues that this landscape really presents, since to an untrained eye, it looks untouched. That landscape presents enormous issues that relate to time and change and transformation and human interventions. That's something to contemplate and to enrich. So how does the designer take that challenge and design an experience for someone to stop them in their tracks; and get them to question their own assumptions about what they're seeing, and to contemplate what was there before, and why what they're seeing there today is there today, and how the future can be shaped by their understanding and actions?

RK   *Sometimes people think contemplation is just visual . . .*

MS   No, it's educational. And its body oriented too; it's intellectual, physical, emotional, spiritual, and much more than purely aesthetic. And it's more than you see right off the bat. There are layers. There are strategies for creating contemplative situations, concealing and revealing – that's part of the palette language of contemplative space, I think. What you see and experience in the immediate then peels away to something else that raises questions, and doesn't always provide answers.

RK   *Are there any places you've visited, spaces you would describe as contemplative spaces, that have had potency for you? That you found really stopped the mind?*

MS   There are some real stunner places – but for me there are many contemplative spaces everyday – quite literally, taking the train from New Haven to New York. The train goes by a whole area of New York that shows you things you would never, ever get to see if you're in a car or even if you live there. From the train, you're traveling, "overviewing" this scale of humanity, and what it has created. And if you really look at it – it is a support network for this metropolis – and here I am living in a pastoral landscape in Vermont for the past 30 years, which has a very different scale of humanity. So at certain times I will take that train, and I'm just overwhelmed by the complexity, but also by the poetry, and where it brings my mind, into issues around my own work, into detail, into issues of the city, the macro and the micro; a truly contemplative space.

Michael Singer

I find a certain power plant in Florida very compelling, it's in Riviera Beach just north of West Palm Beach – although most people have a lot of trouble with it – they hate this facility. Because of the climate, there is no need to enclose the interior operation of this power plant, so when you look at this in the daytime, you're looking through this extraordinary skeleton of structure that has innards, that have innards, that have innards. Birds are living in it; it's this very vertical and very beautiful structure. Down the block is a high-rise condominium that you just want to dynamite, and yet everyone is saying how ugly this power plant is, and how we've got to get rid of it, and I'm looking at it and seeing it as the most elegant thing in the area. I took a photo where you can see the context of the two sitting next to each other – the power plant and the condos – and everyone laughed when I said to demolish the condos instead. But the photo did help them start to see the possibility of a new perspective, when I pointed it out, that a power plant could be beautiful. And then I'm seeing that a power plant for what I could do with it – because its structure is basically an apparatus for possible life – for extraordinary life, for interconnection. So I go to some places like that and I sit and contemplate with my jaw hanging open, and I'm saying, "Do you know how beautiful this thing could really be?"

Notes

1. Michael Singer, "Contemporary Landscapes of Contemplation" symposium, University of Minnesota, October 18, 2002.
2. D. Waldman, *Michael Singer*, Solomon R. Guggenheim Museum: New York, 1984.
3. Michael Singer, "Contemporary Landscapes of Contemplation" symposium, University of Minnesota, October 18, 2002.
4. Ibid.
5. Ibid.
6. Ibid.
7. Ibid.
8. Ibid.
9. Ibid.
10. Ibid.
11. Ibid.

Contemplative landscapes, restorative landscapes

Rebecca Krinke

The scholarly literature on contemplative landscapes is relatively sparse. On the other hand, the pioneering work of environmental psychologists Rachel and Stephen Kaplan, Roger S. Ulrich and others over the last 25 years is building a body of research and theory on restorative experiences and environments.[1] A "restorative" environment provides measurable physical and/or psychological benefit to human health. Research has demonstrated that contact with nature, especially vegetation, has measurable restorative effects.[2] The research and theory on restorative environments provides useful tools for examining contemplative landscapes. Do successful contemplative landscapes have associations with restorative experiences/environments? And if so, can case studies begin to suggest some of the ways that the attributes of a restorative experience become realized in physical form? Examining relationships between restorative and contemplative landscapes contributes to our understanding of how to more consciously design landscapes that assist human well-being and development.

In its most straightforward definition, contemplation is "fixed attention" and contemplative energy can be directed at anything. However, synonyms for contemplation include "reflect" and "ponder," highlighting that contemplation is often seen as a state or activity where we are more consciously focused on our thoughts – and often implying "higher level" thoughts involved with questions of self, relationships, cosmos – than in our typical day-to-day thinking. "Meditation" is also given as a synonym for

Rebecca Krinke

contemplation, which suggests that contemplation may be an activity or process that seeks inner silence, or freedom from thought. There is no single definition of a "contemplative landscape" either, but in this essay, a contemplative landscape is defined as one where the designers have set out to create a space that quiets the mind – facilitating a developmental activity or process where the individual has more choice over their thoughts – perhaps to focus their reflections, perhaps to focus on inner silence. Although many of the most powerful designed places may have a "contemplative effect" of fixing one's attention, there is a lack of focused description and analysis of how those effects are achieved. And beyond this, what about the landscapes that have been specifically designed as contemplative realms, implying that they intend to address developmental stages beyond fixing our attention? For example, how is it that the Reflection Garden at the Bloedel Reserve has a demonstrable impact on so many of its visitors?

This essay examines two case study projects: the National Library of France in Paris designed by Dominique Perrault, (construction completed 1995) and the Reflection Garden at the Bloedel Reserve near Seattle, final design by Richard Haag (1984). Both Perrault and Haag have stated that it was their intention to create a contemplative landscape, and this is the primary reason that these case studies were selected. The projects were also selected for the elements they have in common: both case studies employ one of the earliest expressions of the designed landscape – the enclosed garden – which has been used across time and by different cultures for security and to facilitate contemplation. Both settings employ strategies of ritual, such as restrictions on access and movement to create a place removed from the day-to-day world to facilitate a contemplative response. The case studies were also selected for key differences – providing useful points of comparison – as the locales are quite opposite. A second growth forest dominates the Bloedel Reserve, located on rural Bainbridge Island, while the National Library, located along the Seine in central Paris, contrasts a transplanted grove of mature pines with architectural towers. The projects employ the dialectical landscape archetypes of forest (at the Library) and clearing (at the Reflection Garden) as foci for contemplation. At the Reflection Garden, the interior (the clearing) is serene, surrounded by a "wild" nature, and at the Library, a "wild" nature (the forest) is surrounded by a serene architectural enclosure. Taken together, then, these two very comparable landscapes reveal strategies for creating more informed contemplative spaces, and enlarge our understanding of the emerging principles of restorative landscapes.

Published accounts of visitors to the two projects attest to the success of the projects as contemplative – indicating that both projects are being perceived at the level that they were intended, at least for these visitors. (I didn't find published accounts that countered this assessment.) During my visits to the two projects, I also found them to be successful at creating a contemplative experience/realm. The majority of published accounts by visitors to the case study projects are by landscape architects or other scholars who may have been primed for an "appropriate response" to the project since they knew about its intentions, and I put myself in this category. I did see many visitors to the case study sites who didn't seem to have a contemplative response to the landscapes. This observation raises intriguing questions: By what criteria do we judge if a landscape is able to facilitate contemplation? What role does the landscape play and what role belongs to the visitor? Does a contemplative response depend solely on the participant – and if they are interested in contemplation – then is any landscape contemplative? Are some landscapes able to shift one to a contemplative mode even if one enters this landscape with no knowledge or intention of finding a contemplative experience?

Emerging restorative theory from Stephen Kaplan and a theory of art developed by contemporary philosopher Ken Wilber provide useful vehicles for probing this issue of how, when and why a landscape may be a contemplative landscape. From Wilber's perspective, all artwork is consciously or unconsciously aiming for a certain level of connection with its viewer, and each viewer has a certain level of ability to pick up on the level that the art is transmitting or not. From Wilber's point of view, Richard Haag and Dominique Perrault were each aiming for the third or highest level of knowing, the level of contemplation, and art created at this level can help the visitor to develop their contemplative eye.[3] Wilber's theory draws upon the idea of a "perennial philosophy" which states that there are core ideas and values which are held in common by spiritual traditions worldwide. Humans have three different modes of knowing: "the eye of flesh, which discloses the material, concrete, and sensual world; the eye of mind, which discloses the symbolic, conceptual, and linguistic world and the eye of contemplation, which discloses the spiritual, transcendental, and transpersonal world."[4] These ways of knowing develop sequentially. Kaplan is also investigating the relationship between the individual and the environment, and finds correlation between meditation and restoration. He concludes that "meditation shares the goals of restoration, namely to foster tranquility and allow the mind to rest and regain its capacity to focus."[5] But while restorative theory focuses on the role of the environment, meditation emphasizes the role of the individual. Kaplan's theory has implications for the transaction between the restorative environment and its visitor: the individual can enhance the role of restorative environments through meditation; and an environment that is not particularly attractive or restorative may still yield restorative effects to the individual with meditative skill and experience.[6]

Rebecca Krinke

Introduction: the Bloedel Reserve

The 150 acre Bloedel Reserve is the former estate of Prentice and Virginia Bloedel, who worked for over three decades with many different designers to bring their vision for the landscape to fruition, ultimately creating a stunning sequence of garden spaces set within and adjacent to the forest. After much exploration of his land, Prentice Bloedel developed a deep relationship with the earth and cosmos. He wrote of these investigations:

> Out of these experiences comes an unexpected insight. Respect for trees and plants replaces indifference; one feels the existence of a divine order. Man is not set apart from the rest of nature – he is just a member of that incredibly diverse population of the universe, a member that nature can do without but who cannot do without nature.[7]

Investigating the human connection with the earth became Prentice Bloedel's passion. His philosophy is summarized by a statement in the handout given to visitors to the Reserve:

> The Reserve's primary interest is in the relationship between plants and people. There is a generally acknowledged but little understood ability of plants and landscape to evoke a wide variety of deeply felt emotions, ranging from tranquility to exhilaration .... It is a place in which to enjoy and learn from the emotional and aesthetic experience of nature the values of harmony, respect for life and tranquility.[8]

Richard Brown, the Reserve's executive director, described that Bloedel invited pioneers in the field of people/plant relationships to multi-day symposia that he hosted at his estate in order to deepen his own knowledge and contribute to scholarship in this area that so intrigued him. The invitees included environmental psychologists Rachel and Stephen Kaplan, horticulturist Charles Lewis, and Gordon Orians, Professor and Director of Environmental Studies at the University of Washington. Bloedel corresponded with landscape theorist Jay Appleton and architect Sir Peter Shepherd, and also funded invited symposia in England with Appleton taking a lead role and Charles Lewis serving as advisor.[9] Prentice and Virginia Bloedel provided financial assistance for the writing of the Kaplans' book, *The Experience of Nature* published in 1989, and Charles Lewis' book, *Green Nature/Human Nature* published in 1996. The conferences and publications that the Bloedels supported began to create a body of research on the relationship between people and nature, and the Reserve itself was the living laboratory where the human relationship with nature could be explored in physical form.

The Bloedels, although they deeded the property to the University of Washington in 1970, bought the property back because they didn't want the land to be used for research and education. In 1986, they set up the Arbor Fund, a non-profit organization to manage the Reserve as a landscape of contemplation.

Introduction: National Library of France

At the National Library of France, architect Dominique Perrault's design contains a transplanted grove of mature pines, all from the same forest, as the centerpiece of the library. The building completely surrounds the trees; the forest is open to the sky. The architect explains:

> The inclusion of an "inlaid", sunken garden rounds off the symbolic siting of the project, offering a quiet spot away from the fuss and bother of the city. Like a cloister, this tranquil unruffled space will invite contemplation and a flowering of intellectual endeavor.[10]

Perrault elaborates on his design intentions, "I tried in the library to rediscover emotions built on paradoxes between presence and absence, human and monumental, opaque and luminous. . . ."[11] The library succeeds at being a paradoxical place. Although cutting edge information technology is in operation in the library, the building doesn't physically manifest the qualities of the digital era. The building organization, detailing, and selected materials have ancient overtones. The library block with its towers surrounded by a forbidding rampart of stairs conjures up images of a medieval fortress.

The forest at the National Library is purely a visual and psychological space. A physically inaccessible central planted space will strike many as quite odd – why not allow access to it? Perrault has discussed his goal to create a contemplative realm, and the device of an inaccessible space has been used across cultures as an aid to contemplation. When no one is allowed into the garden, the space is dominated by the "natural" environment, and free of distractions from human visitors. In the case of the Library forest, no one is talking, walking, eating, playing sports, etc. – and the garden remains a quiet oasis – available visually to all. Precedents for the inaccessible Library garden include the traditional Zen gardens of Japan, gardens such as the iconic Ryoan-ji, an enclosed rectangle of raked sand

111

Rebecca Krinke

and rock, functioning not as a space to inhabit physically, but as a mental space and an aid to contemplation. (Monks meditated on a wooden veranda facing the garden.) The National Library and its garden also draw upon the precedent of the rectilinear medieval cloister garden, which was primarily experienced visually, or through movement around its edges. Cloister gardens are open to the sky, but typically surrounded by a covered walkway where monks or nuns would circle the garden over and over to facilitate contemplation. The National Library is surrounded by a glassed interior walkway, a perambulation that echoes this cloister walk of a monastery. And similar to monks preserving books and knowledge through the dark ages, the researchers at the new library hold an elite status. To use the lower level research rooms, one must apply for, and be awarded a researcher's card. Many of the furnishings were designed by Perrault and have an ecclesiastical quality, such as the torch-like lights and the tapestry-like metal mesh screens and window coverings.

Ritual-like aspects of the Bloedel Reserve

Prentice Bloedel stated that the Reserve "breaks the connection with the outside world [and] conditions the mind."[12] In order to facilitate this break with the everyday world and heighten the opportunity for a contemplative response, the Reserve employs aspects from ritual theory, including invitation and authority, restrictions and taboos, and prescribed movements.[13]

The Bloedels believed that fewer numbers of visitors would contribute to the highest quality experience, and in accord with this philosophy, the Reserve requires reservations for visits. One must call the Reserve office to secure a date and an hour of visit. Only 20 people per hour are allowed entrance (although there are usually less than 20 people registered for any one hour slot), and admission is charged. Other restrictions include: no bus tours, no large groups, no eating, no pets, and no rental of the grounds. These restrictions all serve to further remove the Reserve from the everyday world.

Prescriptions on movements heighten the separation of the Bloedel Reserve from the outside world. First, one slowly drives up to a closed gate, and is greeted by a volunteer who asks your name and checks your reservation. You're given a handout to read outlining the rules of visitation, and a small guidebook to read along the walking trail through the property. Intensifying the feeling of entering a rarified realm, parking is well hidden by a skillful manipulation of topography and planting. There is very little pavement – most cars park on a lawn area. A contemplative experience is further facilitated by a narrow mulch path, designed as a one-way loop, so that the visitors will not meet other people as they walk the circuit, and that

Contemplative/Restorative Landscapes

4.1
Bloedel Reserve, Bainbridge Island, Washington. Beginning the three mile walk through the Reserve grounds, with parking just behind

people will not bunch up in large groups (Fig. 4.1). There are no signs that label plants, mark directions or interpret features. Only a subtle paved road winds through the property for maintenance. Careful consideration is paid to the maintenance regimes. In my discussion with Richard Brown, he elaborated that noisy kinds of maintenance are typically done when the Reserve is closed – to maintain the contemplative atmosphere for visitors. The commitment of time to walk the three mile loop through the forests and gardens enhances the feeling of leaving the world behind.

Ritual-like aspects of the National Library

Perrault stated that the approach to the library contains "an initiatory itinerary proceeding away from the hubbub towards the hush"[14] revealing his agenda to separate the library and its forest from the day-to-day world. The National Library employs ritual-like aspects, similar to those employed at the Bloedel Reserve, to underscore the rarified and stratified realm of this place. It could be argued that any institution employs these strategies as rules, but at the National Library, they are powerfully at play and affect the visitors' perceptions and experiences of the library and forest.

Perrault is interested in asking questions about nature and the contemporary city in his design for the Library, and encouraging visitors to do the same. He writes:

> Nature is not captured in a single glance, not contained in a single thought, a single emotion does not suffice. It is an ensemble of "natures", from the most virgin to the most artificial, and far from excluding each other these "natures" enter into friction, due to their proximity or to their combination.[15]

These "ensembles of nature" begin where the library meets the city sidewalk. The visitor is immediately startled and challenged by impossibly steep wooden stairs (Fig. 4.2). They seemed incredibly unsafe, but I was unable to see another way into the library. As I carefully ascended the terrifying staircase, I couldn't really applaud their function, but it was a compelling experience nonetheless – at least to another designer. The dangerous stairs necessitated an intense attention to their ascent, and it was intriguing to see wood in the contemporary city. This unusual material selection underscored Perrault's stated intention to separate the library from the city. Where the stairs meet the top edge of the deck, there are rows of large steel mesh boxes filled with soil and vegetation. These serve to warn visitors of the

4.2
National Library of France, Paris. A steep wooden staircase signals the entrance to the Library
Dominique Perrault, 1995

Contemplative/Restorative Landscapes

4.3
National Library of France, Paris.
View from the roof deck showing the escalators bringing patrons down to the library entrance
Dominique Perrault, 1995

impending drop-off, while displaying Perrault's interest in the presentation of nature and the juxtaposition of materials.

As visitors reach the top of the stairs (deck level), they begin to glimpse the wild treetops of the pine grove for the first time – another of Perrault's presentations of nature. The forest is quite vast – approximately 670 feet long (more than twice the length of two American football fields) by 165 feet wide. Visitors to the library descend down and through the edge of the forest on escalators to the building entrances (Fig. 4.3). (The project site was excavated to allow for a massive amount of square footage for reading rooms underground – and the wooden plinth rises over this underground world – therefore you have to go up, and then down, to enter the library.) Guards and metal detectors inspect visitors and their bags. This level of the library is available to the general public of age 18 and over. Admission is charged, and a ticket is issued. Reading rooms are off the glassed hallway, and the forest is not visible from any of the seats in the reading rooms; you must return to the hallway to see the trees. (A complete separation of the reading rooms and the outdoor world may be because books should not be exposed to direct light, or it may be another expression of Perrault's interest in paradox.) Comfortable leather chairs are positioned along the corridor for viewing the grove. Niches have been created for the chairs to nestle into, separating the chairs from each other and from the carpeted walkway. This strategy works quite well, giving patrons a feeling of privacy from other people and a sense of connection with the forest. The café, which has both indoor and outdoor seating, is also on this level.

The lower level of the library, a two-story space containing over 2,000 reading places, is inaccessible to the ordinary citizen. This level is only available to those who qualify as researchers. There are no public tours of the library or other ways for the public to experience the lower level. This level also contains a glass walkway that surrounds the forest, and while there are some views into the trees from this level, many are partial views.

All the restrictions on entering the lower level probably help to create a contemplative realm for the researchers. For the general public, these many restrictions feel maddening. The process to enter the library and the restrictions within it focus one's attention on a stratified society and the security concerns of the contemporary world, which initially may make a contemplative experience within the library more difficult. The restrictions are helpful to a degree in that when one finally gets inside the library, there is a strong sense of feeling removed from the world.

The Bloedel's Reflection Garden: the archetype of "the clearing"

Landscape scholar Christopher Thacker writes:

> No doubt about it. The first gardens were not made, but discovered. [They were] a natural spot – [such as] a clearing in the forest .... In the oldest accounts, such spots are the gardens of the gods, or those favoured by the gods....[16]

The Reflection Garden within the Bloedel Reserve has become an icon of modern landscape architecture, and it draws its strength from the power of the landscape archetype of "the clearing." (See Fig 4.4 and Plate 15.) The Reflection Garden is an exquisite and mysterious void in the forest where perfectly sheared hedges frame a green-black rectangle of water. Finding or making a clearing as a place for settlement (especially one adjacent to water) is considered one of the first interventions humans made on the land.

The genesis for the Reflection Garden was a photograph that the Bloedels found of a Finnish canal. The beauty and simplicity of this utilitarian landscape captivated the Bloedels, and they commissioned landscape architect Thomas Church to design a space of comparable expression at the

Contemplative/Restorative Landscapes

4.4
Final design, Reflection Garden, Bloedel Reserve, Bainbridge Island, Washington
Richard Haag, 1984

Reserve. Church's investigations revealed that the water table was extremely high throughout the property and he designed a long (approximately 200 feet long, 30 feet wide) rectangular reflecting pool by excavating the ground and bounding its edges, creating a groundwater pool.[17] (See Plate 16.)

Landscape architect Richard Haag, who worked on different aspects of the Reserve from 1978 to 1985, recommended that the pool at the Reflection Garden be enclosed within a hedge and that a lawn be installed from the pool edge to the hedge in all directions. These simple but profound changes made the Reflection Garden into the magically potent setting that it is today. The overlapping lines of 10 foot tall yew hedges serve to hide the path, creating a mysterious entrance from the side of the garden (Fig. 4.5). Presently, there is one bench centered on the pool, but originally the Bloedels' placed wooden benches – timbers from the boat building trades on Bainbridge Island – within the Garden. Haag preferred a more minimal approach. He writes:

> This "clutter" surprised me and I persuaded Mr. Bloedel to relocate two benches to other vista points favored by Mrs. Bloedel. At first, I plotted to remove the remaining benches, but eventually I rationalized the benches – there was an air of nostalgia, a kind of ghostly presence. Who were the benches waiting for?

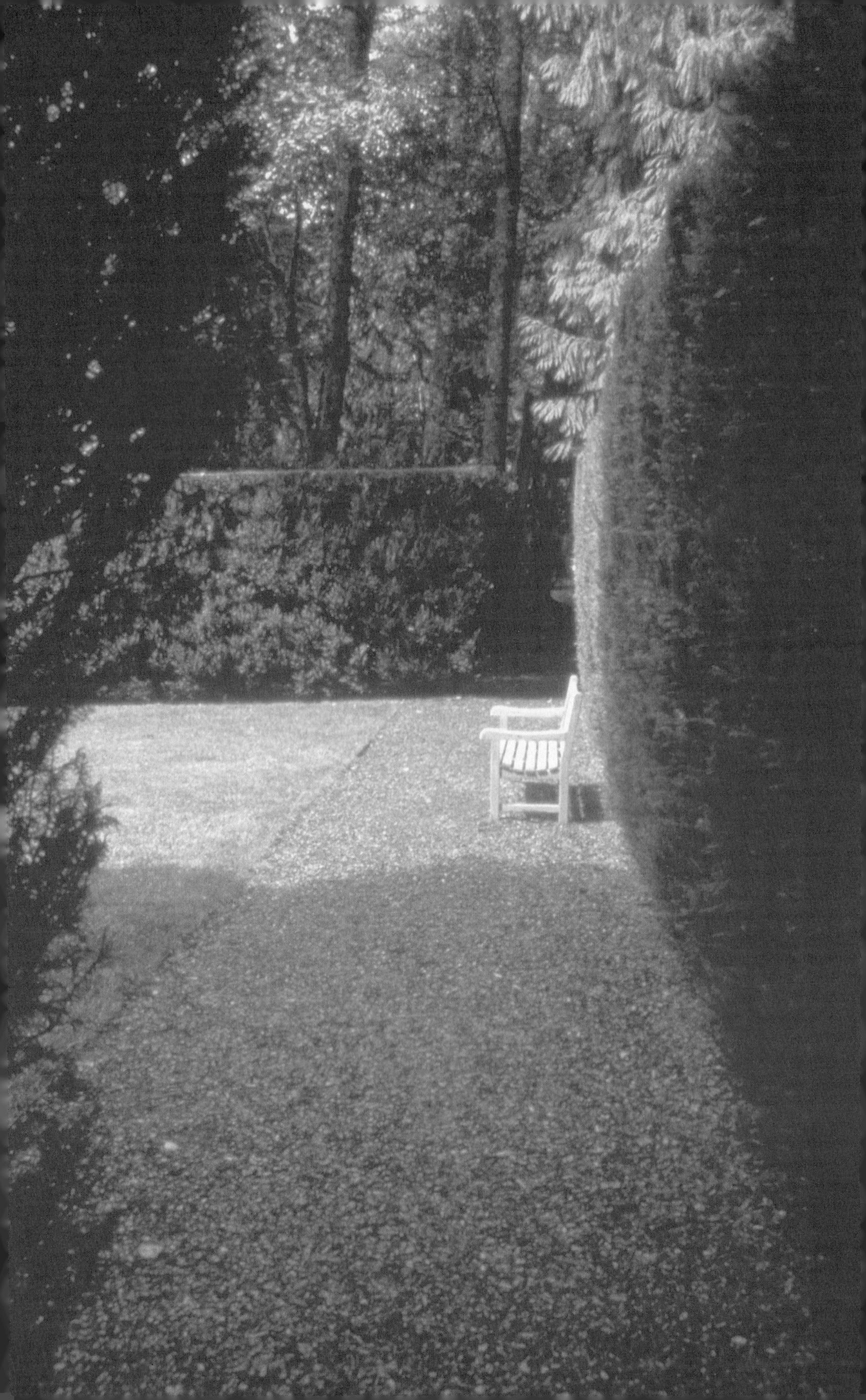

A dialogue between wood spirits and water nymphs. In due time the wood rotted. Today there is one teak garden bench centered at the northerly end of the pool.[18]

In recent years, the mulch path has been extended through the Reflection Garden, since the turf wore down every year under the footsteps of visitors through the space. The mulch extends in perfect lines along the yew hedge. The path was conceived to heighten the separation of the Garden as a meditative space.[19] Most visitors do not step off the path, and if they do, they find the grass to be damp and spongy. The Garden is underscored as an empty center for all to admire. For Richard Haag, the Reflection Garden

> is about selflessness. It's the first time you really realize the woods. . . . The space is nothing. Somebody's been there, but they left. So there's nothing there until you and your spirit enter it, and your spirit just fills it, from wall to wall.[20]

The National Library: the archetype of "the forest"

The inspiration for the forest at the National Library was Perrault's, although landscape architect Erik Jacobsen was enlisted to realize the vision. He recalls an early discussion with the architect:

> [Perrault] wanted to create a place of silence, calm, and serenity for readers: the reading halls therefore could not open onto the rail lines or onto the boulevard alongside the Seine, both too busy and noisy. The idea of a vast interior courtyard emerged, a "well of light" providing daylight to the reading halls on the second level, and in this well, a piece of adult forest should grow, exuberant, diverse, and disorderly, balancing the simplicity and rigor of the surrounding buildings.[21]

4.5
Final design, Reflection Garden, Bloedel Reserve, Bainbridge Island, Washington. Entering the Garden
Richard Haag, 1984

It is Perrault's feeling that the forest would "make the library a place outside time, whose references are universal."[22] Forests do conjure the primordial; "the meaning of the forest predates any language, symbol, icon, or deity."[23] Throughout human history, forests have been seen as both alluring and terrifying, and at the Library, where a piece of forest is framed for our contemplation (Fig. 4.6 and Plate 17), we feel a kind of paradoxically thrilling calm: wildness without danger.

Rebecca Krinke

4.6
Forest at the National Library of France, Paris. An inaccessible, transplanted forest is the centerpiece of the Library
Dominique Perrault, landscape architect Erik Jacobsen, 1995

The architect wanted mature trees in the garden right away, and Jacobsen proposed going to a forest without going through tree nurseries. The nurseries wouldn't have the mature trees they were looking for, and moreover, Perrault was looking for wild trees, not ones raised and pruned in the nursery. A very dense plot of tall thin trees was spotted in a public forest, the Forêt de Bord. The trees had grown to a height of 18 meters or more in search of sunlight. The pine species selected – *Pinus sylvestris* or red pine – is characterized by its exceptional adaptability to different climatic and soil conditions. The forester in charge of this public forest directed them to easily accessible plots of pines 40 years old and more. These 150 trees were planned to be removed anyway in order to excavate the underlying sand and gravel. Due to these soil conditions, the trees had a shallow root system that made it possible for them to be dug out with their root balls intact.[24] Perrault and Jacobsen chose the trees in the forest together. Perrault "... searched for interesting silhouettes, irregular trees with twisted trunks or bends, trunks branching into two parts, the tallest possible.... In the end, the biggest trees are those that have grown the best."[25]

Jacobsen used the Forêt de Bord's "structure ... as a model to help us imagine what the immediate result would be for the National Library."[26] To fulfill the forest's composition, the landscape architect searched the nurseries of France, Germany, Belgium, and the Netherlands for 100 deciduous trees – oaks, birches, and beech trees at least 30 feet tall – to complement the pines. The ground layer consists primarily of vegetation brought in through the root balls of the pines, plants such as ferns, primrose, ivies, honeysuckle, and others.[27] Jacobsen's work is "all based on the same principle: to make others believe that the formations of the landscape and its vegetation have always been there. . . ."[28]

Perceptions of visitors to the Reflection Garden

Published accounts

One of the ways to enhance our understanding of the effectiveness of the case study projects as contemplative realms is to investigate published accounts of visitors. These accounts are primarily by designers and scholars and they overwhelmingly record the success of the Reflection Garden as a contemplative space. The Bloedel Reserve gardens that were developed by Richard Haag won an American Society of Landscape Architects design award in 1986. The jury, comprised of notable landscape architects Peter Walker, Stuart Dawson, and Anne Whiston Spirn and others, wrote that the gardens contain "the one quality you see very, very rarely [which] is the quality of soul or magical response. . . . It is where emotion and intelligence merge."[29]

The work of Haag at the Bloedel Reserve has been interpreted by Patrick Condon in terms of the quest for enlightenment. In an interview with Haag, Condon notes:

> with the consent and participation of [Prentice] Bloedel, [Haag] layered into his design a rich and related set of dialectics in an ambitious attempt to, in Haag's words, 'help the visitor experience something of a *satori*' (roughly translated, "an awakening"), in which the gap between the mind and the material world is bridged.[30]

According to Jory Johnson, the Bloedel Reserve reflects the "maturation of [the Bloedels'] mystical vision, to the assumption of responsibility of sharing that vision with the public."[31] In particular, the Reflection Garden creates a transcendental realm by evoking infinity. Elizabeth Meyer writes: "In less than a quarter of an acre, the simultaneous vastness and closeness, the elusiveness and tangibility of the natural world is inscribed in the thin membranes that frame this outdoor room."[32]

Rebecca Krinke

Observation of visitors

I visited the Bloedel Reserve on May 9 and 10, 2002 to personally experience the landscape and to observe other visitors. Over the course of two days, and more than five hours in the Reflection Garden itself, I observed approximately 30 visitors to the garden without them apparently being aware of my presence, as I was behind the hedge. Most were in groups of two or four people. In general, I was able to discern that the Reflection Garden had a pronounced impact on about half its visitors. A common reaction was to stop short in surprise, and sometimes spontaneously make a comment of pleasure and wonder. For example, one visitor exclaimed, "A new Taj Mahal!"

The other half of the visitors had an outwardly more neutral response to the Reflection Garden; these visitors were focused on gathering data about the space. For example, many entered the Garden while reading out loud from the self-guided tour handbook, and discussing the project with the other members of their party. The pool was the main topic of conversation: How was the pool made? How deep was it? Many of these visitors spoke quite loudly, whereas the visitors that felt an impact from the Garden spoke in quieter tones. Only one person came alone, and this was the only visitor that I observed sitting on the bench for any length of time.

Personal experience

The simplicity of the Reflection Garden contrasts sharply with the wild array of stumps and logs of the Moss Garden that precedes it. The Moss Garden is experienced through movement; there are no stopping points along the path. When one enters the Reflection Garden, the single bench provides a powerful invitation and setting for contemplation. This enticement to rest and reflect is especially welcome since the Reflection Garden is the last space in the Bloedel's sequence of gardens.[33] All during the walk through the Reserve, the visitor is among trees – under them, alongside them, going in and out of the groves – while in the Reflection Garden one sits inside of a clearing: a space carved out of the forest. I found it refreshing to look down and across at the trees reflected in the water, rather than looking up into the canopy. Since this garden is the last in the garden walk, I couldn't help but compare it with the other spaces that I had moved through or stopped at, if there were benches available, such as at the Japanese garden and the Rhododendron Glen. These latter two spaces contained many different plants, textures, and colors, and I found myself more distracted than relaxed.

I was surprised by the strength of the Reflection Garden as a contemplative space. Since I had seen so many pictures of this space, I was both skeptical that the Garden could work magic and desirous that it would. These emotions illuminated another aspect of the contemplative landscape:

Contemplative/Restorative Landscapes

prior knowledge or anticipation of the project may make it difficult for the space to "live up to its reputation." The fact that I found the Reflection Garden so successful given these circumstances, for me, attests to the power of this project as a contemplative space. The Garden's strong geometry and the tranquility of the water had a relaxing, even mesmerizing effect. The pool dramatically reveals moment-by-moment changes in the quality of light, changes that I found almost hypnotic. When it was cloudy, the reflection of the trees and the actual trees seem virtually interchangeable. When the sun emerged, the depth of the forest layers seemed to be even more acutely visible in the water. Sometimes I found myself visually delving into particularly detailed areas of the reflection, and then seeking them out in the actual forest. The pool intensified ones ability to notice changes in the weather, even relatively minute changes. When it was raining lightly, the raindrops spattering the pool changed the texture of the water, and intensified the aroma of the cedar bark mulch.

The Reflection Garden provides a potent meditation on the color green. The pool is the darkest of greens, almost black from the vantage point of the bench. As you move closer to the pool edge, the sky and its colors begin to vividly tint the color of the pool. Small insects on the surface of the water created marvelous ripples. As the pool surface quieted, the grass and hedge became perfectly mirrored. Being surrounded by a vivid chartreuse lawn, juxtaposed with a green-black pool, and enveloped by every other shade of green in the hedge and forest was a very unusual and memorable experience.

Perceptions of visitors to the forest at the National Library

Published accounts

Published accounts of visitors to the National Library reveal that the forest is seen as a contemplative space, conjuring daydreams about nature and time. The forest has been seen by more than one visitor as symbolic of a lost connection to nature and/or the desire to reconnect to nature, for example: "[The towers] stand as sentries and disquieting guardians over a piece of nature, a wood, as the symbol of an aspiration deeply felt by contemporary man."[34] The forest is seen as proposing a new engagement with nature: "The court . . . might return us to an engagement with the world that is more sensual and sensitive to our ecological impacts."[35] The Library forest has been seen as an other-worldly setting, described as "mirage-like" and the "the materialization of a dream."[36] The grove has also been viewed as a transcendental space: "This artificially installed piece of simulated, untouched nature thus becomes a representation of itself; in its unattainability, it is charged with sacrality and is reminiscent of a *hortus conclusus*."[37]

Another critic finds the forest an interesting contemplation, but from a different perspective. He wonders if the juxtaposition of a living forest, with a library made from huge amounts of wood and housing millions of volumes of books (made from paper pulp), is a "mausoleum commemorating the old medium of print."[38] The design of the forest has also been criticized for being inaccessible physically and visually from the reading rooms, "in effect prohibiting the concurrence of work and contemplation of nature. These are sadistic little trifles, perhaps traditional to the design of libraries, where researchers are usually shielded from distractions. . . ."[39]

Observations of visitors

I visited the National Library on April 23 and 25, 2002 to experience and analyze the project. Over the course of two days, and 10 hours in the library, I observed scores of visitors engaged in looking at the forest with varying degrees of intensity. It is impossible to ignore the powerful presence of the trees within the library, the forest feels immense and the circulation system rings it. Library patrons do seem to find the forest a pleasant release from the reading rooms, as they gaze into the trees. Most of the time though, the relationship between patron and grove is seemingly a rather casual one. The most frequented place where patrons observe the forest is from the leather chairs that ring the glassed walkway. Illuminated signs in the corridor say "silence" but no one obeys. Most people talked on cell phones, conversed with a friend, or read, as they observed the grove.

The outdoor café was a popular place to sit and look into the forest. It offers a direct experience of the trees and the outdoors in general. Temperature, humidity, sounds and scents were more vivid, perhaps a useful re-engagement with the world after being immersed in the reading rooms. The café is located on the short end of the garden's rectangle, and by sighting down the length of the garden, the trees present their densest effect. The 30 or so café chairs were generally full throughout the day, with patrons, eating, drinking coffee, talking and smoking, reading, and looking into the trees (Fig. 4.7).

The wooden roof deck holds a huge number of places where one may view the grove: the long ends of the rectangular space are lined by bleacher-like steps (Fig. 4.8). Here, people ate their brown bag lunches, read, conversed in small groups, or simply stared into the garden. From my observations, this deck had the most number of people engaged in directly looking into the grove without being engaged in other activities at the same time. Birdsong was quite prevalent, and across the Seine, the trees of Parc de

Contemplative/Restorative Landscapes

4.7
National Library of France, Paris. Looking through the café towards the forest
Dominique Perrault, 1995

Bercy are visible. A low, wide stainless steel screen provides the safety barrier around the deck's perimeter, allowing better views into the grove than a tall fence would.

It wasn't possible to receive permission to visit the lower level research area of the library and I had to confine my observations of this area to what I could observe from above. The research level contains wooden bleachers focused on the grove, similar to the bleachers of the outdoor deck. In my two days of observation, I only saw one person sitting on the research level bleachers, looking into the trees.

The forest at the National Library provides a place of strong contrast to the settings and activities within the architecture. One typically visits the library to do research, and it is the intellect that is fully engaged. The forest offers a respite from the windowless reading rooms focused on the mind's activities; the forest more directly engages the body and senses. This is quite different than the Bloedel Reserve, where the whole function of the place is to employ the forest and garden in creating a contemplative experience.

Personal experience

The place where the Library forest became the most powerful invitation to contemplation for me was from outdoors, and from where the trees are the

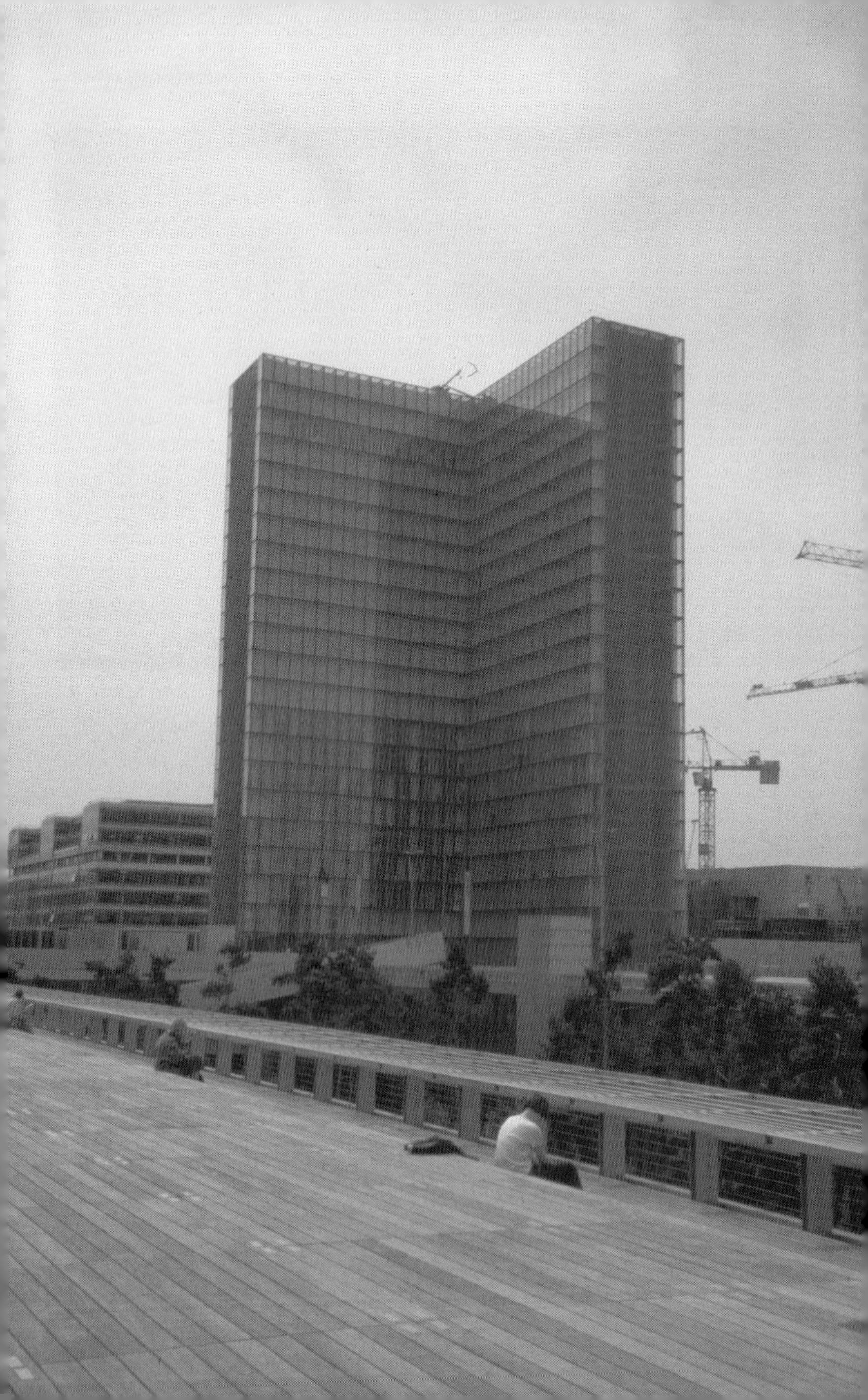

densest and the architecture becomes veiled, for example the views from the café and the roof deck on the short ends of the rectangular space. The wildness of the grove is a relief from the nearby architecture and contrasts beautifully with the stark and monolithic qualities of the building itself. From the outdoor settings, the forest really comes alive as a living, breathing ecosystem: birds flew about the trees, branches moved in the breeze, sunlight flickered across the pine boughs. The grove was less powerful where the vegetation was sparse, although the areas of fewer trees was a deliberate move by the designers, as demonstrated by their planting plans, perhaps to create small clearings in the forest which will change over time. Many of the deciduous trees are still quite small, and as they mature, the forest will become much denser.

I was surprised that I also found the experience of the forest from the interior walkway to be an effective contemplative space, overturning my initial preconception that with the trees behind glass, the forest would seem too remote to capture my attention. The walkway itself is interesting, employing materials and strategies that were successful in helping me tune into my body in a heightened way. For example, the proportions of the all glass walls create an effective unit of measure as you walk down the hall, a carpeted path muffles the sound of footsteps, and wooden floors along the edges provide areas for seating and standing (Fig. 4.9). Chairs against the wall face the forest, and are separated from the carpeted walking path and from each other by short segments of walls so that you do not see long rows of chairs and people. The leather chairs are very comfortable; the way in which they have been designed tips your body back and up which is in strong contrast to the straight backed wooden chairs of the reading rooms. I found the chair placement and design successful at assisting me to enter a relaxed frame of mind. The view into the forest from this walkway juxtaposes trees and architecture. The column-like trunks of the red pines have an affinity with the architectural mullions, both in color and form, and as light and shade play across the vegetation and the glass, I found the view reminding me of Japanese screen painting: nature is segmented by the window frames and presented as pictures.

I discovered the forest at the National Library to be successful as a contemplative space – only when discursive thought returned did I realize that the setting was effective at helping me to move to a contemplative experience. The pictures I had seen of the Library and its trees did not prepare me for the scale of the forest. The sheer strangeness of this huge forest inside the library architecture arrested my attention, and shifted my perceptions.

4.8
National Library of France, Paris. View of the roof deck
Dominique Perrault,1995

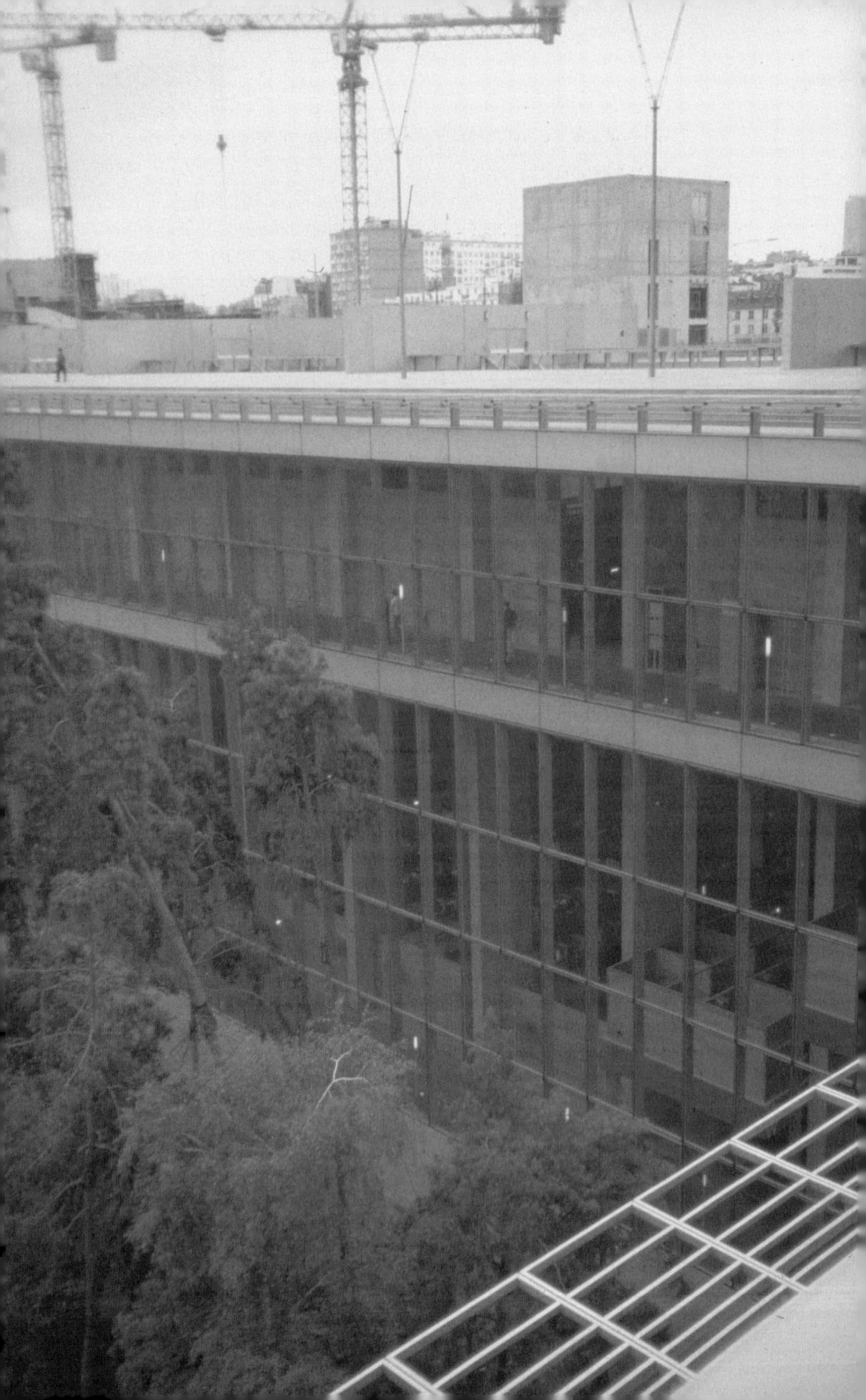

Strategies for creating contemplative landscapes

A comparative analysis of the two case study projects reveals core ideas for creating contemplative landscapes. Both the Bloedel's Reflection Garden and the forest within the National Library are variations on the ancient garden form of the enclosed garden, a form used for thousands of years in both the East and the West for the same basic reasons: it offers protection and promotes contemplation. The cloister garden of the Middle Ages was an enclosed garden, serving as the monastery's central open space and as a symbolic space.

> [T]he cloister was designed to present the onlooker with a highly ordered and selected view of nature. The sky and the plants themselves record the passing of the seasons, while the bounded and restricted view was intended to encourage a reflective mood. The most earnest wish was for the spiritual transformation of the viewer.[40]

In the East, for example in the traditional Zen gardens of Japan, enclosed gardens were located at temples. Physically inaccessible, they served as aids to meditation. Perrault has described his garden as a cloister, and while it has much in common with this garden type, typically, the cloister garden was focused on order: a safe place for reflection with the gardens arranged in geometric planting beds. Perrault's cloister contains a physically inaccessible, seemingly wild grove. The Reflection Garden is enclosed by walls of clipped hedges, not the typical architectural wall that was designed to keep the unpredictable outside world at bay. Here the wild grove looms over the top of the hedge, inviting the undomesticated in, but at a safe distance. Both case study projects successfully transform traditional precedents of enclosed gardens to create contemporary landscapes for contemplation.

The case study projects use the landscape archetypes of clearing and forest to create contemplative realms. These archetypes are strong, clear ideas and are supported in both projects by a minimalist design expression, meaning a simplicity of form supported by a few carefully selected materials. The projects both employ a contrast between static, orthogonal forms (architecture, clipped hedges) and vegetation that grows and changes. The reductive palettes of the projects intrigue the visitor by circumventing expectations in key ways: for example, who has ever experienced a forest inside a library? It is unexpected and exciting, and by magnifying the scale of the forest beyond what seems possible inside a building, our attention is captured. Finding out that it is impossible to actually enter this forest, again,

**4.9
National Library of France, Paris.** Looking into the library and trees from the roof deck shows the glassed walkway that rings the forest
Dominique Perrault
1995

129

Rebecca Krinke

undercuts our mundane expectations, possibly causing frustration to some, but focusing our attention and requiring a shift in how we are to engage this place. The visitor may begin to mull over questions on the role of nature in the city and in their life. The Reflection Garden also startles us from our entrenched perceptions. Finding a place of such perfection (of idea, of form, of maintenance) inside a forest is a very unique experience. Typically we think of large gardens and manicured lawns as attached to residences, or other buildings with specific uses, such as museums, corporate headquarters, etc. The Reflection Garden seems to be a gift to us, a place that invites us to be refreshed by beauty and perhaps stimulated to reflect on self and nature. The case study projects succeed at reinterpreting the ancient landscape archetypes of the forest and clearing to create contemplative space in the contemporary world. Supporting this powerful design idea are reductive, but unusual, design expressions (such as exaggerated scale and unfamiliar settings) that are alluring because they circumvent our day-to-day experience of the landscape. The visitor's attention is captured, and then enticed – through a minimalist design palette that reduces visual stimulation – to disengage from everyday life and relax, encouraging new meditations.

    The case study projects highlight a link between ritual and contemplative space. Rituals and ritual-like activities give "form to the specialness of a site, distinguishing it from other places in a way that evokes highly symbolic meanings."[41] Ritual-like aspects at play in both case study sites helped to remove the visitor from everyday life and activities, encouraging contemplation and reflection. Restrictions on access were particularly effective at both settings to heighten the sense of separation from the outside world. At the National Library, the grove at its center invites all equally to enter the space, although only visually and mentally. And while it was physically possible to enter the Reflection Garden, I observed that almost no one did. These projects also reveal that finding a balance between restrictions that help create a contemplative realm, and restrictions that take away from this feeling is important. When the ritual-like aspects of the projects were overly prohibitive, the visitor begins to feel frustration, rather than anticipation, at entering a place removed from the day-to-day world. For example, at the Paris library, it was cumbersome to gain entrance to the building, and maddening that the lower level didn't have even one area for the general public. However, for the thousands of patrons who will often be at the library and learn how to use it over time, these restrictions will be more manageable, and they will have the opportunity to engage the forest in an ongoing way. The Bloedel Reserve is on an island, virtually assuring that one makes a kind of pilgrimage to visit. This underscores the uniqueness of the site and helps to prepare one for a larger than life experience, although it is possible that many potential visitors may simply decide it is too much work to get there. This in turn may assure that the number of visitors to the Reserve remains fairly low. Those who do make the journey are rewarded with a deeply quiet and inspirational setting, and the project's uniqueness helps it to live on in the visitor's mind. A sense of separation from the everyday world emerges as an important principle to creating a contemplative experience. This may be achieved through careful attention to the initial siting of the contemplative space, and the transitions, entrances and sequences that separate the visitor from the day-to-day world.

Each project employs walking as a means to shift awareness. This attention to prescribed routes or attention to the act of walking itself can be found within meditative traditions, such as Zen Buddhism or Christianity. At the Bloedel Reserve, the long walk through the forest engages the body and all the senses. When one reaches the Reflection Garden and is invited to sit, I found that I was very ready to rest. The physical activity of the long walk helped to quiet the mind as well as intensifying the feeling of leaving the world behind. At the National Library, the long and complex entry sequence, as well as the long walk around the forest, forces you to engage your body, and quiets discursive thought.

Seating emerged as a very important aspect of contemplative space, with insights to be gained from each project. The one bench within the Reflection Garden is a powerful gesture, and has implications for how the space gets used. While the bench invites one to be alone in the Garden, I also found that it can create a sense of unease as well. As I sat on the bench, I occasionally found my thoughts straying to questions about when would the next visitor arrive? Should I vacate the bench or not? While at the National Library, the multiple forms of seating from a variety of vantage points were useful in promoting many possibilities for a contemplative connection with the forest. Even though people were sitting or walking nearby, I knew that once I had found a seat, I could relax; there were plenty of seats to go around. Solitude amongst a crowd was actually quite relaxing.

Published accounts of designers and scholars detail that the case study projects are seen by these authors as successful contemplative spaces, but what conclusions, if any, can we make about the many visitors I observed at these projects who didn't seem to have a contemplative response? Ken Wilber's theory states that art can help the viewer to acquire their contemplative eye,[42] and analyzing visitor responses from his perspective provides useful insights. For example, at the Reflection Garden, about half of the visitors that I saw enter the space were visibly affected by it: their behavior changed abruptly as they stopped talking and gazed. Their attention was arrested and held. This provides some measure that these visitors were receiving the project on the contemplative level that was intended. Wilber's theory proposes that even for the visitor who did not have an outward response to the project, they are in a landscape that was aiming for the highest level of development – the level of contemplation – therefore, even though the visitor may not be aware of or seeking this state, they can theoretically be positively affected by the art/design that seeks and attains this level.[43] Stephen Kaplan posits that an environment specifically designed to support meditation/restoration would be able to move, "even a relatively unskilled individual [to] something approximating meditation with comparatively little mental effort."[44] Another part of the visitor-landscape equation concerns whether one comes alone or with a group. Solitude, either in actuality or a feeling of solitude, may be associated with a contemplative experience. Silence and the freedom of one's own timetable would seem to have a positive relationship on a visitor's potential contemplative response to a landscape. For example, the only person that I observed spending a long time gazing into the pool at the Reflection Garden was the only person that I saw come alone. For designers of contemplative landscapes, simply becoming more conscious of the multiple ways that the visitor, the landscape, and the designer exist in relationship may assist in creating more informed design goals and solutions.

Connections between contemplative and restorative space

In their book, *The Experience of Nature: A Psychological Perspective*, Rachel and Stephen Kaplan describe their research and theory of the restorative experience. Many readers may be familiar with the Kaplans' work in general terms – their research into wilderness experiences as well as of "nearby nature" – that has led them to determine that nature best meets the requirements for a restorative experience. The Kaplans describe the restorative experience as having four attributes: "fascination", "being away", "extent", and "compatibility."[45] It's important to note that these attributes "are properties of a person-environment interaction, rather than of an environment per se. Nonetheless, these properties can be useful for characterizing environments."[46] These four attributes are described in broad terms; physical or spatial qualities of a restorative environment are sometimes implied, but how the attributes may be expressed in physical form is not elaborated. The Kaplans' four attributes of a restorative experience provide a useful tool to deepen our understanding of how the case studies succeed as contemplative realms, and in turn, the case studies can suggest how these attributes of a restorative experience can be facilitated/manifested in physical form.

First, for a setting to be restorative, it must elicit our *fascination*: a state where our attention is intrigued and captured. The Kaplans' sub-

Contemplative/Restorative Landscapes

category – "soft fascination" – is described as the best form of fascination to encourage a reflective mood. Watching clouds, the motion of leaves, or the play of light are given as examples of soft fascination.[47] Our attention is pleasurably, even aesthetically engaged, although no response from us is required. Fascination is critical to eliciting the state of involuntary or non-directed attention that is essential to restoring us from the mental fatigue of our overused directed attention. We use directed attention to manage our jobs and daily lives, and it requires a great deal of energy, not just to focus on the task at hand but to screen out all the various stimuli that compete for our attention. Certainly sleep helps to alleviate this mental weariness but it has been found that sleep is not the whole answer: engaging our non-directed attention during the day is necessary to avoid exhaustion.[48] Research indicates that being in a natural setting, or viewing natural settings, can effectively induce non-directed attention.[49] The National Library seems to employ, either consciously or unconsciously, this idea of directed and non-directed attention in its design. For example, the windowless reading rooms are designed for reading and research only – activities that employ directed attention. Leaving the reading rooms and finding the forest, with its play of light and shadow, encourages non-directed attention, and restoration from fatigue. The term "fascination" also implies the observer identifying with the observed. Both case studies with their selection and intensification of just a few aspects of nature – a long pool of green-black water, an immense grove of primarily one type of tree – are absorbing or fascinating to the eye. The reductive palette of these and many contemplative spaces seem to suggest the validity of "overload" and "arousal" theories that posit that human perceptual systems can become overloaded and stressed in places that have a great deal of complexity or intensity – in visual terms, or through noise or movement. "Both theories imply that restoration from stress or perceptual fatigue should be fostered by settings having stimuli, such as plants, that are low in intensity and incongruity ... that reduces arousal and processing effort."[50]

Second, a sense of *being away* is important to a restorative experience. Being away can refer to a sense of physical separation from your everyday world or a sense of being removed from your everyday activities. Both case study projects have a strong quality of being physically separate from the ordinary world, and both require a significant investment of time to reach. The Bloedel Reserve is on an island, and reservations must be made to visit. The Reflection Garden itself is an enclosed garden at the end of a three mile walk, embedded in 150 acres of forest. To visit the National Library, there is a prolonged entry sequence leading the visitor to interior spaces that remove all trace of central Paris. Both settings eliminate as many activities as possible that don't focus on their core missions – namely contemplative

133

Rebecca Krinke

walking and sitting at the Bloedel and research at the Library – which also serves to make the world of daily life recede.

To describe the third attribute of a restorative environment, the Kaplans use the term *extent*, described as a feeling or quality of being in a different world (physically or perceptually), yet connected to a larger whole. The setting or activity should reveal that there is more to explore than what is easily visible to the eye. Extent implies a balance between order and mystery. Both case study projects embody these qualities through the geometric framework of an enclosed garden juxtaposed with the wildness of trees. The clearly visible hand of human intervention in nature – for example, the pool within the Reflection Garden – provided a resting place for the eye, yet I could also mentally explore the thick forests all around. At the National Library, the immense grove isn't perceivable in one glance, yet the boundaries of it are understood – it is ringed by the architecture – and there are many vantage points to view it from. Extent as a feeling of being connected to a larger whole can also be understood in more conceptual terms, as when an environment assists one in feeling connected to larger systems or ideas, such as nature or natural processes, or the human relationship with nature. The published accounts of visitors to the case study projects highlight that each is seen as a place that activates musings on self, nature, and time.

And the Kaplans' final attribute of a restorative environment is *compatibility*, where the environment supports the visitor and doesn't demand an effort in directed attention. A setting where the individual feels safe, but not bored, is important. Both case study designs are remarkable for their unusual and precise simplicity, which captures one's involuntary attention, and diminishes other thoughts and concerns. The Bloedel Reserve and the National Library are both settings that feel safe for the visitor. They each have similar components that contribute to this quality, such as requirements on entrance, reservations, and admissions. As officiated settings, they each have staff that visibly oversees them, including security at the Library. But beyond these overt aspects of safety, each project employs the archetype of the enclosed garden, a bounded space that offers a sense of protection. The garden wall is one of the most potent symbols of refuge.[51]

The case studies may also owe some of their contemplative and restorative power to the simple fact they are landscapes with an emphasis on vegetation. Research by Roger S. Ulrich and others has shown that contact with nature, especially vegetation, has a restorative effect on human health both physical and psychological; for example, one of Ulrich's most well known studies, "View Through a Window May Influence Recovery from Surgery" (1984) demonstrated that patients recuperated from surgery faster (less pain medication required and earlier discharge) when they had a view of vegetation outside their hospital window rather than a view of a building. The patients were recovering from the same kind of surgery and were matched by other key characteristics for comparison. Additional research by Ulrich found that viewing nature is relaxing and assists one in recovering from stress. Test subjects had higher alpha wave activity when they viewed slide presentations of nature with vegetation, than when they viewed slides of urban scenes lacking vegetation, suggesting that nature is effective in creating a calm, yet alert condition. Ulrich also studied the recovery from stressful episodes by exposure to either a nature or urban video. The nature video produced faster and greater recovery from stress as shown by lower blood pressure, less muscle tension, greater reduction in anger and increased feelings of well-being on the psychological test.[52]

Scholars from both the natural and social sciences have put forth different theories on why people may derive enhanced well-being from contact with vegetation. Some restorative theories emphasize involuntary responses of the human body. Ulrich notes:

> The rapidity of response to nature and its mobilization of so many physiological responses suggest that the parasympathetic nervous system – that is, the component of the nervous system thought not to be under conscious control – must also be involved in the calming effects experienced in response to nature.[53]

These findings have been confirmed in research studies.[54] Evolutionary theories developed by Jay Appleton, biologist E. O. Wilson, and others start from the premise that the long trajectory of human evolution has engendered certain unconscious predilections in our species, including noticing and responding to aspects of the environment that would favor survival, such as the presence of vegetation and water. This premise may support the power of the landscape archetypes of forest and clearing as potent settings and symbols throughout human history. The forest edge is one of the richest places for species diversity, offering food to early humans, and also providing a relatively safe environment since it allowed views of the surrounding landscape. Both of the case study projects draw upon these archetypes of forest, edge, and clearing. While these evolutionary theories dominate the discussion of why nature is restorative, there are other theories that propose that we learn to associate positive experiences with nature, from vacations for example. Many scholars in this area of inquiry find that cultural and learning-based theories are inadequate for explaining the cross-cultural research evidence that supports a preference for scenes of nature over urban scenes,[55] and the preference for savannas or savanna-like settings over other settings.[56]

Besides the spatial and physical aspects of a contemplative or restorative landscape, the amount of time spent in these environments is also a critical variable. The Kaplans have postulated that the restorative experience has four levels of development – each taking increasing amounts of time. The first level is "clearing the head", the second is "the recovery of directed attention", the third is "the recovery of cognitive quiet" and the fourth level of a restorative experience is a "reflections on one's life"[57] which may include "a concern for meaning, for tranquility, and for relatedness."[58] The Kaplans note that this final level "is an aspect of the restorative experience we would never have suspected had it not emerged so clearly in our data."[59] This echoes Ken Wilber's theory that the contemplative experience is also the last in a sequence. Wilber's theory speaks to spiritual developmental, while the Kaplans' theory focuses on the restoration of physical and psychological health – an orientation that speaks to solving a problem. However, both theories point to the same place – the development of a transpersonal awareness.

A very interesting tenet put forward by the Kaplans' is that "increasingly high quality restorative settings"[60] are needed to achieve the highest level of restoration. They don't tell us what these are, besides mentioning that the "sacred groves" of ancient philosophers may offer an ideal starting point.[61] Theory and research on the attributes of restorative environments has shown key overlaps with principles of successful contemplative landscapes. Perhaps landscapes consciously designed and succeeding as contemplative realms, such as the Reflection Garden and the forest at the National Library, are these "highest quality restorative settings." The two case studies highlight specific design elements that can contribute to a contemplative experience, giving us a more in-depth understanding of how to create a contemplative (and restorative) landscape. Landscapes of contemplation will continue to be designed specifically as such, but it also seems clear that strategies for inducing a contemplative state can become a part of other settings, such as schools, parks, prisons, health care centers, and corporate settings, among others. Landscapes designed with the intention of assisting contemplative experiences have the potential make a powerful, positive contribution to contemporary life, contributing not just to our aesthetic and intellectual enrichment, but also to our physical and psychological health.

Notes

1 For example, see R. Kaplan and S. Kaplan, *The Experience of Nature: A Psychological Perspective*, Cambridge and New York: Cambridge University Press, 1989 and R. S. Ulrich and R. Parsons, "Influences of Passive Experiences with Plants on Individual Well Being and Health," in D. Relf (ed.) *The Role of Horticulture in Human Well-Being and Social Development*, Portland, OR: Timber Press, 1992, pp. 93–105.

Contemplative/Restorative Landscapes

2 For example, see R. S. Ulrich, "Effects of Gardens on Health Outcomes: Theory and Research" in C. C. Marcus and M. Barnes (eds) *Healing Gardens: Therapeutic Benefits and Design Recommendations*, New York: Wiley, 1999, pp. 27–86 and the Special Issue on Restorative Environments in *Environment and Behavior*, 33, 4, July 2001.
3 K. Wilber, "In the Eye of the Artist: Art and the Perennial Philosophy," in A. Grey, *Sacred Mirrors: The Visionary Art of Alex Grey*, Rochester, VT: Inner Traditions International, 1990, p. 14.
4 Ibid., p. 9.
5 S. Kaplan, "Meditation, Restoration, and the Management of Mental Fatigue," *Environment and Behavior*, 33, 4, July 2001, pp. 499–500.
6 Ibid., pp. 500–501.
7 L. Kreisman, *The Bloedel Reserve: Gardens in the Forest*, Bainbridge Island, Washington: The Arbor Fund, 1988, p. 45.
8 *Bloedel Reserve Self-Guided Walking Tour*, p. 4.
9 Interview with Richard Brown by the author, May 9, 2002.
10 Perrault quoted in M. Jacques with G. Lauriot-Dit-Prévost (eds) *Bibliothèque national de France 1989–1995: Dominique Perrault, Architecte*. Paris: Artemis, Arc en Rêve Centre d'Architecture, 1995, p. 75.
11 Ibid., p. 48.
12 J. Johnson, *Modern Landscape Architecture: Redefining the Garden*, New York, London, Paris: Abbeville Press Publishers, 1991, p. 54.
13 For example, see C. Bell, *Ritual: Perspectives and Dimensions*, New York and Oxford: Oxford University Press, 1997.
14 Jacques with Lauriot-Dit-Prévost, op. cit., p. 76.
15 D. Perrault, *Small Scale*, Barcelona: G. Gili, 1998, p. 48.
16 C. Thacker, *The History of Gardens*, Berkeley and Los Angeles, CA: University of California Press, 1979, p. 9.
17 Interview with Richard Brown by the author, May 9, 2002.
18 E-mail from Richard Haag to the author, August 18, 2004.
19 Interview with Richard Brown by the author, May 9, 2002.
20 P. M. Condon, "The Zen of Garden Design," in W. S. Saunders (ed.) *Richard Haag: Bloedel Reserve and Gas Works Park*, New York: Princeton Architectural Press, 1998, p. 55.
21 E. Jacobsen, *Forêt et Verger en Milieu Urbain*; trans. E. Cleveland, Paris: Fascicule #1, Éditions SPSP- Paysages Publics, 2000, p. 5.
22 Jacques with Lauriot-Dit-Prévost, op. cit., p. 48.
23 Condon, op. cit., p. 53.
24 Jacobsen, op. cit., p. 7.
25 Jacobsen, op. cit., p. 13.
26 Jacobsen, op. cit., p. 7.
27 Jacobsen, op. cit., p. 31.
28 Jacobsen, op. cit., p. 3.
29 S. R. Frey, "A Series of Gardens," *Landscape Architecture*, September/October 1986, p. 57.
30 Condon, op. cit., p. 46.
31 Johnson, op. cit., p. 57.
32 E. K. Meyer, "Seized by Sublime Sentiments," in W. S. Saunders (ed.) *Richard Haag: Bloedel Reserve and Gas Works Park*, New York: Princeton Architectural Press, 1998, p. 10.
33 A different sequence was proposed by Richard Haag: begin at the Garden of Planes (no longer extant), move through the Moss Garden, to the Reflection Garden, and finally to the Bird Marsh. All of these gardens were designed by Haag, and they embody his ideas of a sequence of spaces that alternate between wildness and order, and the intellect and emotion. See Meyer op. cit.

34 N. Di Battista, "Life is a Dream," in Jacques with Lauriot-Dit-Prévost, op. cit., p. 26.
35 P. Buchanan, "Place and Projection," in Jacques with Lauriot-Dit-Prévost, op. cit., p. 30.
36 C. Slessor, "Grand Gesture," *Architectural Review*, v. 198, n. 1181, July 1995, p. 64 and Di Battista, Nicola, in Jacques with Lauriot-Dit-Prévost, op. cit., p. 26.
37 A. Schmedding, "The Grove under the Pavement," *Daidalos*, 65, 102–103, September 1997, p. 102.
38 P. Buchanan, in Jacques with Lauriot-Dit-Prévost, op. cit., p. 30.
39 F. Edelmann, in Jacques with Lauriot-Dit-Prévost, op. cit., p. 19.
40 N. Gerlach-Spriggs, R. E. Kaufman and S. B.Warner, Jr., *Restorative Gardens: The Healing Landscape*, New Haven, CT and London: Yale University Press, 1998, pp. 9–10.
41 C. Bell, *Ritual: Perspectives and Dimensions*, New York and Oxford: Oxford University Press, 1997, p. 159.
42 Wilber, op. cit., p. 14.
43 Ibid.
44 S. Kaplan, op. cit., p. 500.
45 Kaplan and Kaplan op. cit., pp. 182–95.
46 S. Kaplan, op. cit., p. 482.
47 Kaplan and Kaplan op. cit., p. 192.
48 Kaplan and Kaplan op. cit., pp. 178–82.
49 For example, see Kaplan and Kaplan op. cit. and Ulrich and Parsons, in Relf op. cit.
50 Ulrich and Parsons op. cit., p. 95.
51 J. Appleton, *The Experience of Landscape*, New York: Wiley, 1996, p. 171.
52 Ulrich and Parsons op. cit., pp. 99–100.
53 Quoted in Gerlach-Spriggs, Kaufman, and Warner op. cit., p. 37.
54 Gerlach-Spriggs, Kaufman, and Warner op. cit., p. 37.
55 Ulrich and Parsons op. cit., pp. 95–6.
56 Gerlach-Spriggs, Kaufman, and Warner op. cit., pp. 39–40.
57 Kaplan and Kaplan op. cit., pp. 196–7.
58 Ibid.
59 Kaplan and Kaplan op. cit., p. 197.
60 Ibid.
61 Ibid.

Berlin: topology of contemplation

Lance Neckar

Semiotics of remembrance and reconciliation

The landscape of Berlin has been transformed in the late twentieth and twenty-first centuries by spaces of contemplation. The landscape of the city asks a ubiquitous question: what is the role of remembrance of the past in the space of the present, in the everyday discourse and affairs of the city? A person is almost compelled to ask him or herself, shall I reflect today? This can happen almost anywhere in Berlin.[1] The imminence of the vast apocalyptic effects of the Third Reich, and the postwar world it engendered, dot the urban and suburban landscape of the city. These places are poignant, painful and sometimes too horrible to be sublime. Mostly these places ask questions, and most of these questions are drawn from the period of the crimes of National Socialism (Nazism). What were the crimes and who were the victims? Who were the perpetrators of the crimes, and can one sort their actions into categories of responsibility? What about the bystanders: what was their role?

These questions about the past have led to another level of questions with implications for the future. Berlin asks of us and of itself the most pointed questions of identity: what is remembered, whose memory, who remembers, how shall we remember, and who shall we be? The landscape of the city has become one of the chief media of a larger post-Cold War dialogue. In this historical moment the landscape broaches fundamental speculations on the identity of the city, of Europe, of human existence. So recent are the conflicts represented in its spaces of memory that some have asked, how does one get on with things in Berlin, constantly in the presence of questions? Or, by contrast, as advocates of the various memorials have argued, what future exists without some degree of acceptance of the questions and cultural processing of answers? For them the (paradox-filled) acceptance of the horror and inconceivable "otherness" of the historical record is prerequisite to reconciliation. Interest groups and the local and national governments, particularly in the last ten years, have proclaimed in a series of projects that engagement with the historical record and the feelings evoked by such memories are media of reconciliation. And this commitment is evidenced in the processes and forms of a new topology of contemplation, where places of remembrance evoke these most difficult of memories as part of the everyday landscape of the city.

Given its intimate relationship with public policy and the introspective debates that have led to its making, this emerging topology expresses itself in semiotics, especially morphology and syntax, derived directly from contemporary language. German is a language that is inherently reflexive. For example, in regular German expressions, sentences begin with objects, both direct and indirect, that turn the action back to the actor or the objects of action. This structure and hierarchy lends a certain centering, reflective character to everyday discourse; and when the language becomes a tool of politicians or academics, convolution of the most self-referential order can result. Words assemble into combined forms in German. New and reinvented meaning is made by combination and transformation that makes new names suggestive of metaphysical relationships and synthesis. A counterbalancing aspect of this combinative aspect of the language is disaggregation, embodied in syntactical biases to long sentences with multiple dependent clauses. This tendency is overlaid by the free adaptation of positives as negatives with the simple addition of the prefix *un*. Another particular aspect of naming is the appropriation of verbs to create participial nouns, embodying temporality, action or process in nouns.

Like the German language, the post apocalyptic landscape of Berlin has become a reflexive medium that speaks back to us in processes about our place in the world, as it has also combined meanings and opened itself to analysis. The design of commemorative landscapes in the city has adopted this particularly German syntax to impart new ideas using a vocabulary and a morphology of thought, that have generated new spaces through new forms. New identities are suggested in new expressions of mostly familiar and tangible media. This landscape is an experiment, then, reflective of the questions of a historical moment whose designers seek to enable the depth of these questions to be probed in the quotidian space of the city, sometimes on an individual level, and often, also at a political and cultural level; through historical narrative and locational resonance, and through art and design, sometimes independent of place.

Current public debates about the nature and position of remembrance in postwar Berlin have created a specific vocabulary of discourse, some understanding of the key terms of which is necessary to comprehend the nature of the cultural foregrounding of recent contemplative space-making in the city.

Gedenkstaette

Generically, all spaces and structures of remembrance are today called *Gedenkstaetten,* plural of *Gedenkstaette*, literally a place of thinking and memory, a term that further suggests the reflective activity of remembering by being in a place where something significant happened. This newer term has mostly subsumed the more traditional term, *Denkmal* (literally "thinking sign" or "thinking moment"), as the program of documentation and the aesthetic tone of these places has departed from traditional nineteenth- and early twentieth-century celebratory, literal and, often, monumental modes of expression. Cloaked by this more neutral term is the concept that many of these contemporary places, once experienced, inevitably incorporate in the visitor: the paradoxes of a horror-filled and divided past, sometimes defying the rational explanation implied by the term "thinking." An important distinction about place and time has occurred in the shifting semiotic of these terms, and it illuminates a central debate about the place and form of contemplative space. *Gendenkstaette* focuses on place (*Staette*), on the authentic connection between events and people and a location/space. *Denkmal*, still sometimes used both in places of actual events and more abstract locations of commemoration (but increasingly given the subject matter of victimization, more often transformed to *Mahnmal,* see below), preserves the fusion (or ambiguity?) of time and sign embedded in the suffix, *Mal*. None of these terms, interestingly, has a direct translation in English.

Versoehnung

At the center of the syntax is the hope of the contemporary *Gedenkstaette*, that the studied acceptance of the events of the past will engender *Versoehnung*, the reconciliation with the past that is the presumed basis for the future. Berlin tests the proposition that encounters with the past in the space of the present must involve reflection, and reflection is hypothetically a function of engagement of the mind by both reason and the senses. In the sensual mode, ordinary time is suspended. Thinking combined with the positioning of the body in a space of self – and other – reference merge as experience. Arguably necessary to create this realm of affect, is the fusion

Lance Neckar

of narrative, image, association and space so powerful that it simulates a space of "otherness," that resets one's direction. This effect is the essence of *Betroffenheit*.

Betroffenheit

What Americans might loosely and blandly term "impact," is the Germans' sense of an empathetic response resulting from being struck in a manner to defy words and reason. Historians understand that *Betroffenheit* is induced intellectually by the engagement with the incomprehensibility of acts remembered. Artistic interpretations of the spatial syntax of Berlin, which in many places was so badly bombed as still to have open sites, sometimes carry this weight by the contraction of space, the extreme sense of being bounded. It as if the closing of the horizon simulates the bounding of the future, as if to pick up on the idea of the concentration camps, and the Berlin Wall, but also allowing a certain sense of sublimity, as in a walled garden or in the skylit void of an empty, darkened room. In some of these and other places in more open landscapes there is simply no ordinary reference to location. Such voids, where there is no clear destination, makes a presence of the transmutation of the familiar. In many of these places of simple emptiness, bounded or unbounded, there is only you, yourself stricken, *Betroffenheit*.

Mahnen

The concept of admonition, or warning, the normative playground of the artist and the designer, is perhaps the most difficult semiotic for historians since it involves an abstraction from the memory of facts and empirical academic processes of research, teaching and learning, a certain body of judgments against crimes and their perpetrators.[2] The moral and ethical message is thus clarified, and, at the same time, made ambiguous. One asks, for example, by what process the rational mind, first, incorporates what for many is the unthinkable and, second, develops a revised normative position toward the world? A cognitive process of learning from admonition seems to depend, in the minds of some historians, on the authenticity of experience of the visitor, a condition by which the authenticity of a site and its associations underpin the reception by the visitor.[3] The zone of "authenticity" of the admonition based in historical empiricism, and authentic experience is where the line between the cognitive and the affective, between intellectual preparation and emotions, blurs.

Mahnmal

The evolution of German language with its peculiarly additive richness underpins a double entendre in the semiotic of remembrance in Berlin and endows the landscape with particular, sometimes ambiguous, qualities of twenty-first century meaning. No better example exists of this than the term *Mahnmal*. The double meaning in the word *Mal*, point of time (moment) and sign, as noted earlier, captures essences of both time and space. The transformation of the term *Denkmal* to *Mahnmal*, to incorporate the purposes of admonition and warning with the double meaning of *Mal*, blurs both the warning and the continuities and boundaries of time and space continuum. Blurring, a concept prominent in Peter Eisenman's writing, accords with the common parlance name "*Holocaust Mahnmal*" for his project, the Memorial to the Murdered Jews of Europe. Eisenman has focused on memory as anti-nostalgia, as a function of the "time of the monument, its duration," which he sees as "different from the time of human experience and understanding . . . since no understanding is possible."[4] This is his approach to what has been called in this document "otherness." Eisenman's theories are nevertheless part of a historical "moment" of admonition to future generations at hand in Germany, and it is one of deep anxiety and conflicted intention. Admonition is time-sensitive. Those who remember, whether victims, perpetrators, or bystanders, are dying. And looming also is the passing of the baby-boom generation who were their children and in one way or another, children of the culture of Nazism. That generation's memory is both a construction and a deconstruction of the events of their own collective and individual pasts, inflected by their post-Nazi education, which was a mix of denial and discovery.[5] They have been warned; and some, activists, see themselves as the last direct connection to their parents' generation, and as children of the Cold War, authentic bearers of admonition, of which the *Mahnmal* is the national centerpiece.[6]

Auseinandersetzung

This word often is used to describe the educational and commemorative processes by which one begins to "grapple with" a difficult engagement, here of the effects of state-and culturally-sponsored genocide. It also has a more literal meaning of disaggregation, of setting things apart so that they can be understood; it connotes deconstruction, literal if not literary. In this historical moment in Berlin, *Auseinandersetzung* in some ways speaks (also) directly of the aesthetics of the most recent commemorative spaces, abstracting experience by increasing degrees and disassociation from a literal, symbolic reading of memory, and referencing the disjunctive mood of the age and its affect on the dislocations of those who remember now.

Nachdenken

The German participial, *Nachdenken*, literally, thinking back, in the sense of reflection, is one translation of "contemplation." In this sense of the word, contemplation is conditioned by the past, and is temporal by definition. The unspoken everyday activity of Berlin, *Nachdenken,* puts a temporal frame on the processes of grappling with one's self and one's place in time; and the most evocative simulacrum of this *Nachddenken* is occurring today in the landscape. Like a complex clock or calendar, the landscape registers time on multiple scales and in the mixed media associated with our workings of and on land. Landscape fuses time with place as it positions the oppositional. It mixes organic and inorganic media to speak in a simple, yet eloquent language of temporality. In Berlin empty spaces especially evoke absence, or more precisely, the presence of absence, since usually the space was once populated or built. The imprint of human existence here mixes the residual with the new in sharp relief, the city's voids being filled with connotations of the past.

Destruction, reconstruction, reflection, deconstruction: contemplation

In 1995 Dr. Stephanie Endlich, a historian, and Thomas Lutz, Director of the *Topographie des Terrrors,* wrote *Reflections and Lessons in Historic Places: a Guide to Memorials to the Victims of National Socialism in Berlin,* both an apologia for historical remembrance and a guide to the memorials of all types to the victims of Nazism.[7] As Endlich has declared bluntly, the entirety of Berlin is a "topography of terror."[8] The authors set forth the then emerging position of German educators on the pedagogical role of authentic places of commemoration. The timing of this work has been critical since it has emerged at the 50-year anniversary of the end of the Second World War, also a moment of societal and demographic transition in Germany, only six years after the reunification. Endlich and Lutz have argued persuasively for the acceptance approach, namely that the effects of Nazism on postwar German society are inextricable with the country's history, including the division of the nation into two state entities and, further, that all of the immense cultural formation that had engendered the inhumanities of the Nazi regime were, therefore, still touchstones of German identity today.[9]

Nevertheless, learning about that regime's crimes and the thoughtful acceptance of paradox make a dilemma of reconciliation. This dilemma was heightened after 1961 with the construction of an impassable wall by the German Democratic Republic (DDR) in the East. Berlin became a diagram of Cold War world in the 1960s. The city's landscape with its no-man's land, a "death strip," was divided into zones of schizophrenic development. Their respective political ideological spaces symbolized the devolution of the possibility of reconciliation. Reunification has erased the physical wall, and the DDR has merged with the Bundesrepublik; but as Endlich and Lutz have argued, the cultural palimpsest of these destructive formations remains, embedded in the landscape, tilting the planes on which reconciliation must find footing. The reconciliation process imagined by Lutz in his essay on *Gedenken* (remembering), involves four purposes of these memorial sites and the programming around them: remembrance, admonition, research and learning.[10] Lutz, like many of his contemporaries in academic fields, values the role of objectivist history in cultural formation and distrusts the role emotion would play in admonition.[11] He has advocated the standard of the historical approach: the role of *Gendenkstaetten* is to provide the historical narrative by which one understands cognitively what the effects of Nazism were on its victims, and, further, that out of this cognition empathy for their plight develops, not the other way around. The care with which history needs to be woven with the activities of the various sites takes full advantage of the authenticity of the sites; this nexus is critical to the Lutz's approach.

Yet there have been wide differences across the approaches taken at some *Gedenkstaetten* since the Berlin Wall has fallen. Some, such as the *Topographie des Terrors*, where Lutz is the director, are primarily focused on history and site; and others rely instead on the affective, on aesthetic means. The motivations and expectations for these *Gedenkstaetten* since the 1989 reunification have had their precedence in four decades of experience with these two broad approaches. In the period immediately following the Second World War, as Germans were beginning to rebuild, some were also coping with guilt for having so easily become followers of and bystanders to the Reich, while others were living with denial. The first memorials were an attempt to find and recognize the strength of the good, of those who had been part of the *Widerstand*, the Resistance.[12] The memorial to the 1944 effort by Commander Claus Schenk, Graf von Stauffenberg to assassinate Hitler was (and is) the best known and most central of these resistance activities, and was also the first to be commemorated, in 1953. Stauffenberg and his colleagues had placed a bomb in a barracks where Hitler was to be on July 20, 1944. In 1969, on the twenty-fifth anniversary of the failed attempt, a museum building was dedicated to house documentation of the event. In 1983 the mayor of West Berlin ordered the development of a documentation project on all aspects of the Resistance, and this work took the form of an exhibition opened in 1989 as the *Gedenkstaette* of the German Resistance. This work predicated the historical museum-oriented, place-specific commemoration that would co-dominate with figurative sculpture and the placement of plaques in the next wave of work.

In the period following reunification, the government of Chancellor Helmut Kohl moved reconciliation to the forefront of policy. Among the early, sometimes uncomfortable, efforts of the early 1990s was the rededication of the Neue Wache (New Watch) as the central *Gedenkstaette* of the

Lance Neckar

Bundesrepublik for Victims of War and Totalitarianism. The building (1816), was designed by Karl Friedrich Schinkel as a small castrum with a temple front. It is both an important tourist destination on the restored street, Unter den Linden, in the former East zone, and the place where by ordinary government protocol, officials are brought for certain kinds of rituals such as wreath layings. On the plaque on the exterior; re-dedicated in 1993, the various victim groups are listed: the fallen of the two World Wars, the murdered Jews and gypsies, victims of euthanasia and the *Widerstand*, and those oppressed by Stalinism. This ecumenical dedication is much critiqued by those who have directed their efforts to create projects related to specific sites of Nazi (and other) brutalities as a too-generalized statement about German responsibility for the effects of all war and dictatorships, casting such a wide net as to be either meaningless or offensive to those most recently implicated, especially the perpetrators and bystanders of the DDR regime.[13] In other words, its attempt to do something that accepts all guilt (if not actually honoring the victims), leaves unanswered the questions of the specific acceptance of responsibilities whose convoluted character is opaque to the observer.[14] Aesthetically too its official transformation has been controversial, largely because of the overtly Christian symbolism of the central sculpture in the building, an oversized version of the 1938 pieta by Kaethe Kollwitz (Fig. 5.1).

5.1
Pieta, an oversized version of the 1938 sculpture inside Neue Wache building, Berlin
Kaethe Kollwitz

146

1
Woodland Cemetery, Enskede, Sweden. The lawn (the clearing) under snow; the freestanding stone cross faces the Chapel of the Holy Cross/Monument Hall
Gunnar Asplund and Sigurd Lewerentz, 1915–1940

2
Woodland Cemetery, Enskede, Sweden. The forested landscape of graves
Gunnar Asplund and Sigurd Lewerentz, 1915–1940

3
Salk Institute, near La Jolla, California. The "River of Life" fountain connects the courtyard to the Pacific Ocean and the sky
Louis Kahn, 1959–65

4
The Lightning Field, Quemado, New Mexico
Walter De Maria, 1977

5
***Last Breath,
Principal Financial
Group, Des
Moines, Iowa***
James Turrell,
1990

6
Aerial view of Roden Crater, near Flagstaff, Arizona
James Turrell

7
Roden Crater Project, near
Flagstaff, Arizona. East Tunnel
James Turrell, 1977–present

8
Roden Crater Project, near
**Flagstaff, Arizona. The East
Portal's aperture to the sky**
James Turrell, 1977–present

9
Roden Crater Project, near Flagstaff, Arizona. Inside the rim of the volcano – with the eye of the crater in the center
James Turrell, 1977–present

10
***Ritual Series 5/79*, Wilmington, Vermont**
Michael Singer, 1979

11
Pavilion and Garden, Vermont
Michael Singer, 1992

12
Alterra Institute for Environmental Research, IBN-DLO Wageningen, Netherlands
Michael Singer, 1999

13
Concourse C, Denver International Airport, Denver, Colorado
Michael Singer, 1994

14
Trans Gas Energy Cogeneration Power Plant Proposal, New York City
Michael Singer, 2002

15
Final design, Reflection Garden, Bloedel Reserve, Bainbridge Island, Washington, 1986. Haag's design added the hedges and lawn
Richard Haag, 1994

16
Reflection Garden, earlier design by Thomas Church, Bloedel, Reserve, Bainbridge Island

17
National Library of France, Paris. An inaccessible, transplanted forest is the centerpiece of the library
Dominique Perrault, landscape architect Erik Jacobsen, 1995

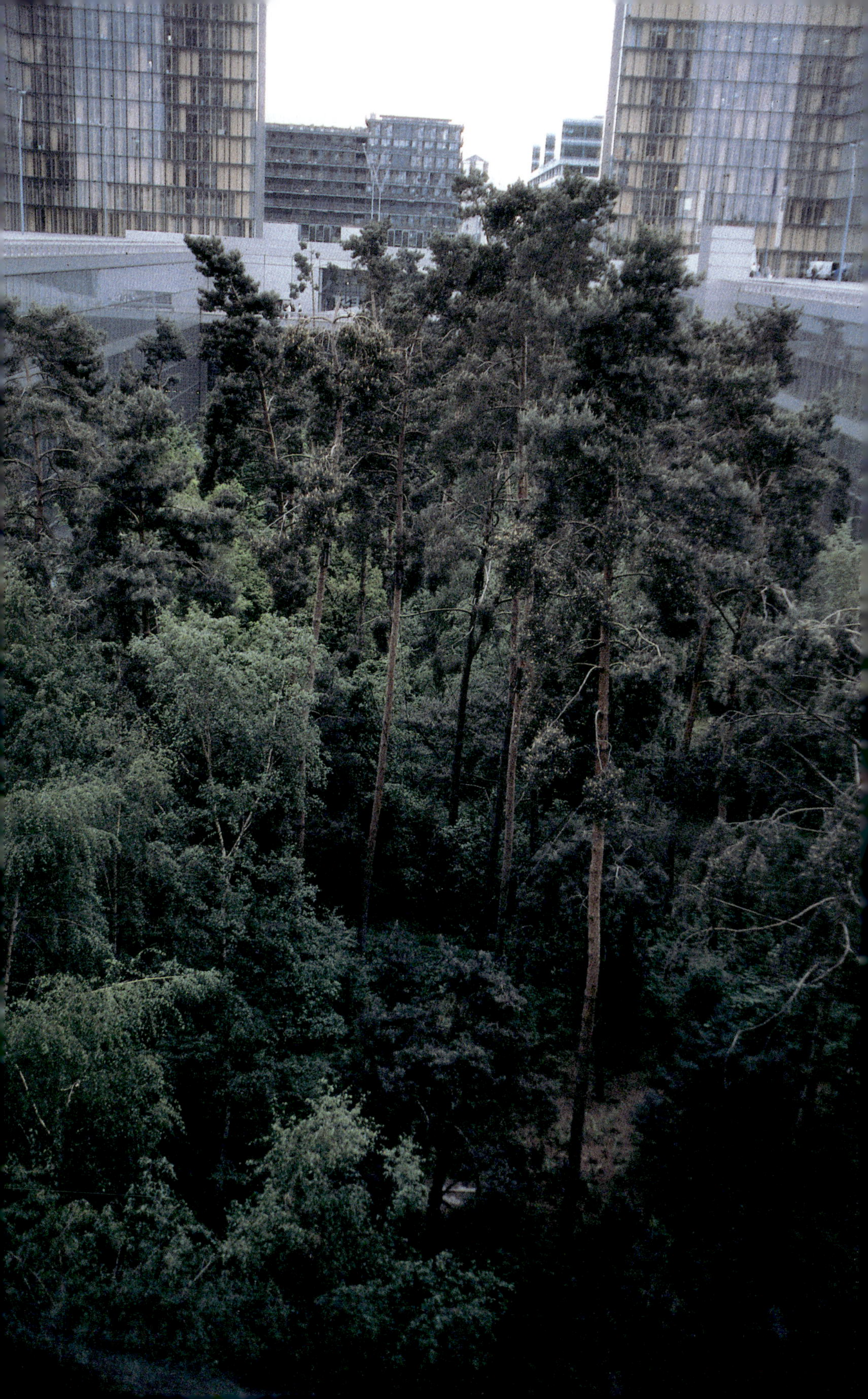

18
Jewish Museum, Berlin. Garden of Exile and Emigration
Daniel Libeskind, 2001

19
***Mahnmal*, Berlin, completion expected 2005**
Peter Eisenman

20
**Swamp Garden,
Spoleto Festival,
Charleston,
South Carolina,
USA**
Adriaan Geuze,
1997

21
**Swamp Garden, Spoleto Festival, Charleston,
South Carolina, USA. Inside the structure**
Adriaan Geuze, 1997

22
***Field Work*,
Spoleto Festival,
Charleston,
South Carolina,
USA**
Martha Schwartz,
1997

Berlin: Topology of Contemplation

Yet if one knows nothing of the wider context of political and aesthetic debates about the Neue Wache, it is one of the most elementally affective sites in the city. From the street edged by the Doric colonnade, one turns to see the door framing a dark mass, barely recognizable as figures in a dark room, illuminated only from above. In the center of the room is an oversized copy, just slightly larger than human scale, of Kollwitz's work, a mother and her dead son. The framing of the bodies brings observers into the space of the pieta in a sequence of movement from the street through the progressive containment of space, first darkening, then illuminating in the time of the eyes' dark adaptation as one approaches the figures in an otherwise dim void.[15] The void, a preoccupation of certain architects since Adolf Loos, becomes positive. The reduction of the dark room to a pure space of brilliant proportional clarity with its domed oculus trains midday light directly on the mother and son. It is an essential essay on war's human damage. The pieta possesses this direct presence. Here another principal strength of the affect is revealed: the character, gesture, scale and positioning of the body in space. Beneath the veneer of Christian iconography is a statement of pure human loss. A mother, brought to ground, holding her dead child, isolated in space, alone.[16]

In the late 1980s and early 1990s, after the Berlin Wall had come down, the reflexive mood of commemoration in Berlin continued to reference the human condition via the body, though less often in strictly figural pieces. As if simultaneously to open the possibilities both of expressive form and of specific sites, many of the most recent *Gedenkstaetten* have used the landscape as more integrated media. In 1992 on the square in front of Rathaus Steglitz, Wolfgang Goeschel and Joachim von Rosenberg appropriated the tradition of the memorial wall (*Gedenkwand*) and the currency of the idea used by Maya Lin of engraving text, especially names, into a reflective surface to make a new kind of literally reflective and dematerializing memorial of the effects of the Holocaust on this district of the city. Another *Gedenkstaette*, *Raum*, ("room," also translatable as "space") an installation proposed by Karl Biedermann in 1988 for Grosse Hamburger Strasse in the Scheunenviertel, a district of a considerable prewar Jewish community amid Catholics and Lutherans, was one of the breakthrough projects of this type. *Raum* consists of a table and two chairs on a floor surface; one chair has been tipped over as if someone had been forcibly dragged away.[17] Another project of 1996–7, by architects Zwi Hecker and Eyal Weizman and artist Micha Ullmann, is an installation of benches in the exact place of the pews of the liberal synagogue on the Lindenstrasse (now Axel-Springer-Strasse) in Kreuzberg destroyed on *Kristallnacht*, 1938.[18]

Lance Neckar

Four other recent projects manifest further development of the landscape strategy as a foundation for the syntax of the unfolding *Auseinandersetzung*. This unpacking of the layered cultural and formal processes, setting the stage for contemplation, focuses on questions of identity. One is a *Gedenkstaette* (added to an original plaque, 1973) that is primarily composed of two sculptural landscape memorials to Jews deported to the concentration camps from the Gruenewald S-Bahn Station, the first by Karol Broniatowski (1991) and the second by the Deutsche Bahn (German Railway, no artist, architect or landscape architect cited, 1998). Another project is Daniel Libeskind's *Juedisches* (Jewish) *Museum* (1998, opened as a museum 2001), the spaces of which were originally largely intended to be an empty memorial structure, including the still empty *Leerraum* (Void Room/Space) of the Holocaust Tower and Garden of Exile and Emigration. The *Denkmal fuer die ermorerdeten Juden Europas*, the so-called Holocaust *Mahnmal* designed originally by Richard Serra and Peter Eisenman now including a documentation center, a project of the latter (scheduled to be completed 2005) in the emerging seam of the reunified city, that until 1991 was the empty death strip between the Brandenburg Gate and Leipziger Platz. Finally, sited on the former Nazi offices of State Security is the *Topographie des Terrors* (temporary exhibition building 1987, now demolished; Peter Zumthor building designed 1993; construction halted for budget reasons in 1995; outdoor exhibition 1997; Zumthor sacked 2004).

The *Auseinandersetzung* has been a process in Berlin by which destruction has led to successive waves of reconstruction, reflection and, now, deconstruction. In this last, current moment, comparative economic stability is the ironic prelude to uncertainty. Change is occurring as a generation dies, another establishes new orders and still another comes of age. The deconstruction of this moment has manifested itself not just as the hyperextension of the convoluted intellectual and emotional processes of grappling with the layered past by intellectual and political discourse and disaggregation, but in the aesthetics of *Gedenkstaetten*. Increasingly these projects have been dug, metaphorically and literally, into the past, into the earth, in many places the last continuous physical medium left after the destruction of the war. Earth is the vessel of reconciliation, the foundation for the future. Excavating and recontouring are syntax and morphology of the emerging topology of contemplation in the city.

Gedenkwand and *Gleis* (Track) 17 at the Gruenewald S-Bahn Station: interruptions of the quotidian

Berlin is dotted with what historian and educator, Annegret Ehmann, calls *"Stolpersteine"* (stumble stones) that recall the past and offer questions, and some guidance for the future. Less visible to political debate than the central

Berlin: Topology of Contemplation

Gedenkstaetten, but having, perhaps, more permanent, daily impact on the average citizen of the city, are the effects of these dispersed, smaller, but in some cases more intense interruptions in the everyday space of the city.[19] These *Gedenkstaetten* are often places of local initiative, of commemoration of actual events, sometimes as here at the S-Bahn station in Gruenewald having wider sponsorship that has evolved with the culture of contemplation.

If you are planning a walk farther afield in Gruenewald using the *Dorling Kindersley Eyewitness Guide to Berlin*, you will be directed to take the S-Bahn to this gracious town, filled with charming early twentieth-century architecture, largely untouched by the war, arranged around a leafy open space system, the "green wood" that is its name. The guide cues you to "take a close look at the station" for its architectural charm. But the *Gedenkstaette* is not mentioned. After the decision of October 18, 1941 to deport Jews to the concentration camps through Gruenewald, trainloads of hundreds of victims were brought through the station on specially scheduled SS-guarded services, all arranged by the Reichsbahn, forerunner of today's Deutsche Bahn. Their passage through the station is marked by the three components of this *Gedenkstaette*. There has been a descriptive historical plaque there since 1973, and since 1991, the fiftieth anniversary of the deportation of Jews to Lodz, a *Gedenkwand* (commemorative wall); and, more recently still in 1998 markers on a track that has no more trains, no more passengers.

Just to the right of the station entrance is the plaque and beyond it, the concrete wall topped by a line of trees (Fig. 5.2). The *Gedenkwand*

5.2
Gedenkwand
Gruenewald, Germany. Concrete wall with negative forms of human figures, 1991

(commemorative wall) wall freezes an expression of human movement in a moment of duress. Loss and instability lie in the voids of the walls. The negative forms into which the human figures seem to have been cast and then removed leave evidence of a procession of an ungainly line of people. Bodies cast in their precarious positions and then dematerialized, leave shadows tipping into and away. Only hollowness remains. The wall is visible to all commuters from Gruenewald, everyday, a warning at the scale and in the form of one's corporeal existence (Fig. 5.3). The wall sits to the side of the station, and the road next to it leads to *Gleis* (Track) 17, the third part of the *Gedenkstaette*. One must choose to go to this platform because no trains run there. One either goes up the street, past the hollow figures, or one climbs the stairs from the tunnel below the tracks toward the light.

On the ballast where the platform used to be, down the space lined by volunteer growth of trees amid the rusting tracks (Fig. 5.4), the deportations are documented in a series of iron plaques in the floor space of the platform. Stand here and you may feel as if you too are waiting to be removed. Stand here and you are in the presence of official, bureaucratic evil, of death. A police van may pull up the road to watch for your safety, or the security of the site, in itself a reminder of difficulty of the *Auseinandersetzung*. But in the relative context of this difficult moment, this is no longer a space of coercion, but rather a place to be warned of the possible interruption of the everyday.

5.3
Gedenkwand
Gruenewald,
Germany.
The memorial's relationship to the station and commuters

5.4
Track 17, Gruenewald, Germany.
The former train platform is a memorial to deportations; names are cast into iron plaques along the tracks, added 1998

Juedisches Museum (Jewish Museum): voids filled

This museum has had an unusual, comparatively fast-tracked history as a *Gedenkstaette*. It grew out of a series of events related to efforts of commemoration by the Jewish community of Berlin beginning in 1975. After the successful mounting of several exhibitions in the 1980s and 1990s (in the Martin Gropius Bau next to the *Topographie des Terrors*), the community secured the support of the city to hold a competition in 1989 for the enlargement of the old City Museum building to house its "Jewish section." Polish-American architect Daniel Libeskind won the competition. Construction took place from 1992 to 1998, and the museum was opened to the public in January 1999; however, the building was empty until 2001. In that year, responsibility for the museum was transferred from the city to the nation and it began to be filled with exhibits.[20]

It is a building shaped, surfaced and filled with symbols. In plan it is "likened to a deconstructed Star of David."[21] It was originally conceived as an empty building that relied on its space and light to achieve an affect of loss, of removal (Fig. 5.5). Since it was also meant (somewhat paradoxically) to house a "section" of the city's history museum, one enters the building today from the neighboring historic structure. The spectacular qualities of the program of the museum and its building have engulfed the city's modest museum.

The museum is a bundle of paradox. Upon entry, one descends a very long flight of stairs to a deep basement. The depth in the ground is emphasized as one traverses the several thematic axes on the tilting planes of this lower, artificially-illuminated level. This axial organization devolves from the "deconstructed" star plan, but it projects unfortunate visual and word associations with the symbols of the Third Reich and the Axis powers. For example, not only does the plan, some details in paving, and some of the fenestration of the building look like lightning strikes (in German, "Blitz" as in "Blitzkrieg,") when the building was empty, its thin section made much of light through windows cut at jagged angles reminiscent of the swastika and Nazi typography. Now, however, as the museum has been filled, the plan challenges the integration of history, exhibits and artifacts into the space of a museum building that is often crowded and where the windows are mostly just another part of a cluttered space. Minus a true collection related to Berlin, generality of interpretation becomes a cover for the underlying desperateness of the curatorial enterprise, less a museum than anxiety-filled voids.

The original intentions of the building can be seen in the *Leerraeume* (void, or literally, empty, rooms/spaces). Left in their original state they are somewhat forced, but uncluttered environments of experience. One is allowed to go into the Holocaust Tower at the terminus of the third axis

5.5
Jewish Musem, Berlin. Outdoor courtyard
Daniel Libeskind, 2001

only when let in by one of the museum staff, who, clad in their (again, oddly discordant) signature black jackets and slacks and red and yellow scarves, open the heavy steel door at intervals of about five minutes.

The Holocaust Tower is dark, illuminated only by a small slash near the roof (Fig. 5.6). It is described in the Museum website in this text:

> This tower is only accessible from underground and is, as are all the "empty rooms" of the museum, made of concrete. It is not heated but neither isolated from the elements; in summer it is cool, and moist. Light comes into the space only by day from a high, narrow slit window. You can hear the street noise clearly, but the outer world is unreachable. It is a space of contemplation that reminds one of the nakedness and emptiness of many Jewish victims of mass murder.[22]

In the space of five minutes in the tower, one might contemplate these specific associations of the Holocaust, given the name of the tower and the context of the entire museum (e.g., names of the concentration

5.6
Jewish Musem, Berlin. Inside the Holocaust Tower
Daniel Libeskind, 2001

camps are stenciled on the walls of this axis), but there is also a more open set of responses that might occur in this minimalist setting, feeling less like a tower than a very deep, dark hole.[23] In this *Leerraum,* by all accounts the most minimal space in the museum, empathy with the effects of deprivation of control is attained (perhaps to its greatest degree in the museum) via a spatial experience of more generalized containment and isolation, a more openly-scripted approach to *Betroffenheit* than some of the more literal spaces, including another tower in which iron faces cover the floor of another otherwise empty room.

One is also let into the Garden of Exile and Emigration from this subgrade level (Plate 18). It is a seven-by-seven grid of 49 tilted stele (six meters in height) that are planters for olive trees. The numerology of the garden is based on seven, the days of the week of the creation, and is intended also to symbolize the year of the founding of Israel (48) plus Berlin, making 49. This garden, another tilted plane, is conceived as a small maze, the passage through which is limited to single people or groups in single file (Fig. 5.7). As in the Gruenewald wall by Broniatowski, the experience of being lined up, or walking alone, this time on a grid, is the only clue to where one is going, here in the space of a hole in the earth, with slivers of the sky and treetops to suggest contact with the rest of the world.

Libeskind's garden, though not the high spatial point of experience in the Museum, does broach the challenge of harnessing the powers of the landscape as a stark garden, one that retains the Edenic references of planting, which encompasses both sign and moment (*Mal*), but puts the plants

5.7
Jewish Musem, Berlin. Inside the Garden of Exile and Emigration
Daniel Libeskind, 2001

out of reach, barely even visible. Nothing is written in the website to convey the intended experience of the garden, although one might safely conclude that if the title and the symbolism refer to emigration to Israel, the experience might be a simulacrum of exile (from Berlin?), and, perhaps, not the Holocaust. Nevertheless, it is impossible not to see the literal relationship of the spatial associations of the grid and confined passage with the design of the *Holocaust Mahnmal*.

Holocaust Mahnmal: simulacrum of the inconceivable

In 1988 Lea Rosh, a television journalist, became chair of the citizen's initiative, *Perspektive Berlin*, and originated the discussion of the idea of a memorial to the murdered Jews of Europe.[24] In 1994 a first competition was sponsored by the *Bundesrepublik*, the city and the Rosh-led group, the *Förderkreis zur Errichtung eines Denkmals für die ermordeten Juden Europas* (Patrons' Circle for the Erection of a Memorial to the Murdered Jews of Europe) for the site, somewhat larger than the current dimensions, south of the Brandenburg Gate. In 1995 the winning submission in the form of an overscaled graveyard, designed by Christine Jacob-Marcks, was vetoed by Chancellor Kohl under pressure from the Social Democratic Party and the Green Party. In 1997 a second competition was held, and four finalists, including Libeskind, Jochen Gerz, Gesine Weinmiller, and the team of Peter Eisenman and Richard Serra, were chosen.[25] The Eisenman/Serra scheme imagined a stark 100m × 100m field of stele with the ground dropping away from the undulating plane established by the tops of these objects. Chancellor Kohl favored this scheme. Then Serra withdrew from the project in an intensified debate about the scale of the stele and the field. With the change in government to Gerhard Schroeder's Social Democratic Party in 1998–9, the new culture minister, Michael Naumann, intervened to amend the project scope to include a documentation center and downsize the site.

      The *Holocaust Mahnmal* debates of the 1990s asked critical questions about the identity of the nation, and principally the nature of public and cultural acceptance of responsibility for the forced dislocation, disenfranchisement, robbery and, principally here, murder, of millions of Jews by the Nazi government. The opponents of the *Mahnmal* asked a question that spoke to the uncharted waters that the project created: "What about a national policy of forgetting and getting on with things?" They seemed to be saying, "Can the project be done with such vivid memories still in place, potentially divisive in their mining of the past?" Is it too obsessed with shame, such that the combined effect is not to mourn the victims or to take heed from their fates, but to embark upon the complex expiation of guilt as the perpetrators and bystanders, our fathers and mothers, die? In this vein is there the downside potential for appropriation of the site by the current politics of anti-Semitism or racism? On the advocates' side of the timing issue has been the worry that the *Mahnmal* (and all of the Holocaust-related sites) is, in fact, becoming too distant in time and direct connection from its events and constituents. Thus unrelated to the experiences of current citizens, it may have no impact of *Betroffenheit*, perhaps being neither meaningful nor controversial at all.[26]

Nevertheless, in June 1999 the project was brought forward for consideration by the German Bundestag. Wolfgang Thierse, Bundespraesident, a member of the ruling Social Democratic Party, made a speech in which he pleaded with his colleagues to make a decision to adopt the project and with this vote recast the idea of responsibility within the nation:

> We must decide today. Do we, after ten years of debate, want to build a memorial to the murdered Jews of Europe? I hear again and again: all arguments have been given, back and forth. But I hear also this: we, the Germans, we, the German *Bundestag*, are not free any longer to make our own decision. The public and international expectation and pressure are so high that the decision is . . . already prejudiced. Nevertheless I say this: this is ours, our very own decision, which we have to make out of a sense of responsibility with a view of our own national history and the conditions of its memory. We must want it – independently of how outsiders judge it. . . . Is not this memorial and our actions on its behalf precisely the opportunity that makes possible a discussion with future generations and who ask us rightfully: why must they bear collective responsibility for crimes for which they were not personally involved? For, that is, of course, correct: the majority of the Germans did not commit murder. But all too many simply watched – whether from fear, from lack of interest, from secret or open sympathy – as their Jewish neighbors were taken away and sent on death marches and death trains.[27]

In another remarkable passage from the speech, Thierse captured the essence of the relationship between Eisenman's idea of the site as a simulacrum of the Holocaust and explained it from a philosophical perspective to his colleagues:

> The Holocaust continues to touch the "borders of our understanding", as it is expressed by Hanno Loewy . . . . I find confidence in the fact that with this memorial the visitor adjusts himself or herself to, as the designer intends, a "terror of the isolation" as it unfolds in the course of a walk. One cannot walk side by side with another

between the stele; there is no entrance, no exit, no center. Though it seems contradictory, in this way it becomes conceivable that the visitor approaches an understanding of the inconceivable. In this way the experience of the memorial approximates that, which Juergen Habermas called the "suitable language" of an uncompromised art, expressed in a "unobtrusive pathos of negatives."[28]

Thierse's political rhetoric, coming from the Social Democrats, had a persuasive role in the adoption of the *Holocaust Mahnmal* in 1999 as an official project of the government. Its adoption expresses the character of a nation that is currently the medium of the postwar generation. The actions of these adults who as children came of age in the last half of the twentieth century shaped their anti-Nazi position in some measure as a manifestation of their shame for their fathers, as Lutz has alluded.[29] And with the vote of the *Bundestag*, came (another) official affirmation of the void as the political and aesthetic evocation of both the isolation of victims and the acceptance of the "otherness" of the acts of the perpetrators, the appropriate stuff of *Betroffenheit* of the moment.

Even with Thierse's eloquent explication, once the Eisenman scheme had been adopted, questions were raised about the public appropriateness of an aesthetic that finds its roots in a particularly personal mode of deconstruction, but emerges from the ground as a (too?) literal representation of a ground of death and mourning, perhaps more nostalgic than its designer had intended. Can this field of stele, so clearly adapted from the Jewish cemeteries of Israel, transcend its own familiar iconographic associations to become what it intends experientially? (See Fig. 5.8 and Plate 19.) In the layered set of meanings that is the contemporary city of Berlin, is there a power in the voids created by the destruction of the city, and can they be enhanced, or preserved, by these new voids? Eisenman's intention is to cast the visitor into a place of absence of the normal, exposed to the sky in a directionless, concrete-studded field, with no apparent hierarchy.[30] As in the image of *The Dancing Skeletons* (1944), the last of Felix Nussbaum's paintings, the idea of the *Mahnmal* is to strip away the paraphernalia of the ordinary, but here, instead of littering the landscape as in the painting, loss presents itself in the form of absence.[31]

Will it be true that the experience of the space with its narrow passages, gridded form – without hierarchy or markings of destinations or entry – can give one the simulacrum of isolation, or, again, of being lined-up? And is this the experience that best calls forth the duration of the camps, of genocide victims and, by extension, the shame of the perpetrators and the bystanders? This is a question that relates the impact of containment of the site to its scale and to the scale of the stele themselves. Is the site both

5.8
***Mahnmal*, Berlin, completion expected 2005**
Peter Eisenman

large and contained enough at the edges and confined enough within the space of passage between the stele to create the intended experience, the *Betroffenheit*? Does too much of the city, especially traffic noise, leak into this space of "otherness"? Is the simple exposure to the sky enough to "stage" a contemplative moment in the context of competing visible activities in this part of the city? The *Mahnmal* also lies at the backs of principal buildings that form its edges. Does this configuration isolate the setting, and is this good since the place is about isolation, or bad, because it is a public space? What will be the nature of the perimeter given a whole array of questions about security? Much of its publicness and the character of its security and the designation of a point of entry may depend on the nature of the design of the American Embassy, the south side of which will be directly across the street from the *Mahnmal*.

The *Mahnmal* site is burdened with deeper paradoxes. It has been sited, in a horrible irony, not on an official place of memory related directly to the victims of the Holocaust, but instead almost directly on the *Hitlerbunker*, probably the last place the *Fuehrer* was alive; his burial plot. Can the feeling one carries to this new ground of remembrance, so obviously like a cemetery, not be tinged by a sense of blasphemy?[32] Of greater concern, what powers of admonition can the *Mahnmal* have as the public learns of the commission to the Degussa Company to coat the concrete stele against graffiti when they will also know that Degussa supplied the chemical used in the gas chambers at Auschwitz? Assuming that visitors are prepared to be admonished, will they accept these paradoxes? If so, the *Mahnmal* will ask unsettling questions of them as befits a critical democratic space, a garden of oppositions of the type that gave it rise, a mirror to and of its makers, projecting through paradox the blurred difficulty of the future whole. Like the cranes over the city skyline, this question hovers over the *Mahnmal* as the promised centerpiece of the political and artistic enterprise of the *Auseinandersetzung*.

The project is filled with these difficult but also more promising paradoxes, and the landscape is perhaps the medium of their revelation and resolution. The *Mahnmal* may be the perfect development to suggest the possibility of a new type of a garden of remembrance in this seam along the space of the former Wall. From the Reichstag to Brandenburg Gate to Leipziger Platz, which is the forecourt to Potsdamer Platz, a series of projects have begun to coalesce new urban forms around significantly redefined open spaces. Until now the focus has been on the grounds of the Reichstag. In 1992 Dieter Appelt and his students at the Berlin School of the Arts created a memorial of 88 rough edged steel plates set on end and inscribed to the memory of murdered and deported members of the Reichstag who dissented from Hitler. This project was initiated by *Perspektive Berlin*, the same group responsible for the *Mahnmal*. Nearby are two other memorials of a less permanent nature. Since the first escapees from the East were killed at the Wall, an individual has made an unofficial memorial of fifteen crosses to recognize their deaths at the southeast corner of the building. Almost adjacent is a semi-official dedication of a garden to gypsies (*Sinti* and *Roma*) killed by the Reich. Around a sign suggesting a more permanent structure in the future is a huge clearing of naturalized tulips just south of the building.

The transformation of the Reichstag itself has been a centerpiece in the *Auseinandersetzung*. In 1995 Christo and Jeanne Claude wrapped the Reichstag, calling attention to the potential beauty of what had been at best a problematic and ironical survivor of the bombing of the city. The wrapping was a prelude to the Reichstag restoration, and, as others point out, the restoration was a necessary prelude to the *Mahnmal*.[33] The Kohl government saw the restoration and particularly the construction of Sir Norman Foster's glass dome (Fig. 5.9), into which politicians, citizens and visitors alike may go, as provision of a literal transparency of the government and on the city. Particularly significant are the views to that area of the city that had been the heart of the Nazi regime, the death strip of the Wall, the revitalized city center, and now the place of the *Mahnmal*. All of this is to be seen from a building whose very name ("Reich" means "empire") and reclamation as the seat of government speaks directly to paradox embedded in transformation.

Lance Neckar

5.9
Reichstag restoration, Berlin
Sir Norman Foster
1999

The Reichstag sits at the edge, but still in the Tiergarten, the immense park of the seventeenth century Elector, Friedrich Wilhelm, transformed for public use by Peter Josef Lenné in the nineteenth century and now restored. The character of the dome owes much to the nineteenth century conservatories of Decimus Burton, J. C. Loudon or Joseph Paxton; and its architect, Sir Norman Foster, must certainly have thought also about observatories. Perhaps subliminally in designing the winding ramp inside the dome, he might have seen in his mind's eye a winding path on a medieval or Renaissance mount such as would have been placed in a garden to gain prospect over it and the surrounding landscape. Seen this way, the Reichstag dome is a glass-covered mount and an observatory dedicated to *Nachdenken*. A nineteenth century panorama of the skyline of Berlin, probably painted from the roof of the Reichstag (in Schinkel's *Neue Pavillon* in Charlottenburg) shows church spires and domes rising from a dense fabric of brick and stone and a few gardens. Today many of the spires and the domes are restored or still improbably present, voids are re-filled as cranes raise glass and steel to form a new skyline. The Tiergarten appears unchanged since the trees today are about the same age as the ones painted 150 years ago. As one contemplates the transformation of the city and the nation reborn in this new transparent state, one also sees one's fellows, including those below who are reflected in mirrors at the center of the dome.[34]

For now one void in the city is still visible from the dome: the *Mahnmal* site, where stele anchor the ground, admonishing. The *Mahnmal* has now become the centerpiece of reconciliation in this possible national garden. What realm of affect is expected from this garden, from the *Gedenkstaetten* and especially from the *Mahnmal*? If it is the acceptance of the "otherness" associated with *Betroffenheit*, must there also be an affirmation of life in any space that is a garden, and, if so, is a garden always defined by these Edenic roots? Given that this is a place of a certain kind of minimalism and closeness of body and object, like the Vietnam Veterans Memorial, will there be items placed here as remembrances and what will they be? Do offerings of flowers, stones, pictures, or perhaps personal effects of the everyday world make a garden? Or less a garden than an abstract cemetery? The more significant question is, what happens to this zone that seams the city and the nation back together if it does not become a garden?

Topographie des Terrors: temporary default garden

Thomas Lutz's museum and documentation center was until the spring of 2004 a private non-profit operation, a *Stiftung* (foundation), with oversight by the state, and semi-official status as a project of the city of Berlin. As of late May, 2004, the nearly decade-long delay of the construction of a new building to the design of Swiss architect, Peter Zumthor, was brought to an end with Zumthor's dismissal. At the same time, the $15 million euro debt of the *Stiftung* was taken over by the nation and with it the management of the project, including the engagement of a new architect.

The museum is currently staged outdoors. In a trench made by the foundation walls of the demolished buildings that housed the offices of the Nazi State Security Service, exhibits have been mounted under a long open gallery roof, running the length of a vestigial section of the Wall (Figs 5.10 and 5.11). The Wall fronts Niederkirchner Strasse, renamed (from Prinz Albrecht Strasse to honor Queen Victoria's brilliant spouse) in the DDR period for a young communist victim of the Nazis. Just visible over the Wall on the other side of the street is the brooding *Luftsministerium* of Hermann Goering and another government building, now part of the offices of the reunified Prussian state and the *Bundesrepublik*.

The *Topographie des Terrors* takes the programmatic stance of a museum and archive, but it is also positioned uniquely as a *Gedenkstatte* on the site of its main interpretive focus. The perpetrators of the Nazi regime are the main story of the exhibits of the *Topographie*, but the vicissitudes of the site also figure importantly in this narrative. The panels have a generally chronological historical organization that begins with the description of the devolution of the site from a small Hohenzollern palace with a nineteenth century garden by Peter Josef Lenné. The narrative describes the construction and occupancy of the Prinz Albrecht Hotel and an applied art school, which included the neighboring Martin Gropius Bau, recently restored as a

Lance Neckar

5.10
**Topographie des Terrors,
Berlin**

5.11
**Topographie des Terrors,
Berlin**

Berlin: Topology of Contemplation

separate museum. In the heyday of this area of the city before and just after the turn of the twentieth century, Kreuzberg was a cosmopolitan quarter of Berlin, ironically with many Jewish residents. Continuing along the trench, the narrative focuses on the events around the conversion of these buildings to the offices used from 1932 to 1945 by the Reich security apparatus who were the agents of the destruction of the Weimar government, the first German republican societal experiment. There were three components of State Security, the Security Service (SD), the Protection Squadron/ *Schutzstaffel* (SS), and the secret police, the Gestapo. The criminal activities of these state and party organizations to promote the persecution, enslavement, deportation and murder of so-called undesirables, degenerates, and enemies of the regime are detailed as are the lives of some of the most notable victims who first distinguished themselves as threats to the Reich and were then either deported to the camps or killed outright.

The museum today is as much a stratigraphy as a topography of terror. Its primary reason for being is its site. After the historical buildings were bombed and demolished to the level of the street, the site was "forgotten" and used as a dump for the debris of bombed buildings and, later, after the construction of the Wall, an off-road driving attraction. What is eerily effective about the *Topographie* is its rawness. It lacks mediation, it is exposed, piled and excavated. The fact of a visit to this museum is that one is mostly in a trench-like space, outdoors at the edge of a dump in the middle of a sophisticated European city. Here in an open basement in the shadow of the Wall that recently divided East and West was one of the most brutal places in the history of the Western world. Wherever one goes on the site of the *Topographie* the brokenness of the land enhances the immediacy of terror that one feels and also understands from the text. It presents a stark contrast with the context of restored and new buildings on its perimeter. The unfinished stairtowers of the Zumthor project, mute slender concrete slabs, now scheduled to be removed, rising amid the grassy debris piles, sharpen the juxtaposition.

Positioned just below the surface of the narrative of the exhibit is the *Mahnen*, a clear warning that never again shall state-supported murder occur. In this, until now privately-funded effort, this has been a measured message, a clear decision to let the facts and the destroyed buildings and the site speak for themselves. The exhibits do not stretch for a mood of *Betroffenheit* although a considerable segment of the exhibit is devoted not just to the perpetrators but to a range of the victims, from political opponents, including communists (e.g., Erich Honecker, former leader of the DDR) to cultural undesirables including gypsies and homosexuals as well as Jews. The word "Holocaust," with all of its normative connotation of our time is, as in Lutz's and Endlich's book, not used since it is also anachronistic and therefore violates the empirical method of the historical narrative in two ways.

Lance Neckar

As the Topographie becomes a project of the nation, the questions of this moment in German history cloud its future as a *Gedenkstaette* just as its financial horizon clears. Its adoption by the nation has the potential to inflect the interpretive rhetoric of this project. Could one imagine a scenario similar to the evolution of the *Mahnmal*? With its adoption by the nation, will there be pressure to have more *Mahnen* and expiation of guilt than objective history of high crimes whose perpetrators are the fathers of today's politicians? What happens as the generation of perpetrators passes from the scene? Substantively, can this be "good" for the museum as it allows more objectivity? Or is it "bad" for the production of historians, assessing a chronology that is already well hidden, only partly written and now subject to national politics? What about pressure on the financial side as the exigency of the moment, reflected in the adoption of the project by the nation, competes for the "memory euro" of the generation of children of the perpetrators and bystanders when so much has already been expended on behalf of the victims? This is the not-too-subtle subtext of the sacking of an expensive star architect whose inscrutable practices have delayed the project so dramatically.

Director Lutz and his staff are, undoubtedly, wondering when their temporary offices in bright orange shipping containers, looking like misplaced cargo of the global economy, perched between the exhibit trench and the debris piles, will be replaced by a permanent structure. One might argue that an essential strength not only of the *Topographie's* message but also its curatorial culture may be lost when that happens. Paradox has rolled in again, full tide. So much time and money has been plunged into the lost Zumthor project, the responsibility for which has been tied in the press to the recalcitrant architect, that the nation has no stomach for another prima donna. Yet the public undoubtedly also expects signature design as a result of the spectacles of the *Juedisches Museum* and the *Mahnmal*. And this last paradox veils as it undermines the substance of the museum enterprise, the *Auseinandersetzung* of an authentic site, the foundation of Lutz's whole career. For now the site is an extreme garden, a default realm of authentic affect. Once the exhibits are contained in a space of complete shelter, no matter how starkly conceived, will not the name and, indeed the whole realm of affect of this place, change? No longer a garden, a topography of terror, but another void to be filled?

Capital city of contemplation: *nachdenken*

Nachdenken in Berlin has become local initiative, public policy, art, architecture and landscape. Berlin is betting on the landscape in some settings to complement spectacle architecture, to operate within the mind of its citizens, residents and visitors. Reflexive imagery and combinations of ideas have been reduced to memorable voids around which the everyday landscape is filled with the ordinary activity of the city. Part of the wager is that a garden demands attention if it is to be sustained. A garden stakes its sustenance on future gardeners. The landscape of the city's *Gedenkstaetten* has made a physical syntax and morphology of remembrance, admonition, and contemplation. Berlin was so recently a city divided, a diagram of ethnic, religious and ideological separateness that has contorted the world's peoples in violence. Today it is a place where the *Auseinandersetzung* with the legacies of the twentieth century is a working hypothesis on the identities of the twenty-first. In this, the Western city most prominently associated with memories of World and Cold Wars; in this once and again the easternmost capital of the West, now enlarged by ethnic diversity previously unheard of; here, in reunified Berlin, a national landscape of reflection and transparency is evolving, a necessary garden of voids in a city being filled.

It can also be said of Berliners that they have embarked on the making of their own unique unofficial gardens of remembrance, *Stolpersteine* everywhere else. It is an experiment uniquely theirs, a developing aesthetic of democratic discourse and introspection, reflexive, combinative and minimalist in its semiotic, an organic topology of contemplation in process (Fig. 5.12).

And so, we end where we began but give the last words about the affect of this topology to a Berliner, Rabbi Walther Rothschild:

> How sensitive, empathetic must one be in Berlin? How open to empathy may one be in Berlin? Is normal life possible? If so, can I have a bit of it? And if not, how long must one wait until one no longer feels empathy?
>
> I regularly visit Kreuzberg, (the district of the city where the *Juedische Museum* and the *Topographie* are) and one day as I was walking along the Paul Lincke esplanade I noticed a small four-cornered bronze or alloy plate in the pavement of the sidewalk at number 41. It looked like a normal water, gas, electricity or telephone cable access cover. Out of boredom or curiosity I read what it said on the plate; not Spandau Iron Foundry or BEWAG, it read:
>
>> "Here lived Horst Lothar Koppel, 24 years old, deported 1943. Transport to the East."
>
> The sun clouded over, the birds stopped singing, the whole noise of the street was suddenly silent.[35]

Lance Neckar

5.12
Stolpersteine, (stumble stones) are dispersed, smaller memorials; in this case a plaque on the street of Berlin names a man who used to live here – and who was deported in 1943

An autobiographical afterword: blurred remembrances of Berlin

As the plans for this essay took shape, I reflected on my previous visits to Berlin for about a year. As I prepared in earnest for this trip, I purchased a *Dorling Kindersley Eyewitness Guide* to the city. On the cover? The Reichstag with its new Norman Foster dome of transparency. Having been to Lisbon earlier in the year, I was struck by the sharp contrast in the tone of the Berlin guide. I fairly devoured the guide in a day as I recalled the city in my mind and began planning my itinerary with the enthusiasm availed to a stimulating new project. I saw immediately that I had not allotted enough time to see all of the memorial spaces even listed in the guide that I would want to have experienced in order to write about this topic. The guide, a superficial, and as I came to understand, unreliable source to the city, nevertheless, is really unlike any guide to other European cities with which I was familiar. It was remarkable for the number of sites that were associated with the memory of some horror or atrocity of twentieth-century life. Here in the city were these concretized memories of evil of the worst and most recent order. What would this feel like, to me, an infrequent tourist? Could I extend my reactions to those more closely involved, the citizens of the capital city, this revitalized country, going about their everyday lives in a new millennium, not imagined in the previous one? After all, I am the Leonard Zelig of Berlin. Like Woody Allen's character I have made, in the larger realm of things, unscheduled visits to the city in the past, popping in as an incidental, sometimes chameleon-like character to observe important events.

In the meantime the whole question of the void as the design mode of memorial to the victims of the 9/11 attack on the World Trade Center rose to the front pages of the *New York Times* and *Metropolis* magazine. As New Yorkers became less comfortable with the naked encounter with nothingness projected by Michael Arad's scheme, the planted minimalism of Peter Walker brought new confidence in the power of the garden to heal.

At the same time the completion of the discordantly Albert Speer-like Second World War memorial on the mall sent me to my own files of photography of the other memorials in Washington, D.C. My approach began to take some general shape. I also looked through my old scrapbooks and journals of my 1968 trip, and I poured over the beautiful *Album von Berlin* that had been a gift to my mother-in-law from her father at the height of the Weimar inflation before they had left their apartment in Charlottenburg for Sibley, Iowa. I began to read the debates about the *Mahnmal* in German, practicing my language skills, preparing hopefully to discover the essence of the expressive moment. What would be the situation now, so long after reunification? Now, with most of the pro- and antagonists of the war era passing from the scene, with a flurry of new investment in the reunified city, and with the proliferation of memorials to the oppressed of the war and of the postwar shadow occupation, what would it be like?

For many reasons, I had purposely stayed away from Germany for almost 20 years, and before that, I had not been there since the spring of 1968. Then, in 1968, I had arrived from Hamburg, itself a city bombed and fast-forwarded into the last half of the twentieth century. I came into Friedrichstrasse Station on a DDR train pulled by a steam locomotive. With a group of fellow student visitors and a handful of older Germans, called *Rentner*, who had free passage between the zones of the country, we passed into the customs area. The *Volkspolizei*, the Vopos, (I think they were) made a very thorough search of all of our luggage, a shocking invasion to young Americans, disarming our cockiness. Endless moments passed as the young customs officer, only a bit older than we, wearing one of those overarticulated brimmed caps of Soviet fashion declension, took each of our passports. With a piercing stare at our faces, one by one, he placed the

Lance Neckar

passports in succession into a worn slot in a wooden wall behind his position, well practiced, never adjusting his fixed gaze on his decadent applicants. I had never seen my passport disappear before, or since.

We stayed in the last wing of the Hotel Adlon, near the Brandenburg Gate. We were told, I believe, that we were also just near the site of the Goebbels's ministry and garden, and then a bit farther, the infamous Hitlerbunker. Who knew then that this would become the site of the *Holocaust Mahnmal*? It was hot in Berlin when we arrived. We looked out of our hotel window to see where an indistinct, maybe Slavic melody was coming from, old music on an old phonograph. As soon as I appeared at the window, the Vopos trained their binoculars on me as if I were planning to make a break for the West, somehow, improbably scaling the Wall, outrunning their guns in the open death strip, to be swallowed in the West among the trees newly planted in the shattered Tiergarten.

One sweltering evening I escaped the stuffiness of the hotel room and went for a walk. The streets were empty, dark. I wanted to see the Platz der Akademie (now, again, the Gendarmenmarkt) with the old Schauspielhas by Schinkel flanked by the nearly matching Franzoesischer and the Deutscher cathedrals, then both in partial ruin. As I crossed the plaza, (or was I really in the Opernplatz farther up Unter den Linden, near the Neue Wache, more likely to be patrolled by goose-stepping Vopos?) my pace was met in the opposite direction by a Vopo, walking, not marching. I could tell even from his dim profile that he carried a small submachine gun. My pulse quickened a bit, I kept walking, sweating even more in the humid night. I am an American; I thought, who can touch me? But then, I remembered the disappearing passport, and it crossed my mind that the streets were empty, of people and cars. Where was everybody? As these nervous thoughts shot through my mind, my opposite suddenly veered at the last minute of recognition. He had seen me for the improbable American tourist I was, playing a stupid game of chicken.

I had already gotten myself into trouble during that trip. It had to do with a memorial of the Holocaust. I had been staying in Celle with some rather liberal hosts, the family of Dr. Erwin Lindner, whose nephew, Anno (I think that was his name, but I am probably confusing him with another Anno or the name of the Lindner's dog), would regularly appear to siphon a few beers from the household supply. One Saturday he showed up to cadge a drive in his uncle's new Fiat. As we drove in the red sports coupe through the flatness of the Lueneberger Heide that reminded me, cloaked in mist, oddly of Iowa, Anno asked if I had been to Bergen-Belsen. I had no idea it was nearby. Like nearly every American schoolchild of that era, I had read the *Diary of Anne Frank*. The diary ends when Anne's family is found in their hiding place in Amsterdam. The wide horror of knowing but not really knowing was my preparation for the experience of Belsen. I had begun to make a kind of quiet reckoning with the facts only after we had made a careful reading of all of the exhibits in a small pavilion. This sober factual preparation for a walk among the lines of mass graves was for a young person, a postwar kid, a kind of opening to the sublime or just plain horror. Maybe it was the language on the stones, somehow mitigating what seemed to be monstrous numbers: Hier ruhet 3,000 – Here rest 3000. (Was that the number?) and as if "to rest" was a resolution, horrible, but somehow comforting and distancing too. Then you remember that Anne Frank was young, like you too. Just the thought that the camp had been opened to the public was, I thought, positive, if both eerie and modern. Anno drove back. I am sure we spoke, but I cannot remember what we said.

    The next week I suggested idly to my fellow American students that we should all see this place. They agreed that this was a good idea. This suggestion sent a wave of painful discord through the community. I had had no idea of the history of the horrible behavior of this conservative town toward its Jewish residents on *Kristallnacht*, the night of the breaking of Jewish life, in 1938, then only thirty years prior. I think no one outside of a few historians and the residents themselves could have known this. The denial about the knowledge of *Kristallnacht*, like the existence of Belsen, had become submerged in a community narrative of those of the *Widerstand*, those opposed to the oppressors. The repercussions of this suggestion to go, officially, to Belsen divided opinion among the children of all of these people, who were variously perpetrators, bystanders and those of the Resistance, now adults in charge of the city. Guilt and shame were countered by the first statements of a need for transparency of these facts, and these discussions were brought close to the surface of everyday life for the citizens of Celle. It was decided after much discussion that we would be taken, officially; we would be guided there. I remember that in the presentation of the decision to me, and discussions with my exchange *Mutti*, Frau Lindner, I was made to feel like an insensitive young American, and, indeed, this was true. Unfortunately for many, especially those who had been bystanders, this would be an era of such incidents. The decision to take the Americans, children of the victors and protectors of the high moral ground, to Belsen was part of an early unfolding interpretation for postwar Germans of a horrific past.

    In 1985 I visited Berlin with my wife and her mother, who had been born in the city in 1904. We spent what in retrospect was a strange week of visits with my mother-in-law's old family friends, especially Hans Gunter Mueller, who had been an officer in the *Wehrmacht* in the Second War and had subsequently (or consequently?) become a successful IBM executive. We had a separate schedule of touring events with his somewhat

Lance Neckar

estranged son, Peter. Anxious to show us the new Berlin, Peter took us to the City Museum, now largely overwhelmed by the Jewish Museum, and to various housing projects that were the warm-up for the IBA exhibition of German urban design, a precursor to new urbanism here in the States. His tour focused on Kreuzberg, specifically the area around the Wall now occupied by the *Topographie des Terrors* and the site of the *Juedisches Museum*. All the while we were being tested, again, for our sensitivity to the situation, callow Americans of the Reagan Era that we were presumed to be now only pretenders to the high moral ground.

When the Wall came down in 1989, I felt a vague loss in not having reappeared. That part of the script is now complete. In late April, 2004, I went.

When I arrived, as in 1968 to an anomalous heat wave, and immediately began to walk the city, and ride the S-Bahn, the shocking facts of its destruction and reconstruction, the sharpness of the city's edges, its incompleteness, ironically especially at the center, where the Wall had been, hit me hard. This time, I picked an apartment hotel on Friedrichstrasse, at the edge of the old Stasi headquarters district and an easy walk to the Potsdamer Platz, the new Adlon, the Brandenburg Gate, Unter den Linden, the Reichstag, the Tiergarten, and, of course, the *Mahnmal* site. I stayed a week, met with people, walked the city, rode the S- and U-Bahn, recorded images, wrote, went to lectures, lectured, and thought about what I was experiencing. This essay is one product of a personal process of remembrance, admonition, reconciliation and contemplation, in and about Berlin, and me.

Thanks to:

Michael Cullen, Thomas Lutz, Annegret Ehmann, Dr. Stephen Feinstein, Sabine Bing, Assoc. Prof. Rebecca Krinke, Prof. Dr. Erich Funke, Prof. Dr. F. A. DuVal, Helene Aielts Smith

Notes

1. See for example, the Center for Holocaust Studies website, compiled by Dr. Stephen Feinstein, available HTTP <http://www.chgs.umn.edu/Visual__Artistic_Resources/Public_Holocaust_Memorials/Berlin_Memorials/berlin_memorials.html>.
2. Holocaust is a word not used, however, in the text. Instead the connotations of genocide are substituted with the more generalized, descriptive term, "*Voelkermordes*" (literally, murder of a people, p. 43) and the more general term "mass murder" (*Massenmord*) for example, p. 19.
3. I asked Thomas Lutz and Annegret Ehmann if there were a survey assessment of affect, especially of "*Betroffenheit*" that had been done of the various sites already established and currently much visited. Not as yet.
4. Eisenman's essay, "Memorial to the Murdered Jews of Europe," in *Blurred Zones* (New York: Monacelli Press, 2003) treats his sense of time as an experience. In attempting to

sever the nostalgic ties of memory, Eisenman removes the "goal" in the space, (p. 314). Perhaps his sense of an experience of "otherness," a blurring of both cognitive and emotional reception is best understood by his particular sense of the temporal in the memory. He presents an idea of knowing "the past through its manifestation in the present,"(p. 314). And so with the addition of "Holocaust" to the common parlance name of the project, a word also used by Eisenman, a judgment has been made to tie a recently coined term for a specific genocide and to emphasize the normative character of the intent of project, while also potentially blurring the impact of the objective record.

5   Annegret Ehmann was particularly forthcoming about the slow evolution of acceptance of Nazi genocide in the 1960s.
6   In the subtext of activist writing on the ubiquity of memorials in Germany, codified by a formal *Netzwerk der Errinerung* (Network of Memory), is a fear that the resources, historical and monetary, of this "moment" of memory will be consumed by gigantic national efforts such as the *Mahnmal*.
7   S. Endlich and Thomas Lutz, *Gedenken und Lernen an Historischen Orten: Ein Wegweiser zu Gedenkstaetten fuer die Opfer des Nationasozialismus in Berlin*, Berlin: Landeszentrale fuer Politische Bildungsarbeit, 1995.
8   Endlich and Lutz op. cit., p. 9.
9   Among the many critical statements of the book were the principles that had emerged as touchstones of German history in the period following reunification:

   1   National Socialism had brought forth the most extreme form of inhumanity, not only in Germany but in the occupied countries.
   2   National Socialism was grounded in motives in the specific history of Germany and the working out of the situation of postwar Germany. It has tied the current society of Germany with entirety of German history, and only through National Socialism can one understand the origin and development of the two postwar German states.
   3   In National Socialism the most extreme versions of modern political rule are shown as manifested in the bureaucratic organizations of the military, justice, police, medicine, media, statistics, sports, art, and science, all of which contribute to our governance culture today.
   4   The modern possibility of malformation and perversion of limits on human behavior via ruling methods was set forth in the system of National Socialism. This system represented the posing of questions, the undermining of fundamental values and norms that give validity to community life in a civil society.
   5   Study of the history of National Socialism involves itself with the recognition of personal connections and the limits of one's behavior are developed as an exposition of the values of the present.
   6   The splitting apart of the society which came with National Socialism offers the possibility of drawing comparisons stemming from concrete examples. The involvement with historical study of National Socialism has claims therefore on the shape of the present.

10   Endlich and Lutz op. cit. p. 16.
11   Prof. Dr. Carola Muysers, E-mail discussion on the emotional/intellectual frameworks of reception of contemporary memorials by her students as contrasted with the generation of the postwar baby boom in Germany, May 2004.
12   Lutz, interview, April 23, 2004.
13   Originally created as quarters for the Royal Watch, this small temple has been reprogrammed and retrofitted several times in the twentieth-century. After the First World War (1930–31) it was dedicated as a memorial to the German fallen. In this incarnation its interior was punctuated by an eternal flame, and a marker for an unknown soldier. The room was illuminated by a domed oculus in the roof designed by architect Hermann Tessenow.

Lance Neckar

In the period of Nazism it became the *Reichsehrenmal*, (a monument honoring the Empire) and a large cross was mounted on the back wall, and wreaths and candles were placed into the composition. After the Second World War, under the East German regime, the cross was removed, and it was rededicated to the victims of Fascism (and later, also Militarism) with a central altar-like glass prism, an eternal flame and text. Endlich and Lutz op. cit. p. 114.

14 An oculus, or more properly, a skylight, figures prominently in a work that engages a specific event in its space, just cross Unter den Linden from the Neue Wache, in the Bebelplatz. Here in 1993, the Israeli artist Micha Ullman created the *Denkmal* to the Memory of the Bookburning of May 10, 1933. In the pavement of the plaza was an skylight to an underground room, "Library," the name of the piece. Passers-by could see both the room lined with 20,000 volumes of forbidden texts and, by day, the reflections of the sky and the neighboring buildings. Bebelplatz, currently under reconstruction for an underground parking garage, could not be visited by the author, and whether this work will be reinstalled is unknown by the author.
15 On the official website of the *Bundesrepublik*, its perfection as a "monumentally void interior hall" is recognized. Online, available HTTP: <http://www.stadtentwicklung.berlin.de/denkmal/denkmale_in_berlin/en/unter_den_linden/neue_wache.shtml>.
16 Although the work here is by Kollwitz, there are other major figural works of the 1960s through to the 1980s by the inheritors of German Expressionism. There may also be a debt to Ernst Barlach, but this is another subject, another paper.
17 *Raum* has apparently been executed, but the author was unable to locate it. Endlich and Lutz op. cit. p. 120.
18 Jane Amidon, *Radical Landscapes: Reinventing Outdoor Space*, New York: Thames and Hudson, 2001.
19 Although this site in Gruenewald is sometimes empty on weekends, not even passed by commuters, it was the place to which Colin Powell, U.S. Secretary of State and other attendees of the April, 2004 conference on anti-Semitism were brought.
20 Online, available HTTP: <http://www.jmberlin.de/>.
21 Wiedza i Zycie, Wydawnictwo *et al. Berlin*, London: Dorling Kindersley, p.143.
22 Online available HTTP: <http://www.jmberlin.de/>.
23 Libeskind has also proposed a 70-foot deep hole for the World Trade Center memorial site, now reduced to 40 feet.
24 Online, available HTTP: <http://www.nachkriegsdeutschland.de/holocaust_mahnmal.html>.
25 Serra's T-4, a curved double cor-ten wall near the Philharmonie, has become a kind of unofficial memorial to victims of euthanasia killings by the SS in the villa that formerly stood on the site of the Hans Scharoun-designed landmark.
26 Like George Segal's "breadline" at the Franklin Delano Roosevelt Memorial in Washington, where people line up to be photographed with the figures in the sculpture, the Mahnmal may become a kind of misunderstood photo-op for the "I was there" crowd.
27 Online, available HTTP: <http://www.bundestag.de/parlament/praesidium/reden/1999/016.html>.
28 Online, available HTTP: <http://www.bundestag.de/parlament/praesidium/reden/1999/016.html>.
29 Thomas Lutz, conversation with the author, March 23, 2004.
30 Of course, since the concrete stele of the initial submission have been lowered, this simulation probably requires visual editing at the edges of the field, since, in fact, the surrounding walls of the city will be visible to most adult viewers.
31 It is horribly ironic that Nussbaum lived in Gruenewald where the deportations were staged. See HTTP: <http://www.berlin-judentum.de/denkmal/grunewald.htm>.
32 Annegret Ehmann, interview, April 26, 2004.

33 Stephen Feinstein, Michael Cullen, most notably in the author's conversations. It should also be noted that several artists, notably Hans Haacke have been creating important works for the restoration, most prominent of these being his *Der Bevoelkerung*, a word play on the changing nature of the Germans, and on the inscription above the portico of the building, *Dem Deutsch Volke*. Another irony of the original inscription, so associated with National Socialism, is that it was made by the Loevy Company, a Jewish-owned business.

34 In his conversation with Thomas Lutz, the author had postulated, again with (simplistic) reference to the *Mahnmal* site, a kind of spatial model to develop a zone of monuments and memorials, separate from but close to the seat of government, and part of a series of potentially linked destinations for citizens and other visitors to the seat of national government as in Washington – a kind of remembrance quarter, made more poignant by the Vietnam Veterans Memorial and, perhaps, the Holocaust Museum. In his first reaction Lutz responded directly to this thought in two (unexpected but critically important) ways that place this kind of general idea on a different plane in the context of Berlin: first, he said that the Vietnam Memorial is still seen by Germans involved in memorials as a memorial to soldiers, not, perhaps, as it is seen by some of my generation as a memorial to victims who happened to be soldiers. Second, he observed that the Washington Holocaust Museum has clarified the need to define the persecution of the Jews in the context of German history. He is less sure that this kind of historiographic framework exists in the thinking about the *Mahnmal*.

35 Online, available HTTP: <http://www.berlin-judentum.de/denkmal/koppel.htm>.

Filling a void

Creating contemporary spaces for contemplation

John Beardsley

What makes a space contemplative? Or what is it about the character of a space that induces contemplation? I might start to formulate an answer with a bit of semantic wrangling. Specifically, I think it would be useful to differentiate contemplation from commemoration, an experience with which it shares some qualities, but from which it is nonetheless fundamentally distinct. Commemoration is linked to specific events or people: it is a remembrance of things past, to borrow the familiar translation of the title of Proust's great novel, or a mindfulness of people whose values or experiences we might seek to emulate. As such, commemoration is a form of contemplation. But the contemplation with which I am concerned here is more abstract: it is generally unhinged from the sorts of specific references we associate with commemoration. It signifies careful consideration or observation, but of things that might be more phenomenal or metaphysical than historical. Indeed, one of the word's roots, the Latin *templum*, suggests divination: it refers to an open space marked out by augurs for interpreting signs and omens. It implies the extrapolation of metaphysical implications from physical phenomena. While contemplative spaces now are not typically prophetic, they often have a sacrosanct quality: they are at least implicitly sacred and inviolable. Contemplative spaces – at least in the context of contemporary art and design – continue to bridge the physical and the metaphysical, providing a heightened awareness of the physical, psychological, and spiritual dimensions of existence.

Given the increasingly global character of contemporary culture, it is perhaps not surprising that designers today draw on both Oriental and Occidental traditions to create effective places for reflection. I want to focus on selective aspects of both Eastern and Western practice to suggest how contemporary space is rendered contemplative. On the one hand, I will examine the use of Japanese precedents. As Marc Treib argues elsewhere in this volume, Japanese landscape traditions provide numerous examples of devices that can induce contemplation by reducing stimuli or "dampening" experience, including enclosure, threshold, and simplification. But I want to add to these observations a discussion of the Japanese conception of *Ma*, which describes the relationship of space and time, and which I think is equally important in inducing a sense of reflection.

On the other hand, I want to look at several aspects of Western practice that are equally important in fostering contemplation. Some of them overlap with Japanese ideas; some are distinct. I want to suggest the importance of pilgrimage – the significance of removing ourselves from everyday life as a vehicle for contemplation. I want to examine the role of isolation – either created outdoors by a sense of great distances or by physical separation of some sort, or achieved indoors by enclosure and sensory deprivation. I also want to look at the role that the distillation of experience plays in inducing reflection, and the equally important effect of a severely reductive formal language.

I want to begin, however, with a few observations on the use of light as a contemplative medium. Light has a long history of use in Oriental and Occidental art as a manifestation of spirit or as an emblem of transcendence – think of the glowing nimbuses behind the heads of divinities in Christian and Buddhist art; or of the shafts of light that signify the Annunciation or that illuminate saints in Italian painting, as in Caravaggio's *Calling of Saint Matthew* (c. 1597–98) in the church of San Luigi dei Francesi in Rome. The emblematic use of light achieved perhaps its most elaborate expression in northern Renaissance art, as exemplified by Matthias Grünewald's *Isenheim Altarpiece* (c. 1510–15), where a nimbus surrounds the dove symbolizing the Holy Spirit in *The Annunciation*, where light spills from God enthroned in the clouds above *The Virgin and Child with Angels*, and where a brilliant halo in a starry sky sets off Christ in *The Resurrection*. Light was also deployed in architecture as symbolic medium – Gothic cathedrals, for instance, used stained glass to suggest the presence of divine light.

In the modern era, the Mexican designer Luis Barragan provides one of the clearest instances of the use of light for contemplative purposes. At times, he used it in specifically religious contexts, as at the Capuchin

John Beardsley

Convent in Mexico City. The convent includes a courtyard, the aisles of which receive light filtered through perforated screens. Barragan was explicit about the effect that diffuse light might have on our contemplative experience:

> Architects are forgetting the need of human beings for half light, the sort of light that imposes a sense of tranquility. . . . About half the glass now used in so many buildings – homes as well as offices – would have to be removed in order to obtain the quality of light that enables one to live and work in a more concentrated manner, and more graciously. We should try to recover mental and spiritual ease and to alleviate anxiety, the salient characteristic of these agitated times, and the pleasures of thinking, working, conversing are heightened by the absence of glaring, distracting light.[1]

If Barrragan recognized the contemplative quality of half light, then he also celebrated its sacrosanct character. The chapel at the Capuchin Convent receives illumination from tall thin panes of yellow leaded glass that are hidden from worshippers behind a diagonal wall. In a manner that anticipates some of the indoor light installations of James Turrell, light spills from behind this wall, creating a kind of veil or scrim of illumination that falls on the altar. From there, light is reflected back on the congregation from a gold-leaf altar panel designed by the artist Mathias Goeritz. The effect is one of a diffuse golden haze, at once serene and celebratory; it is explicitly in the Christian tradition of light as a revelation of the Holy Spirit.

Outdoors, where it is harder to control light, Barragan aimed for a different effect: he sought instead to focus attention on light as a changing phenomenon. This is especially evident at Las Arboledas, a residential subdivision north of Mexico City where Barragan worked in the early 1960s. In an area known as the Plaza and Fountain of the Trough, an elongated black stone water tank, inspired by vernacular agricultural examples, stands at right angles to a tall white wall, the whole shaded by rows of eucalyptus trees (Fig. 6.1). The composition exemplifies the simplified and balanced but asymmetrical geometries of a Mondrian painting; it also focuses our perception of nature. Trees are reflected in the water; shadows play on the surface of the wall. Barragan concentrates our attention through the distillation of experience: he edits both form and phenomena to heighten our awareness of the physical and metaphysical properties of light.

Barragan's reductive aesthetic is also evident in some of his larger landscape planning work. In the late 1940s, Barragan devised a master plan for a residential development at El Pedregal (the stony place), 750 acres of lava southwest of Mexico City. Barragan's plan called for houses to be tucked

6.1
Plaza and Fountain of the Trough, at Las Arboledas, near Mexico City
Luis Barragan, 1958–62

176

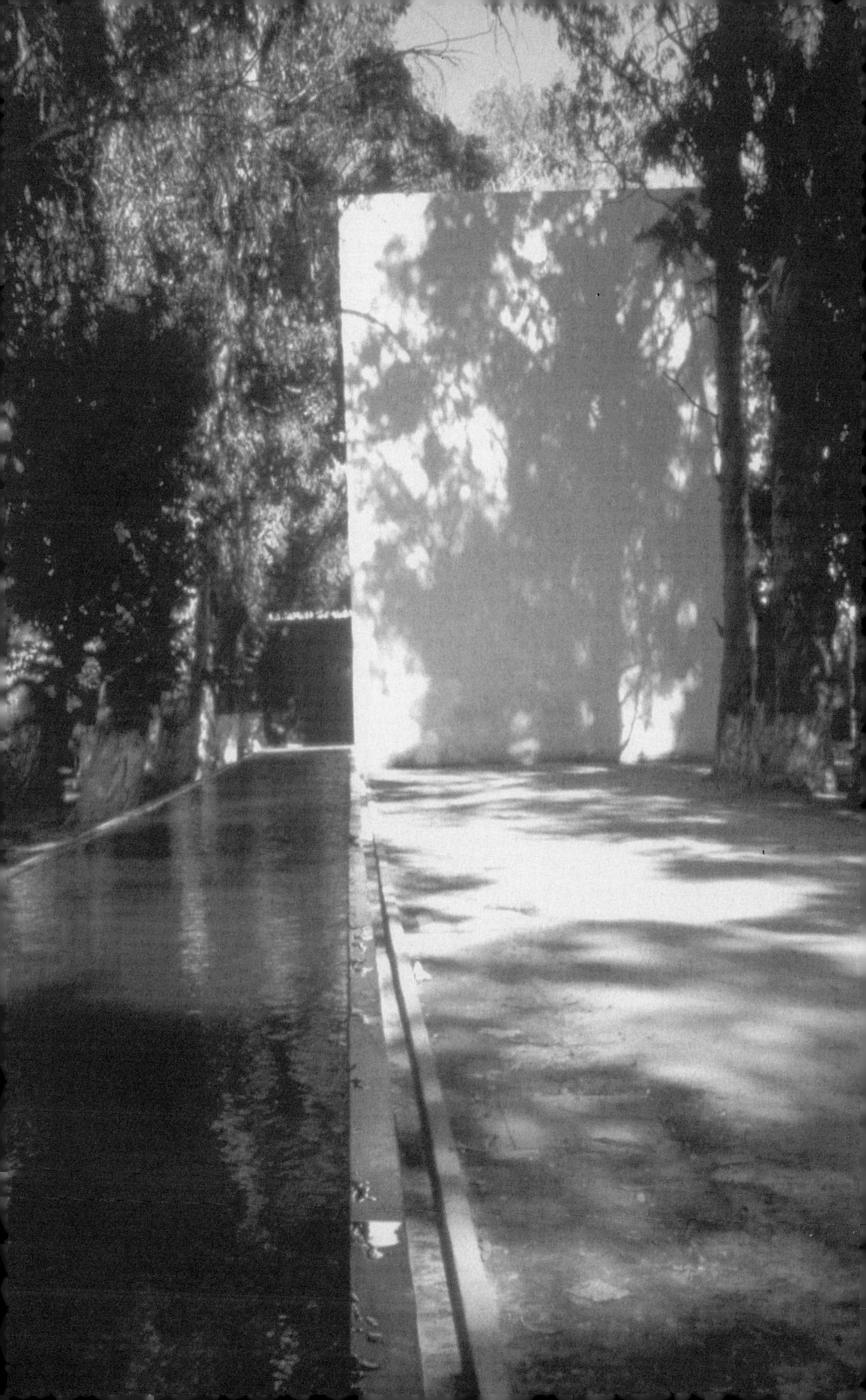

John Beardsley

into the lava field and grouped around parks, with monumental gates, fountains, and plazas at the entries to the development. Little remains of Barragan's plan other than a small, evocative park, where underbrush was removed to reveal the contorted folds of lava. Exposed rock is interspersed with cacti, pepper trees, and occasional areas of grass (Fig. 6.2). Through selectively subtracting elements from this landscape, Barragan was able, in the words of Kenneth Frampton, "to transform a wilderness into a magical place that was part Islamic, part Mayan, and partly evocative of the kind of oneiric landscape one finds in the work of such artists as De Chirico and Max Ernst."[2]

Frampton's appeal to magic is sustained in the words of Barragan himself:

> It is alarming (he noted at an address given when he received the Pritzker Architecture Prize in 1980), that publications devoted to architecture have banished from their pages the words beauty, inspiration, magic, sorcery, enchantment, as well as the concepts of serenity, silence, intimacy, and amazement. All these have nestled in my soul, and, although I am fully aware that I have not done them justice in my work, they have never ceased to be my guiding lights.[3]

6.2
El Pedregal (the stony place), near Mexico City
Luis Barragan, late 1940s

Filling a void

Achieved primarily through the manipulation of light and the simplification of experience, serenity remained one of Barragan's primary goals; he perceived it as implicitly spiritual: "All architecture which does not achieve serenity fails in its spiritual mission."[4] Barragan's work is unquestionably successful in his own terms: even outside of explicitly sacred contexts – as at Las Arboledas or El Pedregal – its serenity induces a meditative experience that most observers would experience as spiritual.

The continued relevance of Barragan's legacy to the creation of contemplative landscapes is demonstrated by a fascinating project completed in 1979 at Ciudad Universitaria (University City) in Mexico City. Called El Espacio Escultorico (Sculpture Space), it was a collaborative project by several artists then teaching at UNAM (the National Autonomous University of Mexico), including Mathias Goeritz, Manuel Felguerez, and Federico Silva, together with the land artist Helen Escobedo.[5] Like Barragan's park at El Pedregal, the Sculpture Space was created by clearing dense underbrush and excavating the volcanic rock hidden beneath the vegetation. The space itself is circular: a sunken ring 120 meters in diameter delineated by a tall basalt rubble wall that is topped by 64 archaic-looking triangular concrete modules, each four meters high and ten meters on each side (Fig. 6. 3). The apertures between these pyramids are consistent except at the points marking the four cardinal directions, where the openings are larger. The physical focus of the

6.3
El Espacio Escultorico (Sculpture Space), Ciudad Universitaria (University City), Mexico City
Collaborative project by artists including Mathias Goeritz, Manuel Felguerez, Federico Silva, Helen Escobedo, 1979

6.4
El Espacio Escultorico (Sculpture Space), Ciudad Universitaria (University City), Mexico City
Collaborative project by artists including Mathias Goeritz, Manuel Felguerez, Federico Silva, Helen Escobedo, 1979

Filling a void

6.5
El Espacio Escultorico (Sculpture Space), Ciudad Universitaria (University City), Mexico City
Collaborative project by artists including Mathias Goeritz, Manuel Felguerez, Federico Silva, Helen Escobedo, 1979

space is the vast void within the ring, where the textures, folds, and extrusions of lava can be observed either from the top of the wall or by climbing down into the circular precinct (Figs 6.4 and 6.5).

The subject of the work might be described as the very creation of the earth – the processes of land formation and the sublime power of volcanoes still active in the Valley of Mexico. Its allusions are to the great sweep of planetary history and to the monumental architecture of pre-Columbian Mesoamerica. Like much contemporary land art, the space suggests a mindfulness of time, both geological and historical; it might be said to derive at least part of its effect from the humbling contrast between the size of the individual visitor and the intimations of vast time and space. The pleasures of this space are exactly those that make Barragan's work so rewarding, chief among them the paradox of a reductive aesthetic making the remaining elements more plainly evident. The void here is filled with the contemplative act – the focusing of attention that in turn creates the serenity so valued by Barragan. Most visitors to this space would, I suspect, find that this serenity invites meditation of a metaphysical sort on the wondrous nature of creation.

Some of Barragan's methods, notably the manipulation of light and the simplification of experience, are likewise evident in the creations of contemporary landscape artists and designers in the United States. Before turning to their work, however, I want to explore the Japanese notion of *Ma*, because it provides another valuable tool for understanding the strategies for rendering space contemplative in contemporary art. *Ma* is a way of conceptualizing the relationship between space and time. Its importance in Japanese aesthetics was affirmed by the architect Arata Isozaki in a 1978 exhibition at the Musée des Arts Décoratifs in Paris, which is when the notion began to gain traction in the West. In both the exhibition and the accompanying publications, Isozaki used the ancient Chinese character *Ma* to describe how he thought space and time were intertwined in Japanese culture. In spatial terms, he suggested, *Ma* is "the natural distance between two or more things existing in a continuity." In temporal terms, *Ma* is "the natural pause or interval between two or more phenomena occurring continuously."[6]

Neither space nor time, in this conception, is fixed; neither exists without the other. Space is experienced through time; time is measured by a movement through space. In all, *Ma* provides a theory to describe the continuity of space and time, to understand them as a single entity. In Japanese landscape traditions, one of the most common devices for heightening this awareness of the relationship between space and time is the stepping stone. Stones establish intervals; they make a person more conscious of movement through space over time. Moreover, movement in Japanese gardens is often indirect: it is frequently interrupted, with places for pauses. At Koto-in, for example, a subtemple of Daitoku-ji built in the Momoyama period (*c.* 1600), there are several right angle turns in the approach walk, causing momentary pauses and reorientations. Stepping up and stepping down are other devices to establish interval and spacing. At the same temple, a gated threshold marks the transit from one realm to another: stepping over the threshold brings an awareness of passing from the everyday to the consecrated or otherwise differentiated environment.

Ma can also be used to express emptiness or void; it sometimes implies a space awaiting occupation by various phenomena. As written, the word is composed of the character for "gate" embracing the character for "sun" (originally "moon"); the implication is that of a void – the gate – being filled with the presence of light. Space is conceptualized as identical with the phenomena occurring in it; we might describe it as empty place where phenomena are made visible over time – where they appear, change, and disappear. *Ma* thus describes the transience of phenomena, or what Isozaki called "the moment of movement."[7] The conception of *Ma* as a void awaiting occupation might seem to describe the so-called Zen or dry stone (*kare sansui*) gardens of Kyoto and, indeed, they may be descended from the ceremonial clearings that identified holy places in ancient Japan. Mountains, stones, and trees have been understood at times in Japanese culture – notably in the Shinto tradition – as emblems of divinity, potentially inhabited by spiritual forces. Spirits might be induced to be present by setting up sanctified spaces – typically vacant – for them to inhabit. But dry stone gardens may have been at least as much pictorial as religious in character: the garden at Daisen-in, for example, also at Daitoku-ji (c. 1500), may have been a translation into three dimensions of contemporaneous monochrome brush paintings of mountains, waterfalls, and sea. Most relevant to my argument, however, dry stone gardens are another means of focusing attention on phenomenal experience. As radically simplified environments, they are places for the staging or the apperception of events: the sound of wind through bamboo; the change in qualities of light; the projection of shadows on raked gravel; the melting of snow, the scattering of leaves.

In all, *Ma* is a complex conceptual construction that is at once spatial, temporal, and phenomenal. The notion suggests that space is not merely three-dimensional; it is four-dimensional. *Ma* is a supple and evocative way of accounting for the introduction of time to constructions of space, rendering them more contemplative in character. It is a way of describing a void that is waiting to be filled with meditative experience.

But how relevant are these notions to contemporary Western landscapes? Japanese aesthetics had a direct impact on the sculptor Richard Serra, who spent six weeks in Kyoto in 1970. Temple landscapes, he later said "completely changed my ideas about sculpture."[8] Serra subsequently began working in the landscape at a large scale, creating linear and later arced sculptures of concrete or steel that were fully revealed only through the viewer's movement through space over time. Walter De Maria's *Lightning Field*, however, provides an even better example for me of the relevance of *Ma* to an understanding of the contemplative experience in contemporary sculpture. Completed in 1977 and located near Quemado, New Mexico, *The Lightning Field* is composed of a rectangular grid of 400 polished stainless steel poles 2 inches in diameter, standing at an average height of just over 20 feet 7 inches, in such a way that the pointed tips are all level (Fig 6.6 and Plate 4). The grid is composed of 16 rows of 25 poles running east to west and 25 rows of 16 poles running north to south; the poles are 220 feet apart, and stretch a mile on the east-west axis and just over a kilometer on the north-south axis.

The Lightning Field was constructed in a vast, semi-arid basin in west-central New Mexico; the site is ringed by distant mountains but has otherwise nearly unlimited vistas. It is a place with a high incidence of lightning activity in the summer, which the piece is designed scrupulously to attract. In this sense, the place is a void awaiting occupation by a potent natural phenomenon; it focuses attention on the approach and passing of storms. But few people are lucky enough to witness lightning strikes. For other visitors, *The Lightning Field* is an experience of more subtle phenomena: the piece virtually disappears in the bright midday sun, becoming fully

John Beardsley

visible only at dawn and dusk, when the poles glow with reflected light. It was very much De Maria's intention to showcase these changing effects: "The light is as important as the lightning," the artist has insisted. *The Lightning Field* is also an experience in the demarcation of space, which is comprehended as a measure of the intervals between poles. The passage from one to the other is perceived both in temporal and spatial terms; the pacing assumes a meditative quality. Reaching the extremities of the grid, the visitor intuits the proportion between its mile and kilometer dimensions and the relation of these explicit measures to the immeasurable distance to the horizon. The time required to walk *The Lightning Field* and the subtle transformations in the quality of light require the visitor to slow down and experience duration in a more intense way, which enhances the contemplative experience.

De Maria's *Lightning Field* was not made to illustrate conceptions of *Ma*; after all, it was conceived and executed before the notions were popularized in the West. Many of its strategies, especially the paradoxical one of editing experience in order to focus concentration, are as much Western

6.6
The Lightning Field, Quemado, **New Mexico**
Walter De Maria, 1977

as Eastern. So too is pilgrimage, which is very much a component of *The Lightning Field* experience. It is a long way from almost anywhere to Quemado, New Mexico, and the typical visit involves a 24-hour stay at the site – where there is a restored homesteader's cabin for shelter – to see the work at all times of the day and night. Removal from the quotidian world is part of the intended effect: "Part of the essential content of the work," De Maria wrote, "is the ratio of people to the space: a small number of people to a large amount of space. . . . Isolation is the essence of land art." But at the same time, *The Lightning Field* demonstrates the relevance of concepts like void and interval to the orchestration of contemplative experience. It is a space coincident with the phenomena occurring in it; it is a place understood through the experience of motion through space over time.

The notion of a space coinciding with the phenomena occurring in it has great relevance to another of the most ambitious works of American land art – the *Roden Crater Project* by James Turrell. Widely known as a magician of light, Turrell has used natural and artificial illumination to control or alter the perceived character of architectural space. The means by which Turrell has created his effects vary greatly – he has used both projected and reflected light, both tungsten and neon. Some of his constructions involve the opening of apertures into spaces suffused with totally uniform fields of color (Plate 5); others use diagonal walls with beveled edges to cast veils of light. He has also employed natural illumination in a series of pieces called Sky Spaces. These are rooms with carefully designed apertures to the sky, which is perceived almost as a scrim on which diurnal and nocturnal events are recorded; the space itself, meanwhile, registers the changing qualities of light.

Turrell's grandest scheme by far is his *Roden Crater Project*, which has been some 25 years in planning and development. It is taking shape in a volcanic cinder cone on the edge of the Painted Desert, about 40 miles from Flagstaff, Arizona (Plate 6). The project will ultimately include a sequence of sky-viewing chambers in both the main crater and a fumarole, or side vent. These spaces are to be connected by tunnels that will collect the light from various lunar and celestial events – moon rises, transits of Venus – and project them into rooms, onto water, and onto polished slabs of stone. The project is being constructed in two phases, the first of which is nearly completed. The rim of the cinder cone has been reshaped to make it into a perfect circle at a level elevation. An 850-foot tunnel has been constructed to link the side vent with the main cone; it rises 150 feet to a space known as the East Portal. Climbing the tunnel (Plate 7), a perfect circle of light appears in the distance; as you approach the East Portal, the circle is resolved into an elliptical aperture to the sky, in a correspondingly elliptical room with sloping roof (Plate 8). The chamber focuses attention on light in several respects: there are vivid projections of light into the room; there are changing qualities of light in the sky; and there are changing patterns of clouds as they pass over the opening.

From the East Portal, another tunnel leads into the heart of the crater, branching in one direction to the Crater's Eye, a circular room with a perfectly circular opening under the center of the bowl: here, the oculus makes the sky look like a dome. Another tunnel leads up a sloping ramp into the crater itself, where there are raised platforms to lie down on (Plate 9). Tipping your head back, you perceive the sky as a celestial vault, contained within the perfect roundel of the crater's rim. The sky becomes oceanic, a vast surface on which clouds are perceived almost as a projected moving image. The empty space of the crater is filled with the consciousness of the visitor.

Turrell's *Roden Crater Project*, like his Sky Spaces, focuses attention on the perception of light, on the way light transforms the experience of space, and on the passage of time. Spatially, it is apprehended by movement through the various tunnels and chambers, punctuated by pauses in the sky-viewing spaces. Temporally, it addresses both the time of individual perception, and the nearly incommensurable time of astronomical events. It requires many hours of silent habitation to perceive the changes in light; eventually, people will be able to spend the night, as at *The Lightning Field*, in a lodge built on the side of the crater. At the same time, some of the phenomena it registers take place only once a year, once in a lifetime, or even once in a millennium; it would require multiple visits – even visits from beyond the grave – to experience all its various phenomena.

It is often said that Turrell's subject is perception itself – that what we see in Turrell's art is ourselves seeing. As we watch ourselves looking, we become aware not merely of what we are seeing, but of how we see over time. The occupation of one of Turrell's sky spaces at the Roden Crater produces a heightened awareness akin to contemplation, which has, according to Turrell, both sensual and metaphysical implications, both conscious and unconscious dimensions. "I want to address the light we see in dreams," Turrell told the *New York Times* writer Michael Kimmelman, allying himself – momentarily at least – with the surrealists:

> It's not about filling a space with stuff. Light is sensual. Anything sensual, while it can attract you toward the spiritual, can hold you from it too; it can keep you in the physical world, and that's an explicit part of my work, which I think is sensual and emotional in the way that music is sensual and emotional.[9]

Turrell's analogy to music is instructive: like light, it is an intangible medium, but one that can fill a space with varying degrees of intensity and with changing tonal and chromatic qualities. Aware of the spiritual connotations of light, Turrell is equally concerned with it as a medium for perceptual and psychological experience. As in Barragan's work, light in Turrell's hands is a physical phenomenon with metaphysical implications.

I want to conclude by suggesting how some of the same strategies that are used to focus concentration in contemporary art are also being deployed by landscape architects. Specifically, I want to examine two projects that were commissioned in 1997 as part of an exhibition I organized for the Spoleto Festival USA in Charleston, South Carolina. Called *Human/Nature: Art and Landscape in Charleston and the Low Country*, the exhibition featured 12 installations by painters, sculptors, and video artists along with landscape architects, all of whom were asked to explore the fluid interactions between nature and culture in the urban and exurban landscapes of Charleston.[10]

One of the projects, *Swamp Garden*, was by landscape architect Adriaan Geuze, a designer from Rotterdam who has built a practice focused chiefly on urban spaces. His preoccupation with what is now called landscape urbanism is perhaps inevitable, given that population densities in Holland approach those of Japan, but it might also help explain his attraction to the solitude of the low country cypress swamps. When he came to South Carolina, he was intrigued by Charleston but seduced by the silent, unpeopled freshwater wetlands of Magnolia Plantation, Middleton Place, and Cypress Gardens. These are both wild and historical places. They are dominated by mature stands of cypress and tupelo and home to alligators, snakes, and fabulous birds. (The swamp garden at Magnolia Plantation was named for John James Audubon, as he collected some of the specimens there for his celebrated 1827–38 book *The Birds of America*.) But they are also cultural artifacts. These wetlands were created by slave labor in the eighteenth century as fresh water impoundments for inland rice cultivation. What looks "natural" in these instances are in fact constructed environments.

The same interplay of built and native elements characterized Geuze's creation at Cypress Gardens, a 170-acre public park once part of one of the largest inland rice plantations in the low country. The structure was distinctly man-made, but it was conceived with the intention of intensifying a visitor's experience of the natural elements of the swamp environment. It consisted of a simple rectangular pavilion, 30 by 60 feet and 20 feet high, built of slender steel posts connected by parallel strands of wire. These were draped with Spanish moss, an epiphyte of the bromeliad family native to the southeast (Fig. 6.7 and Plate 20). Drawing both its moisture and its nutrients from the air, the moss stayed alive on the structure, changing color from an

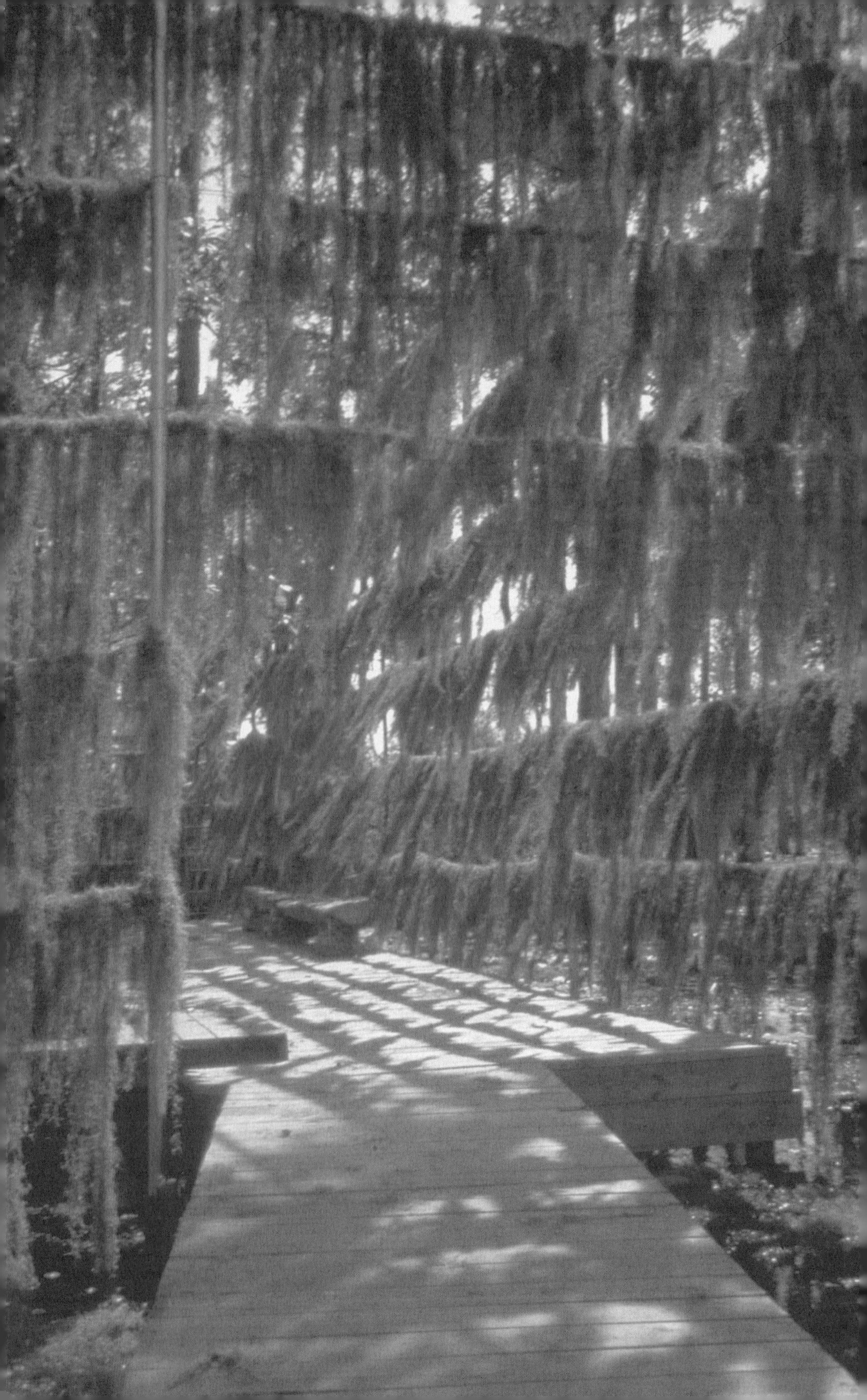

ashen gray when it was dry to gray-green when damp. It was hung in such a way that it formed a semi-transparent veil when the walls were observed head-on. Looking down the length of the sides, it appeared to be opaque.

Approached by a boardwalk that reached 50 feet out into the water, the pavilion contained two wooden decks at right angles to each other, on one of which was a pair of simple log benches made from the split halves of a toppled cypress found in the swamp (Plate 21). The structure enclosed a section of wetlands, including several trees, but it was otherwise open to the sky and the water. Looking from the outside like a rectangle of moss suspended in the air, it was imagined by the designer as contemplative space in emulation of enclosed, dry-stone temple gardens in Japan. As one of Geuze's associates said to a reporter during construction, "The idea is to come inside the pavilion, sit at the edge and meditate. It's modeled after a Zen garden but without the religious inferences."[11] Like those gardens, too, it was at once a reflective space and a pictorial one: it concentrated attention on a composition of trees and water within its walls, and framed vistas through various apertures out into the larger wetlands.

The simplicity of this structure mandated close attention to its details in design. The boardwalk that led out to the piece angled around a tree and changed levels, both to diminish its apparent length and to provide varying perspectives on the structure from the approach. The viewing platforms within the pavilion were given a serrated edge to add visual interest; they too were on different levels. Neither walk nor platform had railings of any kind, to enhance the psychological experience of proximity to the water and its wildlife. Geuze's design was motivated by a conviction that the experience of a landscape is intensified by expansion and contraction of vistas. From a distance, the pavilion drew your eye; it became an object of curiosity and then a destination in the depth of the swamp. From the inside, the sense of enclosure focused your attention on the basic elements of this landscape: aquatic plants, cypress trees, and Spanish moss, all intensified by the reflective quality of black water. Again, we see here a strategy of editing stimuli to focus attention on selective elements of the environment. From the viewing platform, the visitor looked back through the entrance and along a deck out over the open water. These openings provided a visual release from the compression of the interior, allowing one to extrapolate from this segment of the swamp an experience of the whole.

6.7
Swamp Garden, Spoleto Festival USA, Charleston, South Carolina
Adriaan Geuze, 1997

Geuze's project for *Human/Nature* also involved an element of pilgrimage. It was some distance from Charleston – Cypress Gardens is about 25 miles up the Cooper River in neighboring Berkeley County. Within the 170 acre swamp, it was constructed far from the visitor center. It could be approached either on foot or by rowboat; either way, it took some effort to get there. In both cases, the approach was part of the experience. Your pace

John Beardsley

slowed, preparing you for the solitude and serenity of the place. As in so many other projects with a contemplative intent, you arrived at a space awaiting occupation by the perceiving, reflective individual; you experienced a void that was identical with the phenomena occurring in it.

Although located in swamp that was a human construction, this project focused more on the natural environment than on the cultural one; the balance between nature and history in this work was tilted toward nature. The reverse was true in a project in the same exhibition by landscape architect Martha Schwartz: although her work drew on nature in important ways, its primary focus was on the cultural history of the landscape. This resulted in a different kind of contemplation.

Martha Schwartz has earned a reputation as one of the most original and provocative landscape designers at work in the United States today, transgressing some of the traditional boundaries between elite and popular culture, artificial and real versions of nature, and history and contemporary life. Trained as a visual artist and as a landscape architect, she straddles the two worlds, using the unorthodox, often commonplace materials and conceptual underpinnings of contemporary art to challenge some of the conventions of her profession.

Schwartz's project for *Human/Nature* was located on an antebellum plantation across the Ashley River from Charleston. It responded to – even subverted – the principal formal elements of this landscape, a pair of live oak allées that extend along driveways that approach the front and side of the plantation house. Called *Field Work*, the project was composed of plain white cotton fabric panels hung from cables laid out in parallel rows that crossed one of the double lines of live oaks, connecting a row of 1855 slave cabins to a field of sweet grass presently under cultivation for the city's African-American basket makers (Fig. 6.8 and 6.9). The cables were held up by steel posts; they were installed to form a continuous horizontal plane above the surface of the sloping ground. Consequently, the fabric panels were a mere four feet high near the slave cabins but lengthened to about fifteen out in the field. By interrupting one of the dominant axes on the site and by linking the slave dwellings to the meadow, the project suggested the relationship between domestic labor and field work in the lives of the cabins' former inhabitants.

Field Work employed a few of Schwartz's signature strategies. It involved the use of commonplace, mass-produced materials; it featured plots of white painted lawn in front of each cabin, as if the structures were casting shadows toward the sweet grass (Plate 22). It adapted the strategies of other contemporary artists to the interpretation of landscape: in this case, the fabric panels alluded to Christo, both to his materials and to his interest in exploring the social history of a place. But *Field Work* was a sober, sometimes

6.8
***Field Work*, Spoleto Festival USA, Charleston, South Carolina**
Martha Schwartz, 1997

6.9
***Field Work*, Spoleto Festival USA, Charleston, South Carolina**
Martha Schwartz, 1997

melancholy project from an often flamboyant and whimsical artist. It registered the natural phenomena on the site: it took on distinct attributes in different weather conditions and at various times of day. On a still morning, the cloth resembled sheets hung out to dry. On a windy day, the panels – which were tethered at one corner – evoked a fleet of sailboats. In the mist, they suggested row upon row of canvas tents, like some abandoned Civil War encampment.

If superficially distinct from Schwartz's previous projects, *Field Work* manifested deeper analogies with them. Foremost was the concern it demonstrated for the workings of vernacular culture. The sheets, held up by countless wooden clothespins, alluded both to women's work and to domestic labor; it was Schwartz's intent to affirm the value of both. The selection of a cotton material was a deliberate reference to the importance of this plant in the economy of the antebellum South. Schwartz was also deeply concerned about the history of this particular landscape, especially the way its legible form represented the social relationships among plantation residents. She meant to subvert the dominant axis on the site; she wanted to enforce the relationship between the cabins and the field. But the fabric panels and grass paint together had the additional effect of creating a yard around each house. Schwartz was figuratively giving the inhabitants independence and privacy from each other and from the plantation structure. It was here, in the ethereal spaces around the slave cabins, that Schwartz's *Field Work* achieved its most meditative character. The visitor experienced a sense of solitude in these enclosures, but also an awareness of a ghostly presence. The void here was filled not only with the phenomena occurring in it. It was also resonant in this instance with a consciousness of the missing persons in plantation history.

Field Work elicited a considerable amount of controversy among the residents of James Island. Many complained when sections of it blew down in heavy winds. Some called it "Martha's Wash;" a number wrote to the Charleston newspaper, the *Post and Courier*. One ridiculed the idea that clotheslines could be art; another complained that "what appears to be laundry" was "a disgrace, an insult to the late Willie McLeod and should be removed immediately." But an equal number wrote to endorse the project. One confirmed that for some visitors at least, it conjured up the spirits of the plantation's past inhabitants, the sheets suggesting "sails of long-gone vessels that . . . brought the Africans to Charleston as slaves." The writer described Schwartz's effort as:

> a moving tribute to the persistent courage of generations of black slave women who humbly worked, gave birth, and died in the

cabins of McLeod and elsewhere in our beloved South. Like all good art, it points no fingers; it conveys its subtle messages with visual symbols to those of us who try to see.[12]

Field Work may have been fragile and ephemeral, but it signaled an ambition for a tough and durable new form of cultural landscape criticism. The interpretation of any site tends to privilege a master narrative; history is often told from the point of view of the rich and powerful. Schwartz said her intent was to "make it possible to see this landscape again" from a different perspective. She hoped people would recognize the combination of "horror and enchantment" she saw in the graceful allée of oaks sheltering the slave street. She wanted to bring out the ironies of the site: it is human nature to improve a landscape, she noted, but also to make captives of other people.[13] By exhuming some of the African-American history of McLeod Plantation, she was able to suggest the multiple and contradictory narratives disguised in the landscapes of the low country. She gave voice temporarily to those whose stories are seldom told.

In so doing, Schwartz fostered a different kind of contemplation, one in which meditation on the phenomenal qualities of landscape is inseparable from its social history. She used some familiar devices for creating contemplation, notably the concentration or distillation of experience. Her project also exploited the repetition, the strategic use of interval, and the enclosure of a sanctified empty space that are characteristic of *Ma*. But what is different here? We typically think of contemplation as lifting us out of the material into some transcendent realm, but here we have the strategies of contemplation being directed toward the revelation of repressed narratives from the past. *Field Work* anchored its visitors in history. Does this divorce the project from contemplative experience? I don't think so. *Field Work* presented us with something eminently worth pondering, even if the balance in this project was shifted more toward the cultural than the natural or metaphysical.

A consideration of *Field Work* suggests that the line between commemoration and contemplation is not as clear as I might have suggested at the outset. Most recent contemplative landscapes are divorced from specific acts of commemoration. But some memorials are distinctly contemplative. The Vietnam Veteran's Memorial in Washington, D.C., for instance, deploys the spare idioms and the sense of enclosure characteristic of many contemplative spaces; at the same time, its polished black granite surface exploits literal reflection as a metaphor for self-awareness of a moral and emotional sort. Not all memorials achieve a contemplative quality. The Korean Memorial, across the Mall from the Vietnam commemoration, is merely illustrational, with its

John Beardsley

ranks of correctly outfitted soldiers and its wall of contemporaneous photographs etched in stone. But the best commemorations, among which I would include both Maya Lin's Vietnam Veteran's Memorial and Martha Schwartz's *Field Work*, are sufficiently abstract to lift us out of the quotidian, yet sufficiently allusive to remain relevant to the historical episodes they represent. They are both commemorative and contemplative, using the phenomenal qualities of light and space to invite speculation on the metaphysical, but employing historical referents to recall specific events or people.

Contemplation, then, can be of several sorts, all of which are available to the contemporary designer. There is no recipe for creating contemplative space, but there is accumulating evidence that particular strategies are more successful than others in inducing reflection: pilgrimage and isolation, threshold and enclosure, the subtraction of stimuli that concentrates attention on residual elements. Design can induce an appreciation of selected aspects of the natural or physical world, employing the phenomena of nature – especially intangibles like wind and light – to invite metaphysical speculation. Above all, design that encourages contemplation seems to heighten an awareness of time and distance: the time of bodily movement and perception; the historically measurable interval that links us to other lives across time and space; or the indescribable bridge to the great cycles of the cosmos. Design can provide us with the void – the space that is identical with the phenomena occurring within it – but it is not contemplative in itself. It needs to be filled: it awaits the presence of the perceiving individual.

Notes

1. Luis Barragan, quoted in Clive Bamford Smith, *Builders in the Sun: Five Mexican Architects*, New York: Architectural Book Publishing Co., 1967, p. 74.
2. Kenneth Frampton, "The Mexican Other," in Yutaka Saito, (ed.), *Luis Barragan*, Tokyo: TOTO Shuppan, 1992 p. 238.
3. Luis Barragan, from an address given on receipt of the Pritzker Architecture Prize, Dumbarton Oaks, Washington, D.C., June 3, 1980.
4. Luis Barragan, quoted in *Builders in the Sun*, p. 54.
5. For more information on the Sculpture Space at University City, see Mario Schjetnan and David Ramirez, "La Arquitectura de Paisaje," and Oscar Olea, "El Arte Urbano," in Fernando Gonzalez Gortazar, (ed.), *La Arquitectura Mexicana del Siglo XX*, Mexico City: Consejo Nacional para la Cultura y las Artes, 1994, pp. 218–27; 228–33.
6. Arata Isozaki's exhibition was documented in "Ma: Japanese Time-Space," *The Japan Architect* 2, 1979, pp. 70–9.
7. Isozaki, op. cit. p. 78.
8. Richard Serra, quoted in Mark C. Taylor, "Learning Curves," in *Richard Serra: Torqued Elipses*, New York: Dia Center for the Arts, 1997, p. 33.
9. James Turrell, quoted in Michael Kimmelman, "Inside a Lifelong Dream of Desert Light," *The New York Times*, April 8, 2001, p. 34.

10 The Spoleto Festival project was documented in the book *Art and Landscape in Charleston and the Low Country*, Washington, D.C.: Spacemaker Press, 1998.
11 Cyrus Clark, quoted in Warren Wise, "Moss over Black Swamp is Part of Spoleto," *Post and Courier*, Charleston, May 24, 1997, p. 4B.
12 The letters to the editor about Martha Schwartz's *Field Work* can be found in the *Post and Courier* for June 1, 19, 26, and July 15, 1997.
13 Quotations from Martha Schwartz are taken from conversations with the artist, May 1997.

Index

9/11 167
100 mile view 105

Alterra Institute 94, 98
Appelt, Dieter 159
Appleton, Jay 110, 135
Arad, Michael 167
archetypes 5, 129, 134, 135
Arizona 185
art museums 26–7
Asplund and Lewerentz 39, 50, 54, 56, 60
Asplund, Gunnar 39, 50, 58
"arousal" theories 133
attending 14, 19, 28, 30
Auseinandersetzung 143, 148, 150, 159, 164–5

Bachelard, Gaston 46, 47
Barragan, Luis 175–9, 181, 187; El Pedregal 176, 179; and light 175–6, 179; Plaza and Fountain of the Trough 176–8; Pritzker prize address 178; and Salk Institute 71n11
Becton Dickinson Corporation 84, 89
Benson, Dr. Herbert 37
bereavement 19, 50, 59, 67
Bergen-Belsen 168
Berlin: *see* Jewish Museum, light, *Mahnmal*, memorials, memory, reflection, Reichstag, *Topographie des Terrors*, void
Berlin Wall (Wall) 144–5, 147, 159, 161, 163, 168, 170
Bernini, Gianlorenzo, 20
Betroffenheit 142, 154, 156–8, 161, 163, 170
Biedermann, Karl 147
biofeedback 37, 70
Bloedel Reserve 5, 108; philosophy of 110–11; ritual-like aspects of 112–13, 130; *see also* Reflection Garden
Bloedel, Prentice 110, 112, 121

Bloedel, Prentice and Virginia 110, 116
Brattleboro Food Co-op 104
breath (breathing): and contemplation 8–10, 16, 37
Broniatowski, Karol 148, 154
Brown, Richard 110, 113
Built Landscapes of the Northeast 97
Burke, Edmund 29, 33
Bye, A. E. 96–7

Cage, John 31
Caravaggio 175
Center for Action and Contemplation 3, 4
Charleston (South Carolina) 187, 189–90, 192
Chiswick 17, 33
Christian 19; funeral practices 60, 69; symbolism 51, 146–7; tradition of light 175–6
Christianity 131
Christo and Jeanne Claude 159, 190
Church, Thomas 116–7
Claudel, Paul 24
clearing: as archetype 116, 129, 135; *see also* Woodland Cemetery; central clearing
cloister 129
cloister walk 112
cloister garden 5, 112
commemoration 141, 144–5, 147, 149, 151, 174, 193–4
Condon, Patrick 121
contemplation: and commemoration 139–44, 174, 193–4; definitions of 1–4, 13, 15, 30, 36–8, 107–8, 174; effects of 3, 8–9, 37–8; and religious traditions 3; and museums 26–7; and stress reduction 2; and technology 8–10
contemplative landscape: definitions of 4–5, 8–9, 13–14, 36, 108, 174; historical

196

conceptions of 20; strategies for creating 31, 36, 38–9, 69–70, 129–32, 175, 194 *see also* Berlin, Michael Singer, Salk Institute, Woodland Cemetery; and restorative space 132–6; visitor/landscape relationship 15–16, 22, 31, 39, 108–9, 136, 181, 193; virtual 8–9
Concourse C 85, 97
contemporary life: and mediated experience 8; and technology 8–9; and stress 10
convent 20, 176
cosmic cycles 57
cosmic panorama 38, 44, 45, 48
cosmic stage 44, 48
Cypress Gardens 187, 189

Daisen-in 184
Daitoku-ji 182, 183
dampening 15, 19, 27, 30, 175
Dayton, Ohio 74, 82, 89
Davies, Char 8–10
De Maria, Walter 27, 183–5
Denkmal 141, 143
de Zengoita, Thomas 8
directed attention 133–4
divine 17, 20, 111, 175
dry cascade 23
dry landscapes (*kare sansui*) 13, 22, 182–3
Durand, Asher 17
Durback, Robert 3

Ehmann, Annegret 148, 170
Eisenman, Peter 143, 148, 155, 170–1n4
El Espacio Escultorico (Sculpture Space) 179–181
Emerson, Ralph Waldo 36, 49
enclosed garden 54, 108, 129, 133, 134
Endlich, Dr. Stephanie 144,163
English garden 17
enlightenment 13, 22, 31, 122
Escobedo, Helen 179
Experience of Nature, The 12, 110, 132

Farrand, Beatrix 97
Feleguerez, Manuel 179
Field Work 190–4
forest: as archetype 119, 129, 135; *see also* Woodland Cemetery; forest
forest at the National Library of France 108, 111, 115, 119–21; as contemplative space 129–32; perceptions of visitors 123–27; and restorative landscapes 132–6
Forêt de Bord 120
Foster, Sir Norman 159–60, 166
Frampton, Kenneth 178, 195
Friedrich, Caspar David 17
Frolich, Mary 3–4

Gaia foundation 95
Garden of Exile and Emigration 148, 154
Gedenkstaette 141, 145, 147–51, 164
German language 140, 142
Geuze, Adriaan 187, 189
Giverny 2
Glatt, Linnea 98
Goeritz, Mathias 176, 179
Goeschel, Wolfgang 147
Goleman, Daniel 5
Gothic cathedrals 175
Grand Rapids Riverwalk Floodwall project 84, 96
Green Nature/Human Nature 110
Green Party 155
Grünewald, Matthias 175
Gruenewald S-Bahn Station 148–9
Guggenheim (Museum) 75, 77–8, 82, 106

Haag, Richard 108–9, 117, 119, 121, 137n33; *see also* Bloedel Reserve; Reflection Garden
Habermas, Juergen 157
Harriman State Park 74
Hakone Conference 87
Hatch, Stephen 10
Hecker, Zwi 147
Heizer, Michae, 80
Holocaust 143, 147–8, 152–3, 155–8, 163, 168, 170
Holocaust Tower 148, 152, 153

immeasurable 44, 48
inaccessible space 111
Isozaki, Arata 182
Irwin, Robert 29

J. Parker Huber House 84
Jacob-Marcks Christine 155
Jacobsen, Eric 119–121
Japan 13, 31,182, 187, 189; *see also* Japanese gardens; Zen gardens
Japanese gardens 22, 86, 123, 183

Index

Jewish Museum (Juedisches Museum) 148, 151, 164, 170
Johnson, Jory 121

Kabat-Zinn, Jon 2, 3, 10
Kael, Pauline 31
Kahn, Louis I. 38–41, 43–4, 47–8
Kandinsky, Wassily 2
Kaplan, Rachel and Stephen 5, 107, 110, 132, 134, 136
Kaplan, Stephen 109, 131
Kaprow, Allan 77
Kent, William 17, 33
Kiley, Dan 97
Kinsinger Bill, 95
Kohl, Helmut 145, 155, 159
Kollwitz, Kaethe 146–7
Koto-in 182
Korean Memorial (Washington, D.C.) 193
Kristallnacht 147, 169
Kyoto 13, 14, 22, 183, 184

La Jolla, California 38, 40, 84
land art 181, 185
landscape archetype 108, 116, 119, 129, 135
Landscape Park Duisburg North 8
Leasowes, The 17
Le Corbusier 39
Lenné, Peter Josef 160–1
Leerraum 148, 152–4, 164
Leeuw, Geradus van der 38
Lewerentz, Sigurd 39, 50, 58
Lewis, Charles 110
Libeskind, Daniel 148, 151, 154–5
light: in Berlin memorials 147, 150–1, 153; and Luis Barragan 176–7, 181; and James Turrell 28, 30, 185–7; and making contemplative space 70, 194; and Michael Singer 74, 80, 82, 85; at National Library of France 119, 127; at Salk Institute 43, 45–7; symbolic use of in art 175–77; and tea house 25; and *The Lightning Field* 183; at Reflection Garden 123; use of at Woodland Cemetery 58, 63–4
Lightning Field, The 27–8, 30, 183–6
Lin, Maya 147, 194
Long Wharf, New Haven 95–6
Loos, Adolf 147
Lutz, Thomas 144–5, 157, 161, 163–4, 170

Ma 175, 181–4, 193–4
Magnolia Plantation 187
Mahnen 142, 163, 164
Mahnmal 141–3, 148, 155, 157–60, 164, 167–8, 170
mandalas 16
Mankiewicz Paul, 95
mantra 37
McKinnell, Michael 85, 89
McLeod Plantation 193
meditation: classes 10; definition 2, 37–8; effects of 3; and environment 14; practice of 4, 22, 30
memorials: ideas of in contemporary Berlin 140, 144–5; contemporary American 193–4; in Berlin 147–8, 155–6, 159, 165–6; see also *Mahnmal* and *Topographie des Terrors*
Memorial to the Murdered Jews of Europe 143, 155, 170
memorial wall 147
memory: and contemplation 38–9; design strategies for awakening 59, 61, 64, 70; and the Holocaust 155–6, 158–9; ideas of in contemporary Berlin 139–43, 164–7
Meyer, Elizabeth 121
Middleton Place 187
MIT 92, 94
monastery 20, 40, 112, 129
Monastery-Church of Sante-Marie de la Tourette 39
Monastery of San Francesco 40
Monet, Claude 2
moss garden 22
mourning 51, 61, 63, 68, 157
museums 26, 31, 74, 131
Musô, Soseki 22, 23

Nachdenken 143, 160, 164
Nassau County Museum and Park 74, 82–3
National Library of France 108, 111–12; ritual-like aspects of 113–16, 130; see also forest at the National Library of France
National Socialism 139, 144, 171n9
nature, healing effect of, 49, see also restorative landscapes
"nearby nature" 5
Neue Wache 145, 147, 168
New England Science Center (Ecotarium) 100
New Mexico 27, 183, 185

198

Index

Noguchi, Isamu 30
non-directed attention 133
Nussbaum, Felix 157

Orians, Gordon 110
Osmose 8, 9
Ostrum, Meg 95
"overload" theories 133

palimpsest 145
paradise garden, 22, 23, 61
Pavilion and Garden 84
pattern recognition, 16
perception 15, 39; and artwork of Char Davies 9; and artwork of James Turrell 28–30, 186; and contemplation 37, 194; Gaston Bachelard on 46; stages of 16; in work of Luis Barragan 176
"perennial philosophy" 109
Perrault, Dominique 108, 113, 129; ideas of nature 114–15; on the National Library 111, 113; on the National Library forest 111,119–20, 129; *see also* National Library of France and forest at the National Library of France
Perspektive Berlin 155, 159
Phoenix Solid Waste Transfer and Recycling Center 98, 100–102
pieta 146–7
pilgrimage 61, 130, 175, 185, 189, 194
Place to Remember Those Who Survived , A (Memorial Garden), 85
Pond Pavilion 84
postmodern 3, 9, 102
psychological space 111
Pure Land belief 22

reconciliation 139–41, 144–5, 148, 161, 170
reflection (vb): and the artwork of Michael Singer 85, 89; and contemplation 2, 9, 38, 46, 175, 193; and contemporary Germany 141–3, 148, 165; and Woodland Cemetery 59
Reflection Garden 5, 108, 116–19; as contemplative space 129–32; perceptions of visitors 121–3; and restorative landscapes 132–6; ritual-like aspects of 112–3, 130
refuge 2, 134
Reichstag 159–60, 166, 170
restorative landscape 5, 107, 132–6

retreat 3, 5, 20–2, 25, 31, 84
Rikyu, Sen no 25, 39, 40, 42, 44
ritual 39, 47–8, 146, and Buddhism 13, 25, 40 and funeral practices 63, 66, 68
Ritual Series, 74, 82
ritual theory 108, 112–13, 130
Roden Crater Project 29,185–6; *see also* James Turrell
roji 25
Rosh, Lea 155
Ryoan-ji 14, 111

sacred: and contemplative space 44, 102–3, 174, 179; and Woodland Cemetery 19, 51, 62
sacred groves 61, 136
sacred mountain 39, 61
Saiho-ji 22, 23
Salk Institute for Biological Sciences 38–40; approach 41; courtyard 41–2, 44–7; fountain ("River of Life") 42; laboratory complex 43–4; strategies for creating contemplative space 44–48
Salk, Jonas 40, 44
sanctuary 38, 39, 49, 60, 66
satori, 13, 122
Scarpa, Carlo 89
Scheffler, Israel 47–8
Schinkel, Karl Freidrich 146, 160
Schwartz, Martha 190–4
seating: and contemplative space 131; at National Library 115–6; at Reflection Garden 117, 119
semantic landscape 17
semiotics 139
Serra, Richard 95, 148, 155, 183, 195
Shakers 21, 22
Shepherd,Sir Peter 110
Shinto 182
Silva, Frederico 179
silence: and contemplative space 44, 85, 119, 178; and contemporary life 10; and meditation 37–8, 70, 108; and the sublime 17; and Woodland Cemetery 19, 51, 55–6, 59, 67–8
Singer, Michael: and architecture 92, 94; on contemplative space 99–106; and drawing 78, 81; education 77–8; exhibitions 74 5, 82, 92; and the Everglades 74, 80; and Japan 86–7, 89; meditative retreats 84; and New York 73–75, 81–2; and performance

199

Index

79–80;and power plants 99, 104, 106; on public space 99–100; on sacred space 103; and saltwater marshes 74, 80; on sustainability 95–6; and Vermont 73, 75–8, 80–3, 105
Smithson, Robert 80
solitude: and contemplative space 40, 89, 132, 187, 190, 192; at Woodland Cemetery 58, 63, 64
space of absence 60
Steele, Fletcher 97
stepping stones 25, 40, 182
Social Democratic party 155
Spoleto Festival USA 187
Stockholm 17, 39, 49, 50, 60, 65–6, 69
Stolpersteine 148, 165
stress 4, 5, 10, 133, 135
stress reduction 2, 3, 10
stroll gardens 25
Struth, Thomas 31
sublime 17, 29–31, 33, 139, 169
Suzuki, Daisetz 13
Swamp Garden 187–90
symbolic elements 60

tea ceremony 25, 40
tea garden 25, 40, 44
tea master 25, 39
technology 8, 9, 10, 112
temples 17, 22, 130
temporality 39, 49, 59, 140, 144
Thacker, Christopher 116
Thierse, Wolfgang 156–7
Thoreau, Henry David 5
threshold 29, 41, 44, 48, 60, 175, 182, 194
Thurman, Robert 1,2,9
Todd, John 95, 97
Topographie des Terrors, (*Topographie*) 144–5, 148, 151, 161, 163 -5, 170
Track 17 148, 150
transcendence 49, 50, 60, 64–5, 68–9 ,175
transcendental philosophy 17
"trigger devices" 37
Turrell, James 28–30, 176, 185–7; *Roden Crater Project* 29,185–6; Sky spaces 185–6; *Space-Division series* 29; Spaces that See 29

Ulmann, Micha 147, 172–14
Ulrich, Roger S. 5, 107, 134–5
University of Washington 111, 112

Van Valkenburgh, Michael 96
Versoehnung 141
Vietnam Veterans Memorial (Washington, D.C.) 161, 193–4
virtual reality 8, 9
void: clearing as 51, 60–1, 69, 116; in contemporary Berlin 142, 147, 152, 157, 160, 164; in Japanese tradition 182–3; in 9/11 memorial 167; and relationship to observer 181, 190, 192, 194
von Rosenberg, Joachim 147

Walden 5
Waldman, Diane 74, 82
Walker, Peter 121, 167
walking: as aid to contemplation 131; and Berlin memorials 131, 154; and the Bloedel Reserve 111, 134; and *The Lightning Field* 28; in Michael Singer's work 85; and tea gardens 25; and Woodland Cemetery 63, 67
Ward, Alan 96
Weizman, Eyal 147
Wilber, Ken 109, 131, 136
Wilson, E. O. 135
wilderness 5, 17, 89, 132, 178
"wisdom of the body" 37–8
Woodland Garden, 85, 89, 91
Woodland Cemetery 17, 19, 49–50, 68–9; approach 50–1; asymmetry 60; catafalque, 54, 58, 59, 61, 63–4, 68; central clearing, 51, 53, 55–6, 62, 64, 66–7; Chapels of Faith, Hope, Holy Cross 54; Chapel of the Resurrection, 58, 62; children's cemetery 58; and collective life 66–7; columbarium, 51, 53, 62, 65; cosmic linkages 65–6; commemorative rituals 63; crematorium complex 53–4; design strategies for creating contemplative space 59–70; forest, 51, 55–62, 64; forest tombs, 50, 56–9; and individual life 68; lily pond, 54, 61, 65, 68; Meditation Grove, 50–1, 54–6, 59, 61–5, 68; Memorial Ground, 58, 63; Monument Hall, 50–1, 53–5, 61–2, 64–5; orientation 59, 61; and solitude 63–4; and time/timelessness 66–7; and transcendence 59–60, 64, 68–9; Way of Seven Wells 56, 58, 61; Way of the Cross 51, 53–4, 62, 67; willow grove 58; Woodland chapel 58–9, 62, 66
World Trade Center 167

Zen: description of 13–14, 24; and contemporary museum 27; and tea garden 25
Zen garden 4–5, 13, 21, 97, 111, 129, 189
Zen *koan* 17
Zen masters 31
Zen practice 22, 23, 131
Zen temples 13
Zumthor, Peter 30, 148, 161, 163–4

eBooks – at www.eBookstore.tandf.co.uk

A library at your fingertips!

eBooks are electronic versions of printed books. You can store them on your PC/laptop or browse them online.

They have advantages for anyone needing rapid access to a wide variety of published, copyright information.

eBooks can help your research by enabling you to bookmark chapters, annotate text and use instant searches to find specific words or phrases. Several eBook files would fit on even a small laptop or PDA.

NEW: Save money by eSubscribing: cheap, online access to any eBook for as long as you need it.

Annual subscription packages

We now offer special low-cost bulk subscriptions to packages of eBooks in certain subject areas. These are available to libraries or to individuals.

For more information please contact webmaster.ebooks@tandf.co.uk

We're continually developing the eBook concept, so keep up to date by visiting the website.

www.eBookstore.tandf.co.uk